Jackson Hole Cooks!

JACKSON
HOLE
COOKS!

First printing, November 2003
Second printing, December 2003
Third printing, October 2004
Fourth printing, September 2005
Fifth printing, May 2007

ISBN 0-9642423-3-8

Book design and layout by Rebecca Woods

White Willow Publishing
PO Box 6464
Jackson, Wyoming 83002

Acknowledgments

This book would not be in your hands without the help and contributions of many people. I am indebted to the courteous and helpful staff at Teton County Library and the Jackson Hole Historical Society, who assisted with locating archives and microfiche material. Jamie Schoen at Bridger-Teton National Forest generously shared access to many historical pictures used throughout this publication. Jackson Hole facts and items of interest were drawn from numerous sources, most notably Robert Righter's *Crucible for Conservation*, and John Daughtery's landmark *A Place Called Jackson Hole*. Their scholarship has been recognized and enjoyed by many. And, of course—and most especially—to over 120 businesses, food professionals and accomplished home cooks who so generously shared the fruits of their culinary acumen. Bravo!

—Editor Rebecca Woods

Dedicated to the nonprofit
organizations of Jackson Hole and all
those who support their work. Your
generosity, spirit and hard work
enrich the lives of many.

Table of Contents

Bread and Breakfast 1

Beverages 41

Appetizers & Condiments 59

Salads & Dressings 85

Sides 107

Soups & Sandwiches 131

Entrees 159

Desserts 197

Confections 247

Appendix 255

    Ingredient Equivalents 256
    Measurement Equivalents 256
    Metric and Celsius Conversions 259
    Substitutions 260
    Baking Dish and Pan Sizes 261
    Spice Life 261
    A Well-Stocked Kitchen 262

Index 264

Acknowledgments 281

    Contributors 282
    Individual Contributors 287
    Margin Information Sources 289
    Photo Credits 290

Favorite Recipes/Notes 291

Order Form 295

Recipe Notes

All recipes have been home kitchen tested for accuracy but, of course, errors can occur. Please write to White Willow if you encounter problems. Every effort was made to attribute the source of previously published recipes. Nonsourced but previously published recipes identified with release of this publication will be credited in future editions. Recipes without an identified contributor are adapted versions of recipes I and far-flung friends and family members have used over the past decade. We compose the unofficial cookbook committee of this publication!

As with any cookbook, carefully read through each recipe before you begin. Measurements and descriptions are standardized as follows:

Unless specified otherwise, this item: **Equals:**

chocolate chips .... semi-sweet chocolate chips
cinnamon .... ground cinnamon
cloves .... ground cloves
doz .... dozen
egg ....large egg
env .... envelope
flour... all-purpose flour
green pepper .... green bell pepper
heavy cream .... whipping cream
in .... inch
lb(s) .... pound(s)
milk .... whole milk
mustard .... prepared mustard, not dry
oats.. regular rolled oats
oz(s) .... ounce(s)
pepper ....black pepper
pkg ....package
pumpkin........................... solid pack pumpkin, not pumpkin pie filling
sugar.. granulated sugar
tbsp .... tablespoon
tsp .... teaspoon
vanilla .... pure vanilla extract

—The Editor

Bread & Breakfast

Dogsled races, downtown Jackson, C. 1930

Sassy Eggs

This unusual, rich breakfast dish bakes like a soufflé and draws "lots of raves" from the guests at Sassy Moose Inn Bed & Breakfast. It is served with generous slices of ham and oatmeal pancakes.

1   16-oz. pkg. of frozen peaches, defrosted
¼   cup of sugar
½   tsp. salt
1   pint (2 cups) half-and-half
10   eggs
     corn bread mix
     fresh peaches and/or raspberries
          for garnish, optional

1.   Lightly coat a 9x13-inch pan with cooking spray, then sprinkle a light covering of corn bread mix on the bottom.
2.   Spread the defrosted peaches over the cornbread. Evenly sprinkle the sugar and salt over the peaches.
3.   In a separate bowl, beat eggs and half-and-half together until well blended. Pour egg mixture over the peaches.
4.   Bake in a 400 degree oven for 45 minutes, or until the soufflé is lightly browned and set.
5.   Garnish with fresh peaches and/or raspberries, if desired. Serve warm.

Serves 6-8

Wildflower Baked Eggs with Herbs

Delicious, simple and quick.

4   eggs
     fresh basil, chopped fine
     slivers of sun dried tomatoes
     grated Gruyere cheese

1.   Butter two small ramekins for each person
2.   Drop one egg into each ramekin. Sprinkle with fresh basil, slivers of sun dried tomatoes and cover thoroughly with grated Gruyere cheese.
3.   Bake in 350 degree oven for 10-12 minutes, or until bubbly and the eggs are set as you like. The cheese will puff up. Eat and enjoy!!

Serves 2

Eggs

Buy eggs in the grocery store from the back of the refrigerator case. They will be both colder and fresher. Store the eggs in their carton on a shelf inside your refrigerator, not in your refrigerator door. The warmer door temperature invites disease.

Orange French Toast
Nowlin Creek Inn

Porcupine

When Mark and Susan Nowlin operated their charming B&B, this recipe was among their most requested. The Nowlins have turned to other endeavors, but graciously offered to share this breakfast delectable.

1	loaf of French bread, sliced into 1-inch thick slices
¼	cup butter
⅔	cup sugar
2	tsp. grated orange peel
½	tsp. cinnamon
8	eggs
1⅓	cup orange juice

1. Preheat oven to 400 degrees.
2. While oven is warming up, crack eggs into deep mixing bowl and beat slightly. Add orange juice and mix well. Set aside.
3. Place half of the butter in each of two 13x9-inch glass baking pans. Place each dish in the microwave for one minute, or until butter is completely melted. (If using metal pans, melt butter in microwave and pour into pans.)
4. Mix the sugar, orange peel and cinnamon together and sprinkle evenly over the bottom of both baking dishes.
5. Dip bread slices into the egg mixture and place in the sugared pans. (Approximately 12 slices of bread fit into each pan.) Pour any remaining egg mixture over the bread.
6. Bake for 18-20 minutes, removing when slices are browned. Use a spatula to lift the bread slices out of the pan, turning the sugar side up on a warm platter. Serve immediately.

Serves 10-12

Porcupines are protected from their predators by an impressive number of 30,000 quills. The loosely attached quills detach easily, giving rise to the mistaken belief that the animal can throw its quills. It cannot. Porcupines are strict vegetarians, surviving on bark, buds, twigs and leaves.

Amber's Peach French Toast
Martha MacEachern

When the MacEacherns owned and operated The Painted Porch Inn, guests always requested this recipe.

5	eggs
1	cup packed brown sugar
½	cup butter
2	tbsp. water
1	29-oz. can sliced peaches, drained
12-14	slices thick French bread (baguettes are good)
1½	cup milk
3	tsp. vanilla

Mountain Goats

Mountain goats were introduced in the Snake River Range in the 1970s. After a gestation period of 5-6 months, nannies bear one or 2 kids, typically in May. Mountain goats frequent vertiginous cliffs and ledges, where they are safe from predators. They are able to place all four hoofs on a ledge as small as 6-inches long and 2-inches wide.

1. In a saucepan over medium-low heat, stir brown sugar and butter until the butter melts. Add water and continue to cook and stir until the sauce thickens and foams. Pour into 9x13-inch baking dish, spreading mixture evenly over the bottom. Let cool 10 minutes.
2. Distribute peaches evenly over the sauce, then cover with bread slices, trimming if necessary to fit in one layer. In a small bowl, whisk eggs, milk and vanilla together and pour over bread. Cover and refrigerate overnight.
3. Preheat oven to 350 degrees. Bake uncovered for 40 minutes, or until set and golden brown. Cover with foil the last 10-15 minutes if the toast is browning too quickly. Serve with syrup or fresh berries.

Serves 6-8

Honey Pecan French Toast

Chef Tamalpais Roth-McCormick

This fantastic French toast requires advance planning: the bread must soak in batter overnight. Once you make it, you'll be leaving Post-It™ reminder notes on the 'fridge door. It's that good.

4 eggs, beaten
1 cup half-and-half
1 tbsp. brown sugar
1 tsp. vanilla extract
4-8 slices of French bread, 1-inch thick
¼ cup unsalted butter
¼ cup brown sugar
¼ cup honey
¼ cup maple syrup
¼ cup chopped pecans

1. Combine the eggs, half-and-half, 1 tbsp. of brown sugar and vanilla in a small bowl. Mix well.
2. Pour half of the egg mixture into a baking dish or pan large enough to hold bread slices in a single layer. Place the bread in the dish and pour the remaining egg mixture over the top of it. Cover and refrigerate overnight.
3. Set oven to 350 degrees. Melt the butter in a 13x9-inch baking dish. Remove dish from oven and stir in 1 tbsp. brown sugar, honey, maple syrup and pecans. Add the soaked bread. Bake at 350 degrees for 30-40 minutes, or until puffed and brown. Use a spatula to turn syrup side up on a warm platter. Serve immediately.

Serves 2-4

Baked Cinnamon Apple French Toast

Elizabeth Richardson,
submitted by Anne Whiting Richardson

Fragrant and delicious. Think of apple pie for breakfast—only better.

- 6   slices bread or 1 small loaf French bread, sliced
- 2   eggs
- 1½   cup milk
- 2   tsp. vanilla
- 3   large tart apples, peeled, cored and cut into thin slices
- ½   cup sugar
- 1   tsp. cinnamon
- 1   tbsp. butter, cut into small pieces
- ½   cup chopped walnuts (optional)

1. Preheat oven to 400 degrees.
2. While the oven is heating, lightly oil or spray with cooking spray a 13x9-inch baking pan. Arrange bread in pan in a single layer.
3. Whisk together the eggs, milk and vanilla until smooth and well blended. Pour mixture over bread. (This dish can be prepared ahead to this point, then covered and refrigerated for several hours or overnight.)
4. Arrange the apple slices on top of the bread. Combine the sugar and cinnamon and sprinkle on top of the apple slices. Optional: Add nuts. Dot evenly with butter.
5. Bake for 35 minutes or until the apples are soft and the custard has set. Let cool for 5-10 minutes before serving. Serve with maple syrup, or dust with powdered sugar.

Serves 6

Fresh Apple Muesli

The Wildflower Inn

A great way to start the day!

- 1   cup old fashioned oats
- 1   cup good apple juice or cider
- 2   tbsp. vanilla yogurt
- ⅓   cup sliced almonds
- ¼   cup dried fruits bits

Mix all ingredients and chill well. Serve with yogurt and fruit.

Serves 2

Apples

Americans eat an average of 22 pounds of apples per person, per year. Apples should be kept in the refrigerator. Left at room temperature, they lose firmness and flavor 10 times faster.

Fresh Huckleberries with Lemon Cream

This is an adaptation of a recipe submitted to a now out-of-print cookbook compiled by the Junior League in Palo Alto, California. If you are a huckleberry fan, you'll love this recipe! It is a star both at brunch and at the dessert table.

Huckleberry

These popular, sweet berries are found in lodge-pole forests in Jackson Hole and the canyons of Grand Teton National Park up to 8,500 feet in elevation. Bears and man eagerly await their early to mid-August ripening.

1 pint huckleberries
1 tbsp. sugar
½ cup sugar
2 tsp. finely grated lemon rind
½ cup fresh lemon juice
1 cup heavy cream

1. Gently rinse berries. Drain well. Place in a small bowl and sprinkle with 1 tbsp. sugar.
2. Combine the ½ cup sugar, lemon rind and lemon juice in a small saucepan. Bring to a boil over medium heat, stirring constantly, just until sugar dissolves.
3. Lower heat and simmer, uncovered, 10 minutes. Do not stir.
4. Remove lemon mixture from heat and cool completely.
5. Whip cream until soft peaks form.
6. Gently fold in cooled lemon syrup.
7. Divide berries into four bowls and spoon the lemon cream over them. Heaven.

Serves 4

Note: Blueberries or raspberries can be used with equal success.

Fruit and Nut Granola   *Chef Karen Norby*

Wonderful served with yogurt for breakfast, or as a trail snack.

2 cups dried cranberries or raisins
8 cups oats
2 cups bran flakes
2 cups sunflower seeds
2 cups sliced almonds
2 cups flaked coconut
½ cup brown sugar
½ cup vegetable oil
2 cups honey
4 tbsp. cinnamon
4 tbsp. nutmeg
4 tbsp. almond extract

1. Mix everything except oil and honey together in a large bowl.
2. Add oil and honey and mix by hand to distribute evenly.
3. Spread on well-greased cookie sheets and bake in 350 degree oven until mixture just starts to turn golden brown. Cool before storing in covered plastic container. Granola will keep 3-4 weeks.

Yield: 3 pounds of granola.

Super Oatmeal   *The Wildflower Inn*

Easy and delicious, particularly topped with a dollop of vanilla yogurt.

    2   cups old-fashioned rolled oats
    4   cups milk
    ¼   tsp. salt
    1   fresh nectarine or peach, peeled and diced
    1   apple, cored and diced
    1   banana, sliced into chunks

1. Combine above in a saucepan and let soak for 5 minutes or so.
2. Simmer slowly over low heat, stirring often. Cook until thickened and tender, about 10-15 minutes.

Serves 6-8

Yellowstone Nat. Park Tourist Camp, 1903.

Oranges

Navel oranges with the biggest hole, or navel, tend to be the sweetest. If you are peeling oranges for salads, the white membrane is easily removed if you soak the unpeeled orange in boiling water for 5 minutes before peeling

Oranges with Marmalade   The Wildflower Inn

Refreshing!

    3   oranges, peeled and sectioned
    ⅓   cup orange marmalade
    ⅓   cup orange juice
    2   tbsp. Grand Marnier

1. Combine everything in a bowl and fold together well. Chill for 1 hour to overnight. (We sometimes put the bowl into the freezer for a short while.)
2. Serve in a cut glass bowl for a beautiful dish.

Serves 4

Baked Banana   The Wildflower Inn

A great winter dish

    ⅓   cup (⅔ stick) butter, melted
    3   tbsp. fresh lemon juice
    6   firm, ripe bananas, peeled and cut horizontally in thirds
    ⅓   cup brown sugar
    1   tsp. cinnamon or ground ginger
    1   cup grated coconut

1. Preheat oven to 375 degrees
2. Spread the melted better and lemon juice over the bottom of a shallow baking dish large enough to hold 6 bananas.
3. Put the bananas in the dish and turn them until they are well coated with the butter mixture. Combine the sugar and cinnamon or ginger in a small bowl and stir with a fork to blend thoroughly. Sprinkle the sugar mixture evenly over the bananas.
4. Bake bananas for 10 minutes, or until the butter just begins to bubble. Turn the bananas and continue baking for another 5 minutes.
5. Sprinkle coconut over the bananas and cook for an additional 5 minutes, or until the coconut is brown. (Watch carefully; coconut burns easily.)

Divide into bowls and serve warm with a dab of plain yogurt.

Serves 6

Oatmeal-Buttermilk Pancakes
The Wildflower Inn

Jackson Hole in Space

The U.S. Voyager II spacecraft was launched in 1977 to chart and explore unknown portions of the solar system. Its artifacts cargo includes an Ansel Adams photograph of Jackson Hole.

In a whole host of wonderful breakfast dishes, The Wildflower Inn's oatmeal-buttermilk pancakes are a true standout. This is the award-winning Inn's most-requested recipe.

2	cups old-fashioned oatmeal
2½	cups buttermilk
2	eggs lightly beaten
¼	cup butter or margarine, melted and cooled
½	cup all-purpose flour
2	tbsp. sugar
1	tsp. baking powder
1	tsp. baking soda
¼	tsp. salt

1. Combine the oats and buttermilk and let soak for 15-30 minutes.
2. Add eggs and butter. Stir well.
3. Add flour, sugar, baking powder, baking soda and salt. Stir gently, then let rise for 10 minutes.
4. Cook on a medium hot grill. The Wildflower uses a ¼-cup measuring cup to ladle batter onto the grill for perfect size cakes, every time. Serve with warm maple syrup or strawberry butter, below.

Serves 4

Strawberry Butter
The Wildflower Inn

1	cube unsalted butter, softened
3	tbsp. strawberry jam

1. Combine butter and strawberry jam.
2. Roll into a log on a piece of saran wrap. Chill well.
3. Slice into rounds and serve on a pretty plate.

1900 freight team.

Indian Paintbrush

This semi-parasitic plant is the Wyoming state flower. Paintbrush roots penetrate the roots of other plants, particularly sagebrush, to steal a portion of the host plant's food. It has evolved to become so dependent on other plants that it is difficult to transplant. The bright red bracts of paintbrush color the valley floor from June to early August.

Gingerbread Pancakes
Martha MacEachern

A favorite at the MacEacherns' Painted Porch Inn. Serve hot with maple syrup or real whipped cream.

2½	cups flour
5	tsp. baking powder
1	tsp. baking soda
1½	tsp. salt
½	tsp. ginger
1	tsp. cinnamon
¼	cup molasses
2	cups milk
2	eggs, lightly beaten
6	tbsp. butter, melted
1	cup currants (optional)

1. In a large bowl sift together the dry ingredients and spices. Set aside.
2. In a separate bowl combine the molasses and milk; beat in the eggs and the melted butter. Add to the flour mixture and stir until just moistened. Add currants, if desired.
3. Ladle the batter onto a hot, lightly oiled griddle and cook until golden on both sides.

Serves 4-6

Cranberry Ricotta Pancakes
The Wildflower Inn

Very pretty and very delicious

2	tbsp. concentrated cranberry juice
¾	cups milk
6	tbsp. butter
4	eggs
⅔	cups ricotta cheese
1	cup all-purpose flour
2	tsp. baking powder
½	tsp. baking soda
¼	tsp. salt
¼	cup sugar
½	cup chopped cranberries

1. In a small non-aluminum saucepan, heat the cranberry juice, milk and butter until the butter is melted. (The Wildflower does this in the microwave, in a 4-cup measuring cup.) Transfer to a large mixing bowl.

2. Add the eggs, one at a time, beating well after each addition.
3. Fold in the ricotta and cool to room temperature.
4. Combine the flour, baking powder, baking soda, salt and sugar in a large bowl. Fold into the egg batter until just mixed.
5. Toss the cranberries in a small amount of additional flour and add to the batter. Cover the batter and let rest for 15 minutes.
6. Heat the surface of a griddle or skillet. Brush with margarine. Pour ¼ cup batter per pancake on the griddle surface. Cook until the edges are dry and the surface is covered with small bubbles. Turn pancakes over and cook remaining side. Serve the pancakes hot with butter and syrup.

Serves 6

The Old Painted Porch Pancakes   *Martha MacEachern*

When Matt and Martha MacEachern owned and operated The Painted Porch Inn, this recipe was the B&B's all-time favorite.

   1½ cups whole wheat flour
    1 cup unbleached all-purpose flour
    1 cup old-fashioned rolled oats
    ½ cup yellow cornmeal
    1 tbsp. baking powder
    2 tsp. baking soda
    1 tsp. salt
   1½ sticks unsalted cold butter, cut into small pieces
    4 eggs
    4 cups buttermilk
    ½ cup honey
    1 cup chopped pecans

1. Sift together the flour, oats, cornmeal, baking powder, baking soda and salt. Cut in butter with pastry cutter or forks until mixture resembles coarse meal. Set aside.
2. In a large bowl, beat eggs and buttermilk together until smooth and blended. Beat in honey. Stir in flour mixture, mixing well, then fold in pecans. Refrigerate overnight.
3. Ladle the batter onto a hot, lightly oiled griddle and cook until golden on both sides. Serve hot with butter and syrup.

Serves 10

Pancakes

Low-fat milk can be substituted for whole milk in pancakes without sacrificing taste. For pancakes so light they may float away, replace milk altogether with an equal amount of club soda.

11

Buckwheat Waffles

Wonderfully light and crisp…these never stick to the waffle iron. Serve with fresh strawberries and warm maple syrup.

¾ cup buckwheat flour
¾ cup white flour
2 tsp. baking powder
¾ tsp. baking soda
½ tsp. salt
2 tbsp. sugar
3 eggs
1½ cups buttermilk
½ cup butter, melted and cooled

1. Preheat waffle iron.
2. Combine all dry ingredients in a large bowl.
3. Beat eggs, buttermilk and butter together until well combined. Add to the dry ingredients until just blended. The batter will be thick.
4. Cook until the waffle iron stops steaming and waffles are brown and crisp. (An innkeepers secret: if cooking for a crowd, turn your oven on to 150 degrees and place waffles directly onto the rack until you are ready to serve. The waffles will stay crisp!)

Serves 4

Yellowstone River, 1908. Haines Photo.

Chokecherry Syrup

Elaine May

Great over pancakes. Syrup is best served warm.

ripe chokecherries
>Amount will vary according to amount of syrup desired. A gallon of berries yields a quart or less of syrup. Chokecherries ripen after the first fall freeze, typically early to mid-September.

water and sugar

1. Rinse berries and place in large saucepan or stockpot. Fill pan with water until an inch of water covers the berries.
2. Bring to a boil over medium heat. Continue boiling until berries split and water is purple, approximately 20-30 minutes.
3. Strain mixture through colander; discard berry husks. Strain again through cheesecloth to remove fine particles.
4. Add 7-8 cups of sugar (to taste) per gallon of juice
5. Return juice to stovetop. Over low to medium heat, reduce mixture until thickened juice lightly coats the back of a spoon (1-2 hours).

Buttercream Syrup

Golden and buttery. Serve warm over pancakes, waffles, pound cake, fresh fruit or ice cream.

1 cup light corn syrup
2 cups sugar
1 stick butter (½ cup), cut in small chunks
¼ cup water
1 cup evaporated milk

1. Place corn syrup, sugar, butter and water in a medium-sized saucepan over medium heat. Cook and stir constantly until mixture comes to a full boil, about 10 minutes. Boil, stirring constantly, for 3 more minutes.
2. Remove from heat. Let cool 4 minutes. Pour in evaporated milk and stir well to blend. Store unused syrup in a covered container in the refrigerator.

Note: For a nice variation, add 2 tsp. of ground cinnamon to the mixture in step one.

Yield: 2½ cups

Lower Falls

The Lower Falls of the Yellowstone River drop 308 feet, twice as high as Niagara. The volume of water spilling over the falls varies from 63,000 gallons per second at peak runoff to 5,000 gallons per second in autumn.

Grits Soufflé

Joey Woods

This is a very Southern dish, but Yanks like it, too. Serve with fresh fruit salad. Note: Recipe may be easily halved.

   1   quart milk
   1   cup quick-cooking grits
  ½   cup butter
1½   tsp. salt
  ⅛   tsp. cayenne pepper
   3   generous cups shredded Jarlesberg cheese
   6   eggs, well-beaten

1. Preheat oven to 350 degrees.
2. In a large saucepan over medium heat, bring milk just to a boil.
3. Whisk in grits, then reduce heat to a simmer. Stir until mixture thickens into a mush, about 3-4 minutes. Remove pan from heat.
4. Add butter, spices and cheese, beating mixture well with a wooden spoon to thoroughly blend.
5. Add beaten eggs and beat well to incorporate.
6. Pour into well-buttered or sprayed deep 2½-quart casserole dish or soufflé pan. Bake 70 minutes, or until puffed and golden brown. Serve immediately.

Serves 8

Spinach Ham Quiche

Huff House Inn B&B

This tasty quiche is a breakfast favorite at the Huff House. Paired with a crisp, tossed green salad, it also makes a wonderful lunch or light dinner.

   2   10-oz. pkgs. finely chopped frozen spinach, thawed and drained, or 3 cups chopped fresh spinach, rinsed and drained
   2   cups shredded Swiss cheese
   1   lb. chopped, cooked ham
  ½   cup chopped onion
   6   eggs
   2   cups milk
1½   cups Bisquick®
  ¼   tsp. pepper
   1   tsp. salt

1. Spray two quiche pans or two 10-inch pie pans with cooking spray.
2. In a large bowl, beat eggs well. Add milk, Bisquick, pepper and salt. Mix well.

Winter hotel building

..."A misstep to either side plunges the horses floundering into four to a dozen feet of snow, for the only footing is the 6-inch snowpack made by the runner of the freight-laden sleds creeping slowly over it in their long and perilous journey from the railroad station of Gardiner to the site of the new Canyon Hotel by the brink of the famous cataract of the Yellowstone."

—J.H. Raftery, 1912

3. Divide and layer spinach, ham, cheese and onion in the two pans.
4. Pour half of the egg mixture into each pan.
5. Bake in the middle of the oven at 375 degrees for 30 minutes, or until a knife comes out clean.
6. Let cool for 5-10 minutes before serving.

Serves 6-8

Breakfast Casserole

An easy, tasty way to serve a crowd. Pair with fresh fruit salad.

    12   eggs
    1   12-oz. can evaporated milk
    1   tsp. salt
    ½   tsp. pepper
    1   30-oz. pkg. frozen shredded hash browns, thawed
    2   cups shredded cheddar cheese (8 oz.)
    1   large yellow onion, chopped (about 1 cup)
    1   green bell pepper, chopped
    1   cup cooked ham, cut into ½-inch cubes

1. Preheat oven to 350 degrees. Lightly grease or spray with cooking spray a 13x9-inch baking pan. Set aside.
2. In a large bowl, beat eggs until well blended. Mix in the evaporated milk, salt and pepper and stir to blend.
3. Add potatoes, cheese, onion, green pepper and ham. Mix well.
4. Pour mixture into prepared pan. Bake, uncovered until set and a knife inserted in the center comes out clean, about 45 minutes.

Serves 12

Canyon Hotel

Designed by Robert C. Reamer, the "new" Canyon Hotel was built the winter of 1910-1911. The grand building measured a mile in circumference and featured a 200-foot long by 100-foot wide lounge, a 175-foot long by 60-foot wide dining room and a grand Porte-Cochere. Regrettably, it was built on unstable ground. On the east rim opposite the Upper Falls, a series of modern cabins were constructed in 1959 to replace the hotel. After its furnishings were removed, the hotel was sold to a salvage company for $25.

Trumpeter Swan

Poached almost to extinction for their eggs and feathers, these magnificent waterfowl are slowly making a comeback. Numerous pair nest in Jackson Hole. With a wingspan of up to 8-feet, trumpeters are among the largest waterfowl in North America. Their young, called cygnets, hatch covered with soft grey, downy feathers.

Yogurt Poppy Seed Coffee Cake   *Teton Tree House B&B*

Moist and delicious! Sprinkle with powdered sugar before serving.

  1 2-oz. pkg. poppy seeds
  1 cup plain yogurt
  1 cup butter or margarine
1½ cups sugar
  2 cups plus 2 tbsp. flour
  2 tsp. vanilla
  2 tsp. baking soda
  4 eggs, separated

1. Preheat oven to 375 degrees. Grease angel food or bundt cake pan. Set aside.
2. In a small bowl, mix poppy seeds into the yogurt.
3. Cream together butter and sugar in large bowl. Blend in yogurt mixture. Beat egg yolks well and add to batter, stirring to blend. Add vanilla, flour and baking soda and mix well.
4. In a separate bowl, beat egg whites until stiff. Fold into batter.
5. Pour batter in greased pan and bake for 45 minutes. *Do not open the oven* while the cake is baking.

Serves 12-16

Sour Cream Coffee Cake   *Kim McGregor*

Kim inherited this recipe from her great aunt, Ellen Olsen. When Kim's son, Ian, entered it in the Teton County Fair in 1997, it won grand champion honors. It's divine.

Cake
  ½ cup shortening
  ¾ cup sugar
  1 tsp. vanilla
  3 eggs
  2 cups sifted flour
  1 tsp. baking powder
  1 tsp. baking soda
  1 cup sour cream
Filling/topping:
  6 tbsp. butter, softened
  1 cup brown sugar (packed)
  2 tsp. cinnamon
  1 cup chopped nuts

1. Preheat oven to 350 degrees.

2. Make filling. In a small bowl, cream the butter, brown sugar and cinnamon together until smooth, then add nuts. Set aside.
3. In a large bowl, cream the shortening, sugar and vanilla together. Add eggs singly, beating well after each addition.
4. Sift flour, baking powder and baking soda together in a separate bowl. Add to creamed mixture alternately with sour cream.
5. Spread half of batter in a well-greased 10-inch tube or bundt pan. Sprinkle half of filling mixture over batter in pan, then cover with remaining cake batter. Sprinkle remaining filling mixture over top.
6. Bake for approximately 50 minutes, or until a toothpick inserted into the cake comes out clean. May be served warm or cold.

Serves 16

Nutty Coconut Brunch Cake   *Huff House Inn B&B*

Moist, rich and altogether heavenly.

Cake
    4   eggs
    2   cups sugar
    3   cups all-purpose flour
    1   cup salad oil
    2   tsp. vanilla
    ½   tsp. each of baking soda, baking powder and salt
    1   cup buttermilk
    1   cup each of coconut and chopped nuts
Glaze
    ½   cup water
    1   cup sugar
    2   tbsp. butter

1. Preheat oven to 325 degrees. Grease 10-inch tube pan and set aside.
2. In large bowl, beat eggs until thick and lemon-colored. Add sugar, oil and vanilla to the beaten eggs and blend mixture well.
3. In a different bowl, sift together the flour, baking soda, baking powder and salt.
4. Add sifted dry ingredients alternately with buttermilk to the egg mixture, then fold in coconut and nuts.
5. Pour mixture into the greased tube pan. Bake for approx. 1 hour.
6. Shortly before removing the cake from the oven, combine glaze ingredients in saucepan and bring to a full boil.
7. Remove cake from oven and pour glaze mixture over it. Let the cake sit in the pan for four hours before cutting.

Serves 10-12

Wild Rose

This fragrant, five-petaled wildflower blooms in Jackson Hole from late May through July. When the petals fall at the end of the bloom, rose hips, the fruit of the plant, form and remain on the shrub through the winter. The fruit is loaded with vitamin C and is an important food source for birds and hoofed browsers.

Sifting

When a recipe calls for sifting, it is easier and works just as well to place the dry ingredients together in a mixing bowl and stir vigorously with a wire whisk.

Chocolate Chip Coffee Cake *Teton Tree House B&B*

Chocolate for breakfast. What a great idea.

½ cup butter or margarine, softened
¾ cup sugar
2 eggs
2 cups flour
1 tbsp. baking powder
½ tsp. salt
1 cup milk
1 tsp. vanilla
1 cup miniature chocolate chips
½ cup chopped walnuts
1 tbsp. sugar

1. Cream butter and sugar together in a large bowl. Add eggs to mixture and blend together.
2. In a separate bowl, sift together flour, baking powder and salt. Stir flour mixture into butter and sugar mixture, blending well. Fold chocolate chips into batter.
3. Pour into greased 8-inch square pan or round layer cake pan. Sprinkle with walnuts and one tablespoon of sugar.
4. Bake in a 350 degree oven for 60-70 minutes, or until toothpick inserted into the middle of the cake comes out clean.

Serves 8

Cream Cheese Coffee Cake *Teton Tree House B & B*

As good as it sounds.

Cake
¼ cup butter, softened
1 8-oz pkg. cream cheese, slightly softened
1½ cup sugar
2 eggs
2 cups flour
2 tsp. baking powder
½ tsp. salt
1 tsp. baking soda
½ cup milk
1 tsp. vanilla

Topping
¼ cup butter
¼ cup flour
1 cup brown sugar

1. Cream butter, cream cheese and sugar together in a large bowl. Add eggs, milk and vanilla. Mix well.
2. In a separate bowl, combine flour, baking powder, baking soda and salt.
3. Mix about a third of the dry ingredients at a time into the moist batter, blending well after each addition.
4. Pour batter into a greased, 8-inch square pan or a round layer cake pan.
5. In a small bowl, mix topping ingredients together with hands or a pastry cutter until coarse and crumbly. Sprinkle topping mixture over batter. Bake in a 350 degree oven for 20-25 minutes, or until knife inserted in center comes out clean.

Serves 9

Taggart Lake

Nestled at the base of the Tetons, the still waters of Taggart Lake often create a mirror image of the Grand. Ferdinand Hayden named the lake after W. Rush Taggart, the assistant geologist on his 1872 expedition to this area.

Maple Nut Danish   *Charles Wheeler*

A bit complicated, but worth every scrumptious bite. This recipe earned 12-year-old Charles grand champion honors at the 2002 Teton County Fair. It is from his mother Terri's collection.

Filling
   ½ cup sugar
   1 tbsp. cinnamon
   1 tsp. maple flavoring
   ½ cup chopped nuts of your choice
Dough
   1 pkg. Pillsbury® hot roll mix
   3 tbsp. sugar
   1 tsp. maple flavoring
Glaze
   1½ cups powdered sugar
   1 tsp. maple flavoring
   3-4 tbsp. milk

1. Combine filling ingredients in a small bowl, stirring to blend. Set aside.
2. Prepare hot roll dough as directed on the package, adding the maple flavor to liquid ingredients and the sugar to the dry ingredients before mixing.
2. Divide prepared dough into 3 equal balls. Roll out each ball to fit the bottom of a lightly greased round pizza pan.
3. Place the first round of dough on the pan and lightly brush with melted butter or soft margarine. Sprinkle evenly with ⅓ of the filling. Repeat twice, ending with the last ⅓ of the filling mixture on top.
4. Twist a 2-inch diamter glass into the center of the pan to create a

The Bar BC was the second dude ranch in Jackson Hole. Owners Struthers Burt and Horace Carncross hosted their first guests the summer of 1912. In its heyday in the 1920s and 1930s, the Bar BC was a major employer in the valley. Forty-five buildings covered the 577-acre ranch, including dance and recreation halls, a rodeo ground, swimming pool, fish hatchery and water powered electric generating system. The ranch had its own airstrip and fleet of touring cars. When the last direct heir died in 1988, the property reverted to Grand Teton National Park.

circle. Leave the glass in place. Cut through the layers of dough to form 16 equal, pie shaped pieces. Twist each piece 3 or 4 times. Let dough rise, covered, at room temperature until doubled in size. Remove glass.

5. Preheat oven to 375 degrees. Bake rolls for 20 minutes. Remove from oven and set on a wire rack to cool.

6. Mix glaze ingredients together, adding milk a tbsp. at a time until desired consistency is attained. Drizzle glaze over danish while still warm. Serve danish warm or cold.

Yield: 16 danish

Chocolate Chip Orange Muffins — *Chef Karen Norby*

Chocolate and orange is a classic taste combination used to advantage in these flavorful muffins. They are perfect for a special breakfast treat, tea, or a mid-morning coffee break. Don't expect these to last long!

    2¼ cups all-purpose flour
     2 tsp. baking powder
     ½ tsp. baking soda
     ¼ tsp. salt
     3 tbsp. chocolate chips
     ¾ cup sugar (reserve 1 tbs. for topping)
     ⅔ cup plain nonfat yogurt
     1 tbsp. grated orange peel
     ⅔ cup orange juice (reserve 3 tbsp. for topping)
     1 large egg and 1 egg white
     3 tbsp. vegetable oil
    1½ tsp. vanilla

Remains of the Bar BC main lodge.

1. Preheat oven to 350 degrees. Spray a 12-cup muffin tin with cooking spray or line with paper baking cups.
2. In a large bowl, stir together flour, baking powder, baking soda and salt. Add chocolate chips, mixing well.
3. In a medium bowl, whisk together sugar, yogurt, orange peel, orange juice, the egg and egg white, oil and vanilla.
4. Add wet mixture to the dry ingredients and mix until blended. Spoon evenly into muffin cups, filling each almost to the top.
5. Bake 20-25 minutes or until golden brown. Turn out of pan onto a cooling rack.
6. In a shallow bowl, combine reserved juice and sugar. Dip tops of warm muffins into mixture. Dribble any remaining mixture in bowl over muffins. Serve warm.

Yield: 12 muffins

Bar BC boots

Cherry Yogurt Muffins

Teton Tree House B&B

Yogurt enhances the flavor of the cherries in these moist muffins. Yum.

1 cup rolled oats
1 cup plain yogurt
½ cup vegetable oil
¾ cup brown sugar, firmly packed
1 egg
1 cup all-purpose flour
1 tsp. salt
½ tsp. baking soda
1 tsp. baking powder
1 cup chopped frozen cherries
  (or blueberries, cranberries of huckleberries:
  tart berries are best)

1. Preheat oven to 375 degrees. Grease muffin tin or line with paper cups.
2. Soak oats in yogurt for 10 minutes. Add oil, brown sugar and egg. Beat well.
3. Sift in flour, salt, baking soda and baking powder. Before stirring, sprinkle cherries over batter. Stir to blend.
4. Fill muffin cups two-thirds full. Bake for 20 minutes or until muffins are browned and spring back lightly when touched.

Yield: 12 muffins

The Sound of Music

The New York Philharmonic performed four concerts during Grand Teton Music Festival's 1989 summer season. The concerts marked the first summer residency in the Philharmonic's history.

Tender muffins

The secret to perfect, tender muffins is in the lumps. Muffin batter should be gently stirred only until all the dry ingredients are moistened. Resist the temptation to vigorously stir muffin batter until it is smooth. The lumps will disappear during baking. Overstirring creates tough muffins with pointed tops.

Huckleberry Muffins

Marie Ana Deland

Marie's recipe enthralled the judges' tastebuds at the 2002 Teton County Fair, earning her grand champion honors. The perfect way to use summer's bounty!

- 1¼ cups oil
- 1¼ cups sugar
- ½ tsp. vanilla
- 3 eggs
- 4 cups flour
- 1¾ tbsp. baking powder
- 1½ cup milk
- 1 cup huckleberries
- cinnamon sugar

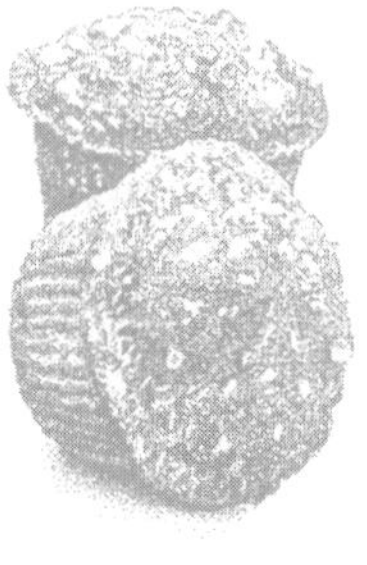

1. Preheat oven to 350 degrees.
2. In a large mixing bowl, mix together oil and sugar until well blended. Add eggs, one at a time, mixing well after each addition.
3. Sift dry ingredients together in a separate bowl. Add dry ingredients alternately with the milk to the oil and sugar mixture.
4. Gently fold huckleberries into the muffin batter.
5. Spoon batter into greased or paper-lined muffin cups until cups are approximately two-thirds full. Generously sprinkle with cinnamon sugar.
6. Bake for 14-16 minutes, or until muffins are lightly browned and tops spring back when gently touched. Let muffins sit for 1 minute in pan, then remove from pan and cool completely on racks.

Yield: 12 muffins

Cinnamon Sugar Muffins

Alta Fischer

Terrific for breakfast or coffee breaks. Their enticing aroma will draw whomever is in your house to the kitchen.

Muffins

- 5 tbsp. butter
- ½ cup sugar
- 1 egg, beaten
- 1½ cups flour
- 2¼ tsp. baking powder
- ¼ tsp. salt
- ⅛-¼ tsp. nutmeg
- ½ cup milk

Cinnamon topping
    6   tbsp. butter, melted
    ¾   cup sugar
    2   tsp. cinnamon

1. Preheat oven to 350 degrees. Paper line or grease small muffin cups. Set aside.
2. Cream together butter and sugar in a large mixing bowl. Pour in the beaten egg and stir to blend.
3. In a separate bowl, sift together the flour, baking powder, salt and nutmeg. Add dry ingredients alternately with milk to the butter mixture, stirring well after each addition.
4. Fill muffin cups half full. Bake 20-25 minutes, or until tops are golden and muffin tops spring back when touched.
5. While the muffins are baking, make topping. Place melted butter in a shallow bowl. In a separate shallow bowl, mix together the sugar and cinnamon. When muffins are done, remove from tin and roll top in melted butter, then dip in cinnamon sugar mixture. Serve warm or cold.
    Note: If using standard muffin tins, fill each cup with approximately 1 tbsp. of batter and proceed as directed.

Yield: 18 small muffins.

Blueberry Bran Muffins *Mary Howley, R.D.*

This yummy recipe has been popular in Mary's nutrition classes. The tasty results are sweetened with date puree and molasses instead of refined sugar.

    2   cups whole wheat flour
    2   tsp. baking powder
    1   tsp. sea salt
    3   cups bran flake cereal, crushed
    6   tbsp. canola oil
    ¼   cup date puree (see recipe, next page)
    ¼   cup blackstrap molasses
    2   organic eggs
    2   cups vanilla soy milk (or equal amount regular milk plus 1 tsp. of vanilla extract)
    1   cup water
    1   cup fresh or frozen blueberries, thawed

1. Preheat oven to 375 degrees.
2. In a large mixing bowl, combine all ingredients except blueberries, stirring well to blend. Gently fold in blueberries.

Doe and fawn

Mule deer in Jackson Hole drop their young in June and July, following a gestation period of about seven months. The spotted fawns are able to walk only minutes after being born.

Wyethia

Commonly known as mule's ears for its green leaves of similar shape, this bright yellow wild-flower blooms from late May to early July on the valley floor. Its genus name recognizes Capt. Nathaniel Wyeth, a fur trader who established Fort Hall near Pocatello. Fort Hall was the first American fort and fur trading post in the North-west.

3. Spoon batter into lightly oiled or paper lined muffin tins until cups are about two-thirds full. Bake 15-20 minutes, or until a toothpick inserted in the center of a muffin comes out clean.

Yield: 17-18 muffins

Date Puree

Mary Howley, R.D.

Instead of sugar and fat in baked goods, Mary uses date puree. She replaces brown sugar with equal amounts of puree and replaces up to 25% of the fat with the same mixture, depending on the desired texture of the item she is preparing. Experiment! This tasty puree is also great spread on toast or crackers.

    1   pkg. whole, pitted dates
        water

1. Placed dates in a small to medium-sized saucepan and add enough water to cover.
2. Bring water to a boil over medium heat, then remove pan from burner and let dates sit, uncovered, for 10 minutes.
3. Using a slotted spoon, remove dates from pan and place in a food processor or blender. Add just enough water so the dates will form a puree when pulsed. Pulse until mixture forms a smooth paste. Store in an tightly lidded container in the refrigerator.

Yield: Approx. 1½ cups

Oatmeal Date Nut Muffins

Fragrant, award-winning muffins.

    1¼ cups flour
    ⅓ cup sugar
    1 tbsp. baking powder
    1 tsp. salt
    1 cup regular rolled oats, uncooked
    ½ cup chopped, pitted dates
    ¼ cup nuts, chopped
    1 egg
    1 cup whole milk
    ⅓ cup butter, melted

1. Preheat oven to 400 degrees. Grease or paper line 12 standard muffin cups. Set aside.

2. In a large bowl, mix together the flour, sugar, baking powder and salt until well blended. Stir in the oats and chopped dates.
3. In a separate bowl, beat the egg. Add milk and melted butter and whisk until well blended.
4. Add egg mixture to flour mixture. Stir only until ingredients are moistened. *Don't overmix: the batter will be lumpy.*
5. Divide batter evenly between the 12 cups. Bake on a rack in the middle of the oven for 20-25 minutes, or until muffins are browned and spring back when lightly touched. Remove muffins from pan. Serve immediately. These are wonderful with orange butter.

Espresso Chip Muffins with Mocha Cream

Your morning buzz in a muffin!

Muffins
- 2 cups flour
- ¾ cup sugar
- 2½ tsp. baking powder
- 1 tsp. cinnamon
- ½ tsp. salt
- 1 cup milk
- 2 tbsp. instant coffee granules
- ½ cup butter, melted
- 1 egg, beaten
- 1 tsp. vanilla
- ¾ cup mini chocolate chips

Mocha Cream
- 4 ozs. cream cheese, softened
- 1 tbsp. sugar
- ½ tsp. instant coffee granules
- ½ tsp. vanilla
- ¼ cup mini chocolate chips

1. Place cream ingredients in a blender, cover, and beat until blended. Place cream in a covered container and refrigerate until ready to serve.
2. Preheat oven to 375 degrees. Grease or line muffin cups with paper.
3. Combine flour, sugar, baking powder, cinnamon and salt in a large bowl. Stir until well blended.
4. In a separate bowl, whisk together milk and coffee until coffee granules are dissolved. Add melted butter, beaten egg and vanilla and whisk until blended.
5. Pour milk mixture into dry ingredients and stir just until all ingredients are moistened. *Do not overmix!* Gently fold in chocolate chips.
6. Fill muffin cups approximately two-thirds full. Bake on a rack in

Removing muffins

If muffins are sticking in their cups, place a wet towel beneath the hot tin for 30 seconds and they will lift out easily.

the middle of the oven until muffins spring back when lightly touched, about 15-18 minutes. Cool 5 minutes then remove muffins from pan and finish cooling of a rack. Serve warm with chilled mocha cream.

Yield: 12-14 muffins

Pumpkin Spice Muffins *Therese Metherell, R.D.*

Yum...pumpkin. With convenient canned pumpkin, these great "harvest" muffins can be enjoyed year-round. Therese shared this recipe in her "Sound Bites" column in the *Jackson Hole News* in October, 2001.

1	cup flour
½	cup whole wheat flour
½	cup wheat bran
2	tsp. baking powder
2	tsp. pumpkin pie spice
1	tsp. baking soda
½	tsp. salt
1	cup solid pack pumpkin (not pumpkin pie filling!)
½	cup grated carrots
½	cup buttermilk
½	cup honey
2	egg whites
1	tsp. vanilla
1	tsp. grated orange zest
½	cup chopped walnuts

1. Preheat oven to 375 degrees. Spray a 12-cup muffin tin with cooking spray and set aside.
2. In a large bowl, mix flours, bran, baking powder, pumpkin pie spice, baking soda and salt together. Set aside.
3. In a medium-sized bowl, whisk together the pumpkin, carrots, buttermilk, honey, butter, egg whites, vanilla and orange zest until well blended.
4. Add pumpkin mixture to the dry ingredients and stir until just moistened. *Don't overmix!* Batter will be thick. Gently fold in walnuts.
5. Divide batter evenly into 12 muffin cups. Bake for 20 minutes or until a toothpick inserted into center comes out clean. Remove muffins from pan and cool on rack.

Yield: 12 muffins

Bison calf

Reddish-brown bison calves spot the valley floor of Jackson Hole by mid-May. A single calf is typically 40 pounds at birth; two calves around 28 pounds. They lose their reddish color after shedding their first coat of hair at three months of age. The calves grow quickly—a necessity to survive Jackson's long, cold winters.

Raspberry Almond Streusel Muffins

With a creamy center and streusel topping, these muffins will remind you of a decadent pastry. They're fabulous.

Muffin
- 1¾ cups flour
- ½ cup + 1 tbsp. sugar
- ½ tsp. each baking powder and baking soda
- ¼ tsp. salt
- ½ cup cold, firm butter
- 1 egg
- ¾ cup sour cream
- 1 tsp. almond extract

Muffin filling
- 1 8-oz. pkg. cream cheese, softened
- 1 egg
- ¼ cup sugar
- ½ tsp. vanilla extract
- ¾ cup raspberry jam, warmed

Streusel topping
- ⅓ cup flour
- 2 tbsp. sugar
- 2 tbsp. cold, firm butter
- ⅓ cup sliced almonds, chopped

1. Preheat oven to 350 degrees. Spray a total of 14 muffin tin cups with cooking oil and set aside.
2. Make filling. In a small bowl, combine the cream cheese, egg, sugar and vanilla. Beat with a mixer until smooth and creamy. Set aside.
3. Make streusel topping. In a separate small bowl, mix together the flour and sugar. Cut in the cold butter with a pastry cutter or two forks until topping is crumbly. Stir in chopped almonds. Set aside.
4. Make muffin batter. In a large bowl, combine the flour, sugar, baking powder, baking soda and salt. Cut in the cold butter with a pastry cutter or two forks until the mixture looks like coarse crumbs. -In a separate bowl, whisk the egg, sour cream and almond extract together until smooth. Add to the flour mixture, stirring until just moistened. *Don't overmix!* Batter will be thick.
5. Fill the 14 greased muffin cups half full of batter. Divide filling mixture and raspberry preserves evenly on top of the batter, and swirl gently with a knife. Cover filling with remaining batter and top with streusel. Bake 20-25 minutes or until a toothpick inserted into the center of a muffin comes out clean. Cool muffins for 5 minutes, then remove from pan and cool completely on a rack.

Yield: 14 muffins

Grand Prismatic Spring

Measuring 250 by 380 feet, Grand Prismatic Spring is the largest hot spring in Yellowstone. The colorful spring discharges over 500 gallons of water a minute. It was named by members of the 1872 Hayden Expedition.

Rhubarb Muffins

Huff House Inn B&B

Cinnamon sugar topping makes these muffins especially delicious.

Muffins
- 2½ cups flour
- 1½ cups brown sugar, firmly packed
- 1 tsp. each of salt, baking soda and cinnamon
- 1 egg, lightly beaten
- 1 cup buttermilk
- ⅔ cup vegetable oil
- 1 tsp. vanilla extract
- 2 cups rhubarb, finely chopped

Topping
- ½ cup sugar
- 2 tbsp. butter, melted
- 2 tsp. cinnamon

1. Preheat oven to 375 degrees. Lightly grease or spray with cooking oil two 12-well muffin tins. Set aside.
2. In a small bowl, mix the sugar, cinnamon and melted butter together. Set aside.
3. In a large bowl, combine the flour, sugar, salt, baking soda and cinnamon. In a separate bowl, whisk together the egg, buttermilk, vegetable oil and vanilla extract until well blended. Add the rhubarb and stir to mix.
4. Add the wet ingredients to the dry ingredients, stirring until just moistened. Fill muffin cups about two-thirds full. Sprinkle topping evenly on top of batter. Bake for 16-18 minutes, or until a toothpick inserted into the center comes out clean. Cool muffins 5 minutes, then remove from pan and cool completely on a rack.

Yield: Approx. 2 dozen

Scottish Oat Scones

Jo Gathercole

These are wonderful served warm with coffee and tea, or a glass of icy cold milk. The recipe originated from the sheepherders of Scotland, who mixed ingredients by hand in one pot. The tasty results were a popular item when Jo owned Grateful Bread, a wholesale bakery still operating under different ownership

- 2 lb. butter (nothing but!)
- ¾ cup honey
- 1 cup milk
- 3 eggs

        3   tbsp. baking powder
     3¾   cups all-purpose flour
        5   cups regular oats
     1½   cups berries, nuts or chocolate chips (your choice)

1. Preheat oven to 325 degrees
2. Cream butter and honey together. Add milk, eggs and baking pow-
    der and blend until well mixed. Add flour and mix well again.
3. Gently fold in oats, adding berries, nuts, etc. at the same time.
    Take care not to mash the oats.
4. Using your hand, scoop a portion into your palm, pulling the mix
    toward the side of the bowl. The scone will be somewhat oblong.
    Place scones in lightly oiled pan.
5. Bake until golden brown, approximately 15 minutes. The scones
    should be firm to the touch.

Yield: Approximately 16 pieces (depends on your hand-size)

Mango Macadamia Nut Bread   *Wyatt Beard*

People who have traveled to Hawaii often come back yearning for a
taste of the tropical fruits and nuts enjoyed on the islands. This recipe
fits the bill perfectly. It earned eight-year-old Wyatt a blue ribbon at
the 2002 Teton County Fair.

        2   cups all-purpose flour
        1   tsp. baking soda
     ½   tsp. ground cinnamon
     ½   cup vegetable oil
        2   cups finely chopped mango
     1½   cups sugar
     ½   tsp. salt
        3   eggs
        1   tsp. vanilla
     ½   cup chopped macadamia nuts

1. Preheat oven to 350 degrees. Grease two 8 ½ x 4 ½-inch loaf pans.
    Set aside.
2. In a large bowl, combine the flour, sugar, baking soda, salt and
    cinnamon. In a separate bowl, beat eggs, oil and vanilla together
    until well blended. Stir into dry ingredients until just moistened.
    Fold in mangoes and nuts. Batter will be stiff.
3. Spoon batter into prepared pans. Bake 50-55 minutes, or until tooth-
    pick inserted near the center comes out clean. Cool for 10 minutes
    before removing from pans to cool completely on a wire rack.

Yield: 2 loaves

Mangoes

Mangoes are most fla-
vorful when eaten soft.
To completely ripen,
keep at room tempera-
ture in a paper bag. Use
ripe mangoes as soon
as possible. Because
mangoes imported from
foreign countries are of-
ten sprayed with pesti-
cides banned in the US
for their known cancer
causing agents, pur-
chase mangoes from
Hawaii or Florida, where
pesticide use is regu-
lated.

Best Banana Blueberry Bread   *Martha MacEachern*

Martha likes recipes that are easy to prepare and produce great results. This one definitely qualifies!

- ½   cup blueberries
- 1½ cups flour, divided
- ⅔   cup sugar
- 1¾ tsp. baking powder
- ½   cup uncooked oats
- 2   eggs
- ½   tsp. salt
- ⅓   cup oil
- 1   cup bananas, mashed (about 3)

1. Preheat oven to 350 degrees. Grease one loaf pan and set aside.
2. In a small bowl, sprinkle blueberries with 2 tsp. of flour, stirring gently to mix. Set aside.
3. In a large bowl, sift together the remaining flour, sugar, salt and baking powder. Stir in oats.
4. In a separate bowl, combine the eggs, oil and mashed bananas until well blended. Add banana mixture to dry ingredients, stirring until just combined. Gently fold in blueberries.
6. Pour into prepared loaf pan and bake 1 hour, or until toothpick inserted into the center comes out clean. Remove from oven and let cool completely on a wire rack before removing bread from pan. Bread is best if wrapped and stored in the refrigerator 24 hours before slicing. It can be frozen.

Yield: 1 loaf

Peanut Butter Bread   *Happy Weston*

This makes a delicious breakfast bread. It is particularly good served warm from the toaster and topped with jam or honey.

- 2¼ cup flour
- 4   tsp. baking powder
- ½   tsp. salt
- ¾   cup creamy peanut butter
- ½   cup sugar
- 1   tsp. vanilla extract
- 1¾ cup milk

1. Preheat oven to 350 degrees. Grease a 9x5-inch loaf pan. Set aside.
2. In a mixing bowl, sift together the flour, baking powder and salt.
3. In a separate, large mixing bowl beat the peanut butter, sugar and

vanilla extract together. Gradually add the milk, beating until well blended.
4. Add flour mixture and beat until smooth. Pour into prepared pan.
5. Bake 1 hour, or until a toothpick inserted into the middle comes out clean. Cool 15 minutes, then remove from pan and continue cooling on a wire rack.

Yield: 1 loaf

Glazed Apple Nut Bread

Lucey Carissa

Red-tailed Hawk

This moist, flavorful quick bread earned 16-year-old Carissa a blue ribbon at the 2002 Teton County Fair.

Bread
- 1 cup butter
- 2 cups sugar
- 3 eggs
- 1 tbsp. cinnamon
- 2 tsp. vanilla
- 3 medium apples, finely chopped (Granny Smith or other tart baking apples are preferred)
- 2 cups walnuts, chopped
- 1½ tsp. baking soda
- ½ tsp. salt
- 1 cup unbleached flour

Glaze
- ¼ cup milk
- 1 tsp. vanilla extract
- 2 cups powdered sugar

1. Preheat oven to 325 degrees. Oil then line three loaf pans with parchment or waxed paper. Set aside.
2. In a large bowl, cream butter, sugar and eggs together until light and fluffy. Add cinnamon, vanilla, apples and walnuts. Stir well to blend. Set aside.
3. In a separate bowl, sift together the flour, baking soda and salt. Add flour mixture in batches to the wet batter, stirring well to incorporate. Batter will be very stiff.
4. Pour batter into three prepared pans. Bake 1 hour, or until a toothpick inserted in the center of a loaf comes out clean. Cool slightly then remove loaves from pans and cool completely on wire racks.
7. While loaves are cooling, whisk together glaze ingredients until light and smooth. Pour glaze over loaves while they are still warm.

Yield: Makes 3 loaves

This large, soaring hawk is found throughout Jackson Hole. Red-tails prey primarily on small rodents, but have also been known to eat birds, reptiles, insects and even carrion. Red-tails often choose the tops of dead trees to perch and look for prey. Perched, they look thick and short-tailed.

Mount Moran

This 12,605-foot peak is one of the most recognizable mountains in Jackson Hole. Its large summit is capped by Flathead sandstone, a vestige of the sedimentary rock that buried the valley floor before the Tetons were uplifted. The peak bears the name of Thomas Moran, a landscape artist on the 1870 Washburn Doane Expedition to Yellowstone. Moran's paintings helped persuade Congress to designate Yellowstone a national park. Ironically, he never travelled through Jackson Hole.

Zucchini Bread with Gingered Cream Cheese
Teton Tree House B&B

Moist and spicy. Wonderful warm, spread with a schmear of gingered cream cheese. Serve in lieu of toast.

      3   eggs
      1   cup vegetable oil
      2   cups brown sugar
      2   cups grated zucchini with juice
      1   cup chopped walnuts
      3   cups whole wheat flour
      1   tsp. salt
      1   tsp. baking soda
      1   tsp. ginger
    1½   tsp. baking powder
      1   tsp. cinnamon
      1   tsp. cloves

1. Preheat oven to 350 degrees.
2. Mix eggs, oil, sugar, zucchini and vanilla in a large mixing bowl.
2. In a separate bowl, mix the flour, salt, baking soda, baking powder and spices.
3. Add roughly a third of the dry ingredients at a time to the zucchini mixture, blending well after each addition.
4. Pour batter in one large or two smaller well-greased loaf pans. Bake for approximately 40 minutes, less if two small pans are used. Bread is done when a toothpick inserted into the middle of the loaf comes out clean.

Gingered Cream Cheese

      1   3-oz. pkg. of cream cheese, softened
      2   tsp. gingerroot, peeled and minced fine

1. In a small bowl, blend the softened cream cheese and gingerroot.
2. Chill for 30 minutes to blend flavor.

Yield: 1 large or 2 smaller loaves.

Bishops Bread
Lois Ruosch

A traditional holiday bread, rich with chocolate, nuts and fruit.

    2½   cups unsifted flour
      3   tsp. baking powder
      ½   tsp. salt

    1   6-oz. pkg. milk chocolate chips
    2   cups chopped nuts
    ¾   cup currants
    ¾   cup raisins
    4   eggs
  1¼   cups sugar
    6   tbsp. oil
    ¼   tsp. vanilla

1. Mix the flour, baking powder, salt, chocolate chips, fruit and nuts together. Set aside.
2. In a separate bowl, beat the eggs well, then add oil, sugar and vanilla. Blend well.
3. Add wet ingredients to the dry ingredients. Mix well.
4. Pour into a greased loaf pan. Bake for 1 hour and 30 minutes in a 300-degree oven. Let cool before removing from pan. Sift powdered sugar over the top, if desired, before slicing.

Yield: 1 loaf

Amish Friendship Bread   *Teton Tree House B&B*

This is one of Teton Tree House's most requested recipes. It takes fore-thought and planning to prepare the starter, but the results are worth it!

Starter ingredients
    1   cup sugar
    1   cup flour
    1   cup milk
Bread ingredients
    1   cup starter ***
    ⅔   cup oil
    1   cup sugar
    3   eggs
    1   tsp. vanilla
    ½   tsp. baking soda
    2   cups flour
  1¼   tsp. baking powder
    1   tsp. cinnamon
    ½   tsp. salt
    1   large box instant vanilla pudding
    1   cup chopped or sliced almonds

1. Combine starter ingredients. Stir with wooden spoon and leave in a covered plastic container on your kitchen counter. (Don't use metal spoon and don't refrigerate!) Stir once a day for a week. Your starter is now ready.

Ouch!

The February 18, 2002, issue of USA Today noted that the median cost of a home in Jackson Hole is $625,000.

2. To make the bread, preheat oven to 350 degrees.
3. Combine 1 cup starter, oil, sugar, eggs and vanilla in a large bowl. Mix well. Add baking soda, flour, baking powder, cinnamon, pudding mix and almonds. Mix well again.
4. Pour into a greased and floured loaf pan and bake in 350 degree oven until the top is golden brown and bread springs back when gently touched, approximately 40-45 minutes. Serve warm or cold.

***After making bread, replenish your starter by adding 1 cup sugar, 1 cup flour and 1 cup milk to existing starter. Store mixture on your counter or in your cupboard, stirring occasionally. *Do not refrigerate!*

Yield: 1 loaf

Dr. MacLeod, 1958

When Dr. Charles Huff, the valley's only physician, died in 1937, Dr. Don MacLeod was asked by Jackson hunting friend Emil Feuz to take his place. MacLeod, a young doctor practicing in Sheridan, travelled to the valley and quickly found a home and office. He returned to Sheridan and loaded the family car with his wife, sister-in-law, two kids, a dog and a bird and drove to Jackson. The entourage arrived on Halloween night. Dr. MacLeod practiced in the valley for many years and called Jackson Hole home for the remainder of his life. A lake in the Gros Ventre Range is named in his honor.

Glazed Lemon Pecan Bread
Sue Enger

"This is a Minneapolis, friend-of-mother's type recipe."

    1   cup sugar
    ½   cup butter or margarine
    2   eggs
    1   lemon (juice and rind)
    1½ cups flour
    1   tsp. baking powder
    ½   tsp. salt
    ½   cup milk
    ½   cup chopped pecans

  Glaze
    ⅓   cup sugar
        juice of one lemon

1. In a large bowl, cream butter and sugar together. Add eggs and mix well. Add rind and juice of lemon and blend well again.
2. In a separate bowl, sift together the flour, baking powder and salt.
3. Alternately add portions of the dry ingredients and portions of milk to the lemon mixture, mixing well after each addition. Add chopped nuts to batter.
4. Bake in 350 degree oven in a loaf pan lined with wax paper for 1 hour, or until bread is a golden brown and a toothpick inserted into the middle comes out clean.
5. Shortly before bread is done, mix glaze ingredients together well to dissolve the sugar.
6. Remove bread from oven and pour glaze over it. Cool in pan 15 minutes before removing.

Yield: 1 loaf

Cranberry Orange Raisin Bread

Jean Jorgensen

This makes a wonderful holiday gift...and you can keep one loaf for yourself!

Orange mixture
- 2   tbsp. butter
- 1   beaten egg
       juice and rind of one orange
       water

Bread ingredients
- 2   cups flour
- 1   cup sugar
- 1½   tsp. baking powder
- ½   tsp. baking soda
- ½   tsp. salt
- 1   cup chopped nuts
- 1   cup chopped, fresh cranberries
- 1   cup raisins

1. Make the orange mixture. To the juice and rind of one orange add 2 tbsp. of butter and enough boiling water to make ¾ cup of liquid. Cool mixture in a small mixing bowl, then add one beaten egg. Set aside.
2. In a large bowl, combine the bread ingredients and mix well.
3. Add the orange liquid to the dry mixture and blend thoroughly.
4. Pour into two greased and floured loaf pans. Bake in a 325 degree oven until golden brown and a toothpick inserted into the middle comes out clean, about 1 hour.

Yield: 2 loaves

The seeds for Jackson's first hospital were planted in a barroom conversation the summer of 1915. Episcopal Rev. Royal Balcomb had joined friends for a drink, and talk eventually turned to the valley's beloved and overworked doctor, Charles Huff. Balcomb said the good doctor needed a hospital. The conversation soon included all the establishment's patrons, and everyone at the bar began to dig in their pockets for donations. One of the men agreed to give a lot for the building if an adjoining lot was purchased for $87.50. Sold! This happened on a Friday night. Monday morning Jackson residents started to cut logs up Cache Creek for the building. The four-room hospital was completed and opened for business in 1916.

String Lake, 1934

Barely 10 feet deep and just over a football field in width, shallow String Lake connects Jenny Lake to the south with Leigh Lake to the north. String Lake is believed to be an old river channel.

Sourdough Baking

Sourdough bread rises by the addition of a starter that contains natural fermentation—a product used hundreds of years before packaged yeast was sold in markets. Not all sourdough tastes sour. (The recipe for Amish Friendship Bread on page 33 is a great example of sweet tasting "sour" dough.) Jedediah's Original House of Sourdough in Jackson Hole specializes in sourdough baking. The recipes that follow use their starter, a living organism over 100 years old. It is available for purchase locally or through mail order. If you'd like to make your own starter, follow recipe instructions below.

Sourdough Starter

> 2 cups warm water
> 2 cups unbleached flour

1. Blend ingredients together with a wooden spoon.
2. Pour into a wide-mouth glass jar with a rubber and wire seal. A loosely lidded small pottery crock or plastic container made by Rubbermaid™ or Tupperware™ are also okay. Do not use a metal container, enamelware or unglazed stoneware.
3. Place starter in a warm place (your kitchen counter is fine). Every 24 hours, feed your starter by discarding half of it and adding a half cup each of flour and water. Stir well after each new addition.
4. Repeat once a day until the mixture develops frothy bubbles on top and has a sour smell. This typically occurs within 3-4 days to a week. Your starter is now ready.
5. Pour out the amount the recipe calls for and set aside. Replenish your starter by adding equal amounts of flour and water.

Starter regeneration and care

Regeneration varies with the temperature at which it is stored and how much of the starter is used. If half has been used, it will take 24 hours to regenerate at room temperature. If you plan to use your starter daily, keep it at room temperature. If you wish to use it once a week or so, store your replenished starter, covered, in the refrigerator. If you seldom use it, be sure to feed it once a month by pouring out half of the starter and adding new flour and water. Remember to allow room for expansion!

Starter often separates, and a dark liquid called "hooch" rises to the top. Simply stir it back in the starter.

French Bread

Jedediah's Original House of Sourdough

Yeast

The shelf life of yeast is extended if the packet is kept refrigerated. Bring to room temperature before using.

Wonderful! This sourdough recipe, used with permission, is included in Jedediah's *The Artistry of Sourdough Cooking* cookbook.

Yeast mixture (optional)
- 1 cup warm water
- 1 tsp. sugar
- 1 pkg. dry yeast

Bread ingredients
- 2 cups sourdough starter
- ¼ cup sugar
- ¼ cup salad oil
- 2 tsp. salt
- 6 cups flour, divided

1. Combine yeast mixture ingredients in a small bowl and set aside. (Note: Sourdough provides all the levitation necessary, but Jedediah's recommends novice sourdough bakers include yeast.)
2. In a large bowl or mixer, combine starter, sugar, salad oil, salt and 3 cups of flour. Blend thoroughly.
3. Add yeast mixture to the dough. (If you choose not to use the yeast mixture, substitute one cup of warm water.) Add 2 additional cups flour and stir well.
4. Knead in approximately 1 more cup flour, adding a small amount at a time, until the dough is fairly stiff. Cover and let rise for 30-40 minutes.
5. Punch dough down and knead again. Form into two loaves and place on a lightly greased baking tray. Use a knife to score 4-5 ¼-inch diagonal slices across the top. Let dough rise until double in volume, approximately 35-45 minutes.
6. Near the end of the dough's rising time, preheat oven to 400 degrees.
7. Place bread in oven and bake for 30 minutes, or until golden brown. For a crisp, heavier crust, place a small pan of water in the oven while baking.

Yield: 2 loaves

**Black-capped
Chickadee**

This plump little sparrow-sized bird needs no introduction: its call is its name. A frequent winter visitor to bird feeders, chickadees are often observed feeding upside down. In summer, chickadees are found among conifers, where they search for insects and eat pinecone seeds.

Molasses Bran Bread

Jedediah's Original House of Sourdough

Serving this easy-to-make, tasty bread with soup or stew makes a filling, satisfying meal.

1	cup sourdough starter
1	egg
⅓	cup salad oil
½	cup molasses (preferably unsulfered)
¼	cup buttermilk
1½	cups bran
1	cup whole wheat flour
¾	tsp. salt
1	tsp. baking powder
½	tsp. baking soda

1. Preheat oven to 375 degrees.
2. In a medium bowl, whisk together the starter, egg, salad oil, molasses and buttermilk.
3. Stir in remaining ingredients. Mix well.
4. Pour batter into lightly oiled 9x12x2-inch pan and bake for approximately 20 minutes, or until bread springs back when lightly touched.

Yield: 1 loaf

Sourdough Buttermilk Biscuits

Jedediah's Original House of Sourdough

A great addition to breakfast, lunch or dinner!

Yeast mixture (optional)
½	cup warm water
1	pkg. dry yeast

Biscuit ingredients
½	cup shortening
4	cups flour
2	tsp. sugar
1	tsp. salt
1	tsp. baking powder
1	tsp. baking soda
1	cup sourdough starter
¾	cup buttermilk

1. Combine yeast mixture ingredients in a small bowl and set aside.

(Note: Sourdough provides all the levitation necessary, but Jedediah's recommends novice sourdough bakers include yeast.)

2. In a large bowl, combine flour, sugar, salt, baking powder and baking soda. Stir well to blend.
3. By hand, mix shortening into the flour mixture, making marble-sized nuggets.
4. Pour in the starter, buttermilk and yeast mixture (optional). By hand, mix ingredients together just until large, sticky lump of batter forms. Do not overmix; batter will have small lumps throughout. Spoon golfball-sized drops of batter on two lightly greased cookie sheets. Let sit 30 minutes.
5. While dough is rising, preheat oven to 425 degrees.
6. Place cookie sheets in center of oven and bake for approximately 35 minutes or until golden brown. (If you use two racks, rotate sheets halfway through.)

Yield: 2 dozen biscuits

Beer Biscuits
Erin Dann

These easy-to-make, tasty biscuits are great with Erin's Southwest Grilled Chicken, page 160. She copied this family-favorite recipe from an airline magazine years ago.

    2   cups Bisquick™
    3   tbsp. sugar
    ¾   cup warm beer

1. Preheat oven to 400 degrees.
2. Combine ingredients in medium-sized bowl and mix well.
3. Spoon ample dollops on non-stick baking sheet, leaving room between the biscuits. Bake in for 20 minutes, or until golden brown.

Yield: 1 dozen biscuits

Remains of the Whitegrass Ranch.

Tower Falls

Yellowstone National Park's Tower Falls was named by members of the 1870 Washburn Expedition for the large rock formations that tower above the 132-foot plunge. A large boulder perched on top of the falls crashed into the canyon below in 1986.

Cloud Biscuits

Sue McGuire

"My mother gave me this recipe a long time ago. It's the best biscuit recipe I have ever found, and it works really well in a Dutch oven on camping trips." Serve with Sue's Green Chile Stew, page 148.

- 2 cups flour
- 1 tbsp. sugar
- 4 tsp. baking powder
- ¼ tsp. salt
- ½ cup shortening
- 1 egg, beaten
- ½ cup milk

1. Preheat oven to 425 degrees.
2. In a large bowl, sift together the dry ingredients.
3. Cut in shortening by hand until the mixture resembles fine crumbs.
4. Combine the egg and milk, then add to the flour mixture all at once. Stir until the dough follows the fork around the bowl.
5. Turn dough out onto a lightly floured surface; knead gently by hand about 20 strokes (not more!!).
6. Press dough to about ½-inch thick and cut with a biscuit cutter.
7. Place on lightly oiled cookie sheet and bake for 10-14 minutes, or until golden brown.

Yield: 1-2 dozen biscuits, depending on the size of your biscuit cutter.

Easy Herb Bread

This couldn't be easier or more delicious. Serve with grilled meats and a salad for a complete meal, or with soup and stew for lighter fare.

- 1 tbsp. extra-virgin olive oil
- 1 green onion, chopped, green top included
- 1 tsp. each crumbled dried rosemary and dried thyme
- ½ tsp. each finely crumbled dried sage and dried parsley
- 1 lb. frozen white bread dough, thawed in covered container in refrigerator (allow 6-12 hours)
- ½ tsp. pepper

1. Heat oil in small skillet over medium heat. Add onion, rosemary, thyme, sage and parsley and sauté 5 seconds. Remove from heat.
2. Place dough in medium bowl. Add herbs and pepper. Knead until herbs are evenly distributed throughout dough, about two minutes.
3. Grease 8½ x 4½-inch loaf pan. Stretch dough into a rectangle,

then roll it up into loaf shape and place in pan, seam side down. Cover and let rise in oven set to "warm" or at room temperature until doubled, approximately 45 minutes.

4. Preheat oven to 375°F. Bake bread until the top is golden brown, about 25 minutes. Turn bread out onto rack and cool completely before serving.

Serves 8

Garlic Bread

Hot, crusty and delicious—and it couldn't be simpler! This disappears in a flash. Serve with spaghetti and salad.

½ cup butter, melted
3-4 garlic cloves, finely minced
1 lb. loaf French bread, cut in half lengthwise
2 tbsp. fresh parsley, minced

1. Preheat oven to 350 degrees.
2. Combine melted butter and garlic in a small bowl.
3. Place bread halves, cut side up, on a baking sheet. Brush generously with butter mixture then evenly sprinkle with fresh parsley.
4. Bake in the middle of the oven for 8 minutes, then place on a rack 4-6 inches from the top broiler and broil for 2 additional minutes, or until crusty and golden brown. Watch carefully. Cut into 2-inch slices. Serve warm.

Serves 8

Square biscuits

It's not a law that biscuits have to be round. Save time by rolling dough into a rectangle and cutting out biscuit squares, so you don't have to keep rolling the dough.

Focaccia
Pat Opler

This wonderful one-rise Italian flat bread is superb served with a crisp salad and grilled meat, or as an accompaniment to a hearty soup. Pat included it in her *At Home on the Range* cookbook. She perfected the recipe while teaching with fellow chef Richard Nelson in Astoria, Oregon, and graciously granted permission for it to be included in this cookbook.

2½ cups all-purpose flour
½ tsp. salt
¾ tsp. dry yeast
1 cup warm water
cornmeal or Wondra® flour
2 tbsp. good-quality olive oil

Badger

Short-legged and pigeon-toed badgers burrow throughout the valley floor and at the foot of the mountains in Jackson Hole. They feed primarily on other small burrowing mammals but opportunistically eat young ground-nesting birds and eggs as well. While badgers sleep through most of the winter, they're not true hibernators. They emerge from their burrow to hunt when outside temperatures are moderate. Badgers give birth to one to five hairless young between late April and mid-June.

2 cloves garlic, thinly slivered
¼ cup mozzarella, thinly sliced
⅛ cup fresh herbs, finely chopped
(Pat likes basil and rosemary. Green onions and parsley will do nicely if others are unavailable.)
coarsely ground salt
fresh ground black pepper

1. Combine flour, salt, yeast and water in a mixing bowl. Blend well.
2. Knead dough until it is elastic and cleans the kneading surface.
3. Turn dough into a bowl greased with olive oil and lightly cover. Let dough rise until doubled, about 1½ hours.
4. Put cookie sheet in oven and preheat both at 425 degrees.
5. While oven/cookie sheet are preheating, press risen dough into a 14-inch circle on another cookie sheet sprinkled with cornmeal or Wondra flour.
6. Rub surface of dough with olive oil. Sprinkle herbs, salt and pepper over the dough.
7. Remove preheated cookie sheet from oven and slide dough onto it. Place in middle rack in oven and bake 12-15 minutes, or until unevenly golden and slightly puffy.
8. Remove and cut into wedges. Serve hot.

Perfect Corn Bread   *Anne Whiting Richardson*

1 cup sifted all-purpose flour
¼ cup sugar
4 tsp. baking powder
¾ tsp. salt
1 cup cornmeal (yellow or white)
2 eggs
1 cup milk (evaporated milk is okay)
¼ cup vegetable oil

1. Preheat oven to 425 degrees.
2. In a medium bowl, sift flour with sugar, baking powder and salt; stir in cornmeal.
3. Add eggs, milk and shortening. Beat with a wooden spoon until smooth.
4. Pour into greased 9x9x2 inch pan. Bake 25 minutes, or until bread is slightly golden on top and a toothpick inserted into the center comes out clean.

For Corn Sticks: Spoon batter into greased corn-stick pans, filling ⅔ full. Bake in 425 oven 12-15 minutes. Makes 18.

Serves 9

Beverages

Wranglers in front of the Reed Hotel, 1920

Peach Smoothie

The Wildflower Inn

"Summer in a glass."

> 3-4 small peaches, sliced, fresh or frozen
> 1 tbsp. sugar
> juice of ½ lemon
> 1 cup vanilla yogurt
> ¼ cup milk
> a few ice cubes if using fresh peaches

1. Combine all ingredients in a blender and puree until smooth.
2. Serve in wine goblets for a pretty presentation

Serves 4

Sparkling Apple Cider

A refreshing, nonalcoholic drink.

> 1⅓ cup apple juice
> 1 tsp. fresh lemon juice
> 12 oz. chilled club soda

1. Mix apple cider and lemon juice together in a serving pitcher. Slowly pour in club soda and gently stir.
2. Pour into tall tea glasses filled with ice and serve immediately.

Serves 4

Ginger Lemonade

Keith Peters

Tart, refreshing and good for you. Heat to soothe a sore throat.

> ½ cup honey
> 2 cups hot water
> 1 2-in. piece gingerroot, or to taste
> juice of six lemons

1. Dissolve the honey in the hot water. Grate ginger and add the pulp and juice to the honey water. Stir.
2. Juice the lemons and add the juice to the mix. Pour mixture into a half-gallon container and add water to fill. Chill.

Serves 8

Mint Iced Tea

Becky Woods

Holly Lake

Holly Lake lies at the bottom of a glacial cirque below 11,555-foot Mount Woodring in Grand Teton National Park. This beautiful glacial tarn is reached by a steep trail up Paintbrush Canyon. It is named after Holly Leek, son of one of the valley's earliest residents, rancher Stephen Leek.

"My husband and I toured Grove Farm, an historic sugar plantation, on Kauai a number of years back. At the end of the visit, guests were invited into the plantation's kitchen for mint iced tea. They received so many requests for the recipe that they finally printed it for mass distribution. This cool, refreshing tea has become a summer tradition."

Minted Water
> Prepare fresh mint leaves ahead of time by breaking apart the leaves and stems and placing them in a colander that has been placed inside a larger pot or bowl. Pour 2 quarts boiling water over the leaves and allow them to steep for about an hour in the hot water. Strain the minted water into a container. Refrigerate the concentrate.

To make a pitcher of iced tea, use the following portions:

    2   cups minted water
    4   cups water
    4   tbsp. Lipton Iced Tea Mix

1. Combine ingredients and stir well to dissolve the tea mix.
2. Pour into four tea glasses filled with ice. Garnish with a wedge of lemon and sprig of fresh mint, if desired. Enjoy!

Serves 4

Southern Iced Tea

Becky Woods

"This recipe comes from my aunt Joey, who knew how to beat the dog days of North Carolina summers with a minimum of fuss. It's delicious and easy to make."

    2   teabags of black tea
    1½   cups sugar
    1   cup unsweetened pineapple juice
    ½   cup lemon juice concentrate

1. Bring two quarts of water to boil. Remove from heat.
2. Steep teabags in water until it is cool, approximately 20 minutes. Remove bags.
3. Add the sugar and juices, and stir well to dissolve sugar.
4. Serve in glasses filled with ice cubes. Garnish with twist of lemon or orange, if desired.

Serves 8

Lucas Garage

Geraldine had a garage built on her property after her son, Russell, sent her a 1924 Buick Touring car. In the winter, she travelled around the valley with a sled and a team of dogs, also a gift from her son.

Sparkling Spiced Iced Tea

Bring on the fizz! This refreshing version of ice tea gets its punch from ginger ale.

 4 Constant Comment,® apricot ginger or tea of choice teabags
 1 qt. (4 cups) boiling water
 ginger ale
 fresh lemon juice
 lemon slices for garnish

1. Place teabags in a teapot. Add boiling water and steep for 10 minutes. Remove teabags.
2. Fill four tall glasses with ice. Fill two-thirds full with brewed tea. Fill remainder of glass with ginger ale. Add fresh lemon juice to taste and garnish with lemon slices.

Serves 4

Watermelon Cooler

A different, thoroughly delicious warm weather drink.

 6 cups seeded watermelon, cut in 1-inch cubes (approximately 4 lbs. with rind)
 1 cup loosely packed fresh mint leaves
 1 cup boiling water
 ¼ tsp. ground cinnamon
 ½ cup skim milk
 watermelon balls on skewers or watermelon wedges

1. Prepare watermelon and spread on cookie sheet. Place in freezer till frozen, 1-2 hours.
2. While watermelon is freezing, place mint leaves in a bowl and pour boiling water over them. Cover and steep 10 minutes. Drain mint liquid through strainer and place reserved liquid in refrigerator to chill. Discard leaves.
3. Place frozen watermelon cubes in blender with cool mint liquid, cinnamon and milk. Blend on highest speed till smooth, about 15 seconds.
4. Serve in tall glasses garnished with skewered watermelon balls or wedges.

Serves 6

Sports Energy Drink

Therese Metherell, R.D.

Drinks with electrolytes may be better than water during and after strenuous exercise—both because studies show people tend to drink more fluids when they are flavored, and because the sodium, potassium and chloride in electrolytes help tissues absorb liquid. Therese's "recipe" is much cheaper than commercial sports drinks, such as Gatorade®. She shared it with readers in her *Jackson Hole News* "Sound Bites" column.

    1 can frozen lemonade
    6 cans water, or double water amount specified on can
        salt to taste

1. Mix together. Pour into water bottles and refrigerate until ready to use. If you are participating in extended activity, freeze one water bottle. Allow space in the bottle for the liquid to expand as it freezes.

   Note: You may also use your favorite fresh lemonade recipe. Simply double the water quantity and recipe specifies.

Yield: Varies with can size/recipe.

Geraldine Lucas Homestead south of Jenny Lake.

Raspberry Mint Crush

Anne Whiting Richardson

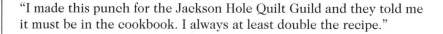

"I made this punch for the Jackson Hole Quilt Guild and they told me it must be in the cookbook. I always at least double the recipe."

¼ cup sugar
½ cup lightly packed fresh mint leaves
1 cup boiling water
1 10-oz. package frozen red raspberries
1 6-oz. can frozen lemonade concentrate

1. Combine sugar, mint leaves and 1 cup boiling water; let steep for 10 minutes. Strain mint liquid through sieve into large pitcher or punch bowl. Discard mint leaves.
2. Add raspberries and lemonade concentrate; stir till thawed. Add 2 cups cold water and stir. Pour into glasses filled with ice cubes. Garnish with fresh mint leaves if desired.

Serves 8

Chai (Tea Latte)

Paul Scialabba

"This is unbelievably addicting. I developed this recipe through trial and error. It took a few tries, but I actually compared it to the chai served at a local gourmet coffee shop, and I couldn't taste a difference. I did my research on the net, and picked the coffee shops' brains for a few secrets. It's far cheaper than $2.75 a cup, and all the ingredients can be found at a typical supermarket."

4 1½-in. slices fresh ginger (use vegetable peeler)
1 2-in. cinnamon stick
4 whole cloves
½ tsp. powdered cardamom
1 6-in. vanilla bean (cut up into 1-in. pieces)
   dash nutmeg
1 heaping tbsp. sugar
¼ cup honey
3 Bigelow Darjeeling Blend tea bags
2 cups water
2 cups milk

1. Bring 2 cups water to a boil and toss in teabags then all other ingredients except milk in the order listed above. Reduce heat and simmer about 5 minutes, stirring occasionally.
2. Add milk and bring to boil, then remove from heat. Strain through sieve lined with a coffee filter.

3. Serve hot or in a tall glass filled with ice. Unused portion may be refrigerated. Reheat in a microwave, on top of the stove, or froth with a cappucino maker.

Serves 4

Vanilla Iced Coffee

At only 72 calories, this is light and refreshing: the perfect cooler for a hot afternoon.

1 cup fresh brewed coffee
1 cup 2% skim milk
¾ tsp. pure vanilla extract
1 tbsp. granulated sugar
ice cubes
ground cinnamon

1. Mix the coffee, milk, extracts and sugar together in a pitcher. Stir well to combine.
2. Place ice cubes into two ice tea or other tall, 12-oz. glasses. Pour coffee mixture into the glasses. If desired, lightly sprinkle with ground cinnamon.

Serves 2

Iced Toffee

A perfect dessert beverage, worth every calorie!

1 1³⁄₁₆ oz. Heath Bar
2 cups vanilla ice cream, softened
½ cup cold, strong coffee (regular or decaffeinated)

1. Place softened ice cream and coffee into blender cup. Top with Heath Bar® broken into pieces. Cover and blend until mixture is smooth and thick.
2. Pour into two chilled, 12-oz. glasses. Garnish with shaved chocolate, if desired. Serve with a spoon.

Serves 2

Yellow-bellied Marmot

This member of the squirrel family is the size of a porcupine without its quills. The shrill alarm emitted when danger approaches has earned it the nickname "whistle pig." Marmots typically inhabit subalpine meadows studded with large boulders, denning in burrows at the base of the rocks. On sunny days, they can be seen basking on top of boulders or logs. Marmots hibernate in late September/early October. They emerge in early spring to begin breeding. Average litters of 4-5 are born roughly five weeks later. While there are rare reports of cannibalization of their young, marmots typically feed on herbaceous or grassy vegetation.

The Ultimate Mocha

Your guests will rave over this sweet delight. It is easy to prepare and is an elegant way to end a meal. Just remember to plan ahead.

> 2   cups freshly brewed espresso (regular or decaffeinated)
> ½   cup superfine granulated sugar
> 1   1-oz. square semi-sweet chocolate, chopped
> 2   cups finely crushed ice
> ¼   cup whipping cream

1. Stir hot espresso, sugar and chopped chocolate together until sugar has dissolved and the chocolate has melted. Refrigerate a minimum of three hours or overnight.
2. Whip the cream until it is just thick enough to mound on a spoon. Set aside.
3. Finely crush ice and divide between four wine glasses. Pour cold coffee over the ice and top each glass with a spoonful of whipped cream. Top with chocolate shavings and garnish with a fresh mint leaf, if desired. Serve with a straw.

Serves 4

Mocha Frappuccino

A cool, easy-to-make treat for coffee aficionados.

    1   tbsp. hot fudge sauce
    ½   cup espresso
    2   cups milk
 ¼ - ⅓   cup sugar, to taste
    1½   cups ice

1. Combine in a blender and blend until ice is crushed.
2. Serve immediately.

Serves 2

Mexican Chocolate   *Happy Weston*

Nicely spiced with cinnamon, vanilla and nutmeg, this recipe will forever banish commercial hot chocolate mix from your home.

    4   ozs. sweet chocolate
    1   cup hot water
   5 ½   cup milk
    ½   cup heavy cream
    1   tbsp. cinnamon
    ⅛   tsp. vanilla extract
         cinnamon sticks

1. Combine chocolate and hot water. Melt over hot water in top of double boiler, stirring to mix.
2. While chocolate is melting, combine the milk, cream, cinnamon and nutmeg in a 3-quart saucepan, beating with a wire whisk to blend. Place pan over medium heat and heat until bubbles form around the edge of the pan, stirring occasionally.
3. Remove milk from heat and stir in the melted chocolate and vanilla. Use an electric mixer or wire whisk to beat until foamy.
4. Pour into cups and serve with a cinnamon stick.

Serves 6

Shooting Star

This beautiful wildflower is found in moist, open sites in Jackson Hole from May through June. The hanging flower derives its name from the 180-degree backward bend of its petals and sepals.

Hot Vanilla

A nice alternative to hot chocolate.

        2   cups milk
        4   tbsp. sugar
        1   tsp. vanilla
            nutmeg

1. Combine the milk, sugar and vanilla in a small saucepan. Stir until hot, but do not boil.
2. Divide between 2 mugs and sprinkle a little nutmeg on top.

    Note: For a foamy version similar to steamed milk atop a cappuccino, pour the hot mixture through the feed tube of a food processor while it's running. When frothy, transfer to mugs.

Serves 2

White Hot Chocolate   The Wildflower Inn

This is a heavenly drink.

        3   oz. high-quality white chocolate, chopped
            (The Wildflower uses Lindt)
       ½   tsp. pure vanilla extract
        2   cups milk (or half and half)
            grated nutmeg or chocolate sprinkles for garnish

1. Warm milk over medium heat until warm.
2. Melt chocolate in the warm milk, stirring frequently. Add vanilla. Stir until smooth.
2. Heat until hot, but not boiling. Serve immediately with a dusting of nutmeg or chocolate sprinkles.

Serves 2

Cranberry Tea Punch   DeAnn Sutton

DeAnn shared her favorite holiday punch with *Jackson Hole Guide* readers one Christmas. It tastes great and, garnished with frosted cranberries, makes a gorgeous presentation.

punch
        2   32-oz. bottles cranberry juice cocktail

Raccoon

Once scarce in Jackson Hole, the population of raccoons has increased as human population in the valley has grown. Raccoons are easily recognized by their bandit-like mask and striped tail. They den in hollow trees, rock crevices and even inactive construction sites. Regrettably, available human garbage supplements their natural diet of insects, rodents, fish, young birds, nuts and berries. Raccoon young, born in April or May, leave their mother in the fall to establish their own home, typically within a 30-mile range.

½ cup brewed tea
¼ - ½ cup sugar, to taste
¼ cup lemon juice
½ tsp. cinnamon
¼ tsp. ground cloves
1 small lemon, thinly sliced
  lemon leaves, for garnish
frosted cranberries
2 cups fresh cranberries
1 cup sugar
1 egg white

First Neon Sign

The first neon sign in the valley was installed in 1932 at Bruce Porter's Jackson Drug Store on the square.

1. 90 minutes before serving, make frosted cranberries and set aside. Place cranberries in colander and rinse with cold running water. Pat dry with paper towels. Place sugar in a sturdy bag. In a small bowl, whip egg white with a fork until frothy. Dip several dry cranberries a time into the white, letting excess drip off, then put in bag and shake until completely coated with sugar. Place coated cranberries in a 13x9-inch baking pan to dry, about 1 hour. Repeat until all cranberries are frosted.
2. 15 minutes before serving, pour cranberry juice, tea, sugar, lemon juice, cinnamon and cloves in a 4-quart saucepan. Cook over high heat, stirring occasionally, until sugar is dissolved and punch is hot.
3. Pour punch into heat-proof punch bowl set on a large, round tray. Float lemon slices on top of the punch. Arrange lemon leaves and frosted cranberries around the base of the punch bowl. Serve warm.

Yield: 10 full or 20 half-cup servings

Teton Tea
The Wildflower Inn

The spicy aroma of this super "tea" greets The Wildflowers' fall and winter guests as they return from a day's outing. It's sure to become one of your favorites!

4 cups cranberry juice
2 cups orange juice
½ cup lemon juice
¼ – ½ cup sugar, to taste
2 1-in. sticks whole cinnamon

Combine in a large pan on the stove. Heat, then simmer for 15 minutes to blend flavors. Remove cinnamon and enjoy!

Serves 4-6

Rudolph "Rosie"
Rosencrans

Austrian native Rudolph
"Rosie" Rosencrans be-
gan working for Teton
National Forest in 1904.
He ran the Buffalo Rang-
er District from then un-
til 1927, when failing
eyesight led to his deci-
sion to retire. Rosie
mapped much of the
area and constructed the
Blackrock Ranger Sta-
tion, now on the National
Register of Historic
Places. Rosie was an
accomplished skier, of-
ten skiing from Moran to
Jackson. He died on
September 22, 1970,
just three months shy of
his 95th birthday. He is
buried near his beloved
Blackrock Ranger Sta-
tion, where a ridge bears
his name.

Perfect Hot Toddy
Chef Tamalpais Roth McCormick

A great way to end a wintery day.

> 1 tbsp. whole unsalted butter
> 1 tsp. light brown sugar
>   pinch of cinnamon
> 1 twist of lemon with 3 whole cloves secured through it
> 4 ozs. apple cider
> 2 ozs. dark rum

1. Heat butter, brown sugar, pinch of cinnamon, lemon twist with cloves and cider over moderate heat until hot.
2. Add dark rum just before serving.

Serves 1

Hot Buttered Rum
Jeanne Houfek and Sandy Bommer

Jeanne and Sandy shared the recipe for this classic winter warmer with *Jackson Hole Guide* readers. It is also included in *The Hole Thing Cookbook*, a publication that benefits St. John's Hospital. For information, please see the acknowledgments section.

> 1 qt. vanilla ice cream, slightly softened
> 1 lb. light brown sugar
> 1 tsp. nutmeg
> 1 lb. pkg. powdered sugar
> 1 lb. (4 sticks) butter, at room temperature
> 1 tsp. cinnamon
>   rum

1. In a large bowl, cream together the butter and sugar. When well blended, stir in the nutmeg and cinnamon.
2. Add ice cream to mixture. Mix well. Place mixture in freezer-proof, tightly-lidded containers and freeze until ready to use.
3. To serve place 1-2 heaping tsp. of mixture and 1 jigger of rum in a cup or mug. Fill with hot water. Top with whipped cream, if desired.

Yield: Enough for an entire ski season!

Old Fashioned Christmas Egg Nog   *Rip Woodin*

A holiday tradition. This is an original recipe from Rip's grandmother, Olivia. He says it "makes enough for a good party or several days of hoarding."

    1   doz. eggs
    12 tbsp. sugar
        one-fifth of bourbon
    ½   pint whipping cream
        nutmeg

1. Separate eggs one at a time, placing the yolks in the bowl that will be your final serving bowl. (Tip: Use a punch bowl or the largest bowl you have.) Save the egg whites in a bowl large enough to beat all 12: whites double in size when whipped.
2. Beat the egg yolks, adding the sugar a tbsp. at a time, until all the sugar is incorporated and the yolks are a pale yellow. Gradually stir in the bourbon until well blended. Set aside.
3. Beat the whipping cream; set aside.
4. Beat egg whites until stiff but not dry. Add the beaten whites to the yolk mixture, stirring to blend, then fold in the whipped cream. Chill, covered, until serving time. Sprinkle with nutmeg before ladling into serving glasses.

Buffalo Bill & Rosie

Rosie reportedly came to America because he had seen Buffalo Bill touring in Europe and was very impressed by him. It was one of Rosie's greatest honors as a ranger to escort Buffalo Bill through the forest in 1914. When Buffalo Bill asked Rosie what he could give him, Rosie asked for a lock of his hair—which Buffalo Bill promptly cut off with a hunting knife. It was a prized keepsake for the remainder of Rosie's life.

Skiing at Blackrock Ranger Station, early 1900s.

The largest summer em-
ployer in Teton County is
Grand Teton Lodge com-
pany. Jackson Hole Mtn.
Resort is the largest winter employer. Both hire
approximately 1,000
people each season.
The largest year-round
employer in the valley is
St. John's Hospital.

Lucilla and Diego's Orange Margaritas

Christy Walton

Consider yourself warned: This is very tasty, and very easy to drink!

½ gallon fresh orange juice
1 cup tequila
½ cup orange liqueur. Mexican Controy and Quantro are good

1. Mix together.
2. Pour into tall glasses filled with ice. This is very pretty presented in a pitcher frosted in the freezer with orange slices floating on top.

Serves 6-8

Amaretto

Echo Taylor

This version of the famous, classic almond liqueur netted Echo grand champion honors at the Teton County Fair.

8 cups water
6 cups sugar
6 ozs. pure almond extract
½ quart Everclear alcohol
5 drops yellow food coloring
2 drops red food coloring
1 drop green food coloring

1. Bring water and sugar to a boil, then cool completely.
2. Add remaining ingredients to sugar mixture and mix well.
3. Pour into bottles.

Yield: 2½ quarts

Kahlua

Echo Taylor

Good by itself as a dessert cordial, or served over ice cream. With pretty bottles and decorative labels, this makes a nice gift.

12 cups water
6 cups sugar
3 cups regular-grind coffee (not instant)
2 ozs. pure vanilla extract
⅛ scant tsp. baking powder
1 quart Everclear alcohol or vodka

1. In a stockpot or other large pan, bring the water to a boil. Add the coffee. When the mix has returned to a boil, add the baking powder and stir well. Remove from heat and let stand 45 minutes, stirring occasionally.
2. Strain coffee from liquid. Add sugar, stir and return pan to stove. Bring to a boil over medium heat. Continue to boil for 20 minutes, stirring constantly
3. Remove from heat and cool completely before adding vanilla and alcohol. Mix well.
4. Pour mixture into sterilized bottles.

Yield: Approx. 1 gallon

Coyote

The adaptable coyote lives in a wide variety of habitats in the valley. It typically travels a 10-mile hunting route, but will range up to 100 miles when food is scarce. Rodents, rabbits, carrion, plants, frogs and insects all satisfy a coyote's voracious palate. A short gestation period of two months yields a litter of five to seven pups.

Cranberry Liqueur

A hit around the holidays, when fresh cranberries re-appear. This beautiful liqueur keeps indefinitely.

1 lb. fresh cranberries
4 cups white sugar, divided
3 cups 80 proof vodka
1 cup water

1. Combine cranberries with 2 cups sugar. Add water and boil 4-5 minutes or until skins start to pop. Remove from heat and cool.
2. Put cooled berries in a quart mixing jar. Add vodka and shake vigorously. Cover and let infuse for a week, stirring once a day.
3. At the end of the week, pour liquid through strainer and discard berry residue. Let the mixture rest, covered, for 3 or 4 days.
4. Strain liqueur through a paper coffee filter placed in a mesh sieve until the liquid is clear.
5. Add 2 cups white sugar and shake vigorously until sugar is dissolved. Let clear overnight, then pour into sterilized bottles.

Yield: 1 quart

Rufous Hummingbird

This occasional visitor to the valley is observed spring through fall. Male rufous hummers are distinguished by their predominantly red tail, reddish-brown back and green crown.

Peaches and Cream Liqueur

This is simply too good to give away. Save it for yourself.

1	14-oz. can sweetened condensed milk
1	cup peach Schnapps
1	cup heavy or whipping cream
¾	cup vodka
4	eggs
1	tsp. vanilla
¼	tsp. almond extract

1. Combine all in a blender until smooth.
2. Pour into sterilized bottles and refrigerate overnight.
3. Shake well before serving. Stores up to one month.

Yield: 2½ pints

Appetizers & Condiments

John Wort in buggy, late 1890s

Red Fox Kit

Red foxes den in a burrow, often made by expanding a marmot or badger hole. Kits are born in a litter of 1-10 in April or May, following a gestation of about seven weeks. They grow quickly and are weaned when they are only a month old.

Stuffed Mushrooms

Jean Jorgensen

"I always double or quadruple this recipe. These go fast!"

½ lb. mushrooms
2 tbsp. melted butter
2 tbsp. soft butter
1 minced garlic clove
3 tbsp. shredded Monterey Jack cheese
2 tbsp. red wine
1 tbsp. soy sauce
⅓ cup fine cracker crumbs

1. Clean mushrooms with brush. Remove stems and finely mince 3 tbsp. of the stems into a bowl. Discard the remainder, or save for other uses. Brush mushroom caps with melted butter.
2. Add other ingredients to minced stems and stir well to mix.
3. Turn on oven broiler.
4. Stuff caps and place in shallow pan or lidded cookie sheet Broil 3 minutes or until hot and bubbly. Best served warm.

Yield: 17-18 caps

Mushrooms Hana

Joanne Hennes

Stuffed with chicken, curry and coconut, these inspired stuffed caps are savory bites of heaven.

2 cups minced, cooked chicken (if pressed for time, can use canned, chunk chicken that has been minced)
24 large, fresh mushroom caps
1-2 tbsp. curry powder, to taste
1-2 tbsp. brandy, to taste
1 tsp. Accent®
1 tsp. mayonnaise
¼ tsp. lime juice, or less, to taste
2 tbsp. crumbled bacon
1 minced hard-boiled egg
2 tbsp. flaked coconut
2 tbsp. fresh chopped parsley or chives

1. Preheat oven to 350 degrees.
2. Mix the chicken, curry, brandy, Accent and mayonnaise together in a medium-sized bowl until well blended.
2. Stuff mushroom caps with chicken mixture and place on a baking pan large enough to hold them in a single layer. Set aside.
3. In a small bowl, mix the bacon, egg, coconut, parsley and lime

juice together until well blended. Carefully top each cap with an equal amount of this mixture.

4. Bake until very warm, about 5-7 minutes. Serve immediately.

Yield: 24 caps

Sausage Cheese Balls

Linda Bourett

Linda saw this recipe featured on a package of Jimmy Dean sausage and in numerous magazines one Christmas. It has become a family favorite.

  2 lbs. bulk sausage, uncooked
1½ cup Bisquick® mix
  4 cups shredded sharp cheese
 ½ cup finely chopped onion
 ½ cup finely chopped celery
 ½ tsp. garlic powder

1. Preheat oven to 375 degrees.
2. Mix all and form into 1-inch balls. Bake on ungreased cookie sheet for approximately 15 minutes, or until golden brown. Skewer with toothpicks and arrange on platter. Serve warm.

Yield: 48 balls

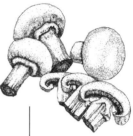

Mushrooms

Choose mushrooms with caps closed around the stem. Exposed brownish gills indicate mushrooms are past their prime. Store refrigerated until used, which should be as soon as possible.

Mexican Pinwheels

Incredibly easy. Incredibly good. Consider doubling or tripling this recipe if you have a crowd.

1 pkg. large spinach or tomato flour tortillas
1 8-oz. pkg. of cream cheese, softened
1 4-oz. can chopped black olives
1 4-oz. jar chopped red pimientos
1 4-oz. can chopped green chiles
3 tbsp. chopped green onions

1. Mix everything but tortillas together.
2. Spread mixture on tortillas and roll up tightly. Wrap each tortilla up individually in plastic wrap.
3. Store in refrigerator until ready to serve. Slice into ½-inch pinwheels.

Yield: Approximately 64 pinwheels

Elk antler arches

Crabmeat Hors d'oeuvres

Rita Stephanou
submitted by Erika Muschaweck

These easy-to-prepare, tasty bites can be prepared ahead of time and heated as needed.

1	6-oz. can crabmeat (drained)
6-7	English muffins
1	5-oz. jar Old English cheese (room temperature)
1	stick butter (room temperature)
1	heaping tbsp. mayonnaise
½	tsp. garlic powder

1. Combine butter, cheese and mayonnaise. Blend well. Add crabmeat and garlic powder and blend well again.
2. Separate muffins and spread each half with crabmeat mixture. Place on a cookie sheet and freeze, then store in the plastic muffin bags.
3. When ready to serve, place on cookie sheet and broil for 7 minutes or until hot and bubbly. Cut into quarters.

Yield: 24-28 pieces

Gingered Chicken Satay

Mouth-watering skewers that are easy to make.

1½	lbs. chicken tenders or 1½ lbs. boneless, skinless chicken breasts cut into ½-¾-in. wide strips.
¼	cup plus 2 tbsp. soy sauce, divided
2	tsp. sesame oil, divided
2	tbsp. plus ½ cup ginger preserves, melted, divided
1	clove garlic, minced
2	tbsp. rice wine vinegar
¼	tsp. red pepper flakes

1. Turn on oven broiler.
2. Place chicken tenders, 2 tbsp. soy sauce and 1 tsp. sesame oil in large, heavy-duty zip lock plastic bag. Seal and shake to coat. Place bag in refrigerator and chill for 10 minutes.
3. While tenders are chilling, melt ginger preserves by heating over medium-low heat, stirring constantly, until mixture is smooth. Remove from heat.
3. Thread chicken tenders on skewers, one per skewer (will be between 12-14 skewers, depending on size of chicken tenders).
4. Place skewers on rack set in broiler pan and brush with 2 tbsp. of the melted ginger preserves. Broil for 12 minutes, turning skewers

once, or until the tenders are no longer pink and juices run clear.
5.   While tenders are cooking, combine the remaining ½ cup soy sauce, 1 tsp. sesame oil and ½ cup melted ginger preserves in a serving dish. Stir in the garlic, vinegar and red pepper flakes. Blend well. Serve the ginger sauce with the chicken tenders.

Yield: 12-14 skewers

Chinese Spring (Egg) Rolls — *The Spice Merchants*

"In China these are a special treat available only in the spring, hence the name. In this country they are normally called egg rolls and are available all year. We think that is a good deal. Who wants to wait till spring to enjoy them?" If you can't find ingredients in the Asian section of your supermarket, order them from The Spice Merchants online. See acknowledgments for information.

    1   pkg. egg roll wrappers
    2   cups cooked ham or cooked salad shrimp
    2   stalks green onion, cut to 1" length, shredded
    1   cup Napa Cabbage, thinly shredded
    2   stalks celery, thinly sliced
    1   cup bamboo shoots, shredded
    ½   lb. fresh bean sprouts
    ⅔   cup sliced black mushrooms (dried foods section), soaked
        vegetable oil for deep frying
    1   egg, beaten
Sauce mixture
    1   tsp. salt
    1   tsp. sugar
    2   tbsp. oyster sauce
    2   tbsp. Hoisin sauce
    1   tbsp. corn starch
    ¼   cup chicken broth
Suggested dipping sauces
        hot mustard
        sesame chili oil
        plum sauce

1.   Soak the black mushrooms until soft, about 20 minutes. Slice the vegetables as listed above. Rinse the bean sprouts under cold water and drain well.
2.   Mix the sauce ingredients together in a cup, whisking to blend. Set aside.
3.   Heat 1 tbsp. oil to very high temperature in your wok or Peking pan and add green onions, celery and Napa cabbage. Stir fry for about a minute then add the remaining vegetables. Stir fry an ad-

ditional minute, mixing well. (The vegetables are cooked briefly to blend the flavors. Keep the cooking time short so the vegetables do not get limp.) Add the ham or salad shrimp and toss to mix well.

4. Add the sauce mixture. Mix well to coat the vegetables. Continue cooking until the sauce thickens and clears, about half a minute. Remove the filling to a bowl and allow to cool to at least room temperature before making the spring rolls. If you try to use the filling when it is hot, the steam will soften the wrappers and cause trouble.

5. Put about ⅓ cup of the cooled filling on a wrapper. The wrapper should have one of the points aiming toward you and the filling should be placed on the lower ⅓ of the wrapper. Bring the bottom point over the top of the filling. Tuck the side points on top of that and roll toward the point farthest away. Seal the top flap with beaten egg.

6. Slide eggrolls carefully into hot oil (about 350 degrees) The rolls should turn a light golden brown in about two minutes. If they brown faster, the oil is too hot. When done remove from oil and drain on a rack or paper towels. Cut each roll into three or four pieces and serve with dipping sauces.

Serves 6

Old Jenny Lake Store in GTNP.

Sicilian-Style Caponata

Chef Tamalpais Roth-McCormick

Even people who aren't wild about eggplant love this dish. Serve by itself or with warm, crusty bread.

Jenny Lake Ranger Station

Jenny Lake Ranger Station was built before July 1929 by Lee Manges as a homestead cabin for his claim near Cottonwood Creek. The building was moved to its present site the summer of 1930, where it served as the Jenny Lake Museum and Visitor Center for over 20 years. It became the home of the Jenny Lake Ranger Station when the old ranger station was moved to the Lupine Meadows housing area in the 1950s.

2	medium eggplants
2	large red onions, halved and sliced very thin
4	celery stalks, cut into ½-inch dice
¾	cup olive oil
4	small zucchini, quartered and cubed
10	very ripe tomatoes, roughly chopped
1	cup brine-cured green and black olives, preferably Sicilian, pitted and coarsely chopped
1	tbsp. crushed garlic
4	tbsp. capers
⅓	cup red wine vinegar
1	tbsp. granulated sugar
½	cup chopped fresh basil
½	cup chopped flat-leaf parsley
	salt and freshly ground black pepper

1. Remove stems from eggplant, peel and cut into ¾-inch dice. Place eggplant in colander, sprinkle liberally with salt, and let drain for about an hour.
2. While the eggplant is draining, blanch celery by placing it in a saucepan of boiling water for about 1 minute. Drain and set aside.
3. In a large skillet, heat ¼ cup of the olive oil over medium heat until hot but not smoking. Add the onions and cook until they are very soft but not browned, about 5-7 minutes. Add tomatoes, olives, capers and garlic. Season to taste with freshly ground black pepper. Lower heat and simmer for 15 minutes, then remove from burner.
4. Rinse eggplant and pat dry. Set aside.
5. In another large skillet, heat remaining ½ cup olive oil over medium heat. Add zucchini. Cook until browned but still firm, stirring frequently. Season with salt and pepper, then remove zucchini with a slotted spoon and place in large bowl. Repeat with eggplant in three batches, cooking until eggplant is browned but firm. Add the browned eggplant to bowl holding zucchini.
6. Add celery to the skillet and cook until soft but not browned. Remove with slotted spoon and add to tomato mixture.
7. Add bowl of zucchini and eggplant to tomato mixture. Cook uncovered over medium heat for 10 minutes. Stir in vinegar, sugar and fresh herbs. Season with salt and pepper. Remove from heat and cool to room temperature.

Serves 8

Magpie

Magpies possess one of
the longest tails of North
American birds. Road,
winter and predator-
killed large mammals
provide a ready food
source for this attractive
scavenger.

Bruschetta

A perennial favorite. This easy version is hard to beat.

1   baguette (French bread) or loaf of Italian Bread
2   firm Roma (plum) tomatoes, seeded and chopped
2   cloves minced garlic
½   cup fresh basil, chopped
1   tsp. fresh lemon juice
1   tbsp. oil
1   tsp. balsamic vinegar
¼   cup fresh grated Parmesan cheese

1. Combine the tomatoes, garlic and basil in a bowl. Toss lightly to mix. Add the lemon juice, oil, balsamic vinegar and pepper. Mix together. Set aside.
2. Slice bread lengthwise. Place halves on baking sheet, cut side up and toast under the broiler. (Watch closely so the bread doesn't burn.) Remove bread from oven and lower oven temperature to 350 degrees.
3. Spread toasted bread with tomato mixture, then sprinkle with Parmesan cheese.
4. Return bread to oven for several minutes to warm topping and allow cheese to melt. Slice and serve warm.

Yield: Approximately 28 slices

Roasted Garlic

Roasted garlic has a wonderful nutty taste. It is superb spread on lightly toasted slices of French bread or crackers.

4   whole garlic bulbs
    olive oil
¼   tsp. salt (sea salt preferred)
1   tsp. fresh ground black pepper
1   whole French baguette sliced

1. Prepare garlic by removing any parchment-like skin that comes off easily. Cut approximately ¼-inch off the tops of the bulbs to expose the top of the cloves. Place heads snugly together in a garlic baker or small baking dish. Brush each bulb lightly with olive oil and sprinkle with sea salt.
2. Cover dish with foil and bake in 350 degree oven for 30-45 minutes. Remove foil, brush with more oil and bake uncovered for an additional 30-45 minutes, or until garlic is tender. Remove from

oven and sprinkle with fresh ground black pepper.

3. To serve, squeeze the warm cloves out of their skins. Spread on crackers or slices of French bread (baguette). To make an appealing platter, place the warm garlic heads on a board or plate with slices of goat cheese; roasted red, green and yellow bell peppers and Greek olives. Garnish with sprigs of chives, cilantro or Italian parsley.

Serves 8

Cucumber Rounds with Sour Cream and Chutney

This "perfect little something" was developed by the California Culinary Academy. It is virtually work-free and fantastic.

English cucumbers
sour cream
chutney

1. Wash cucumbers, pat dry, and score flesh lengthwise all the way around the cucumber with a fork.
2. Slice cucumbers into ¼-inch thick rounds.
3. Top each slice with 1 tsp. sour cream and ½ tsp. purchased chutney.

Yield: Make desired quantity. One cucumber makes about 32 rounds.

Dare-Deviled Eggs   *Judy Eddy*

The use of garbanzo beans instead of egg yolks make these tasty deviled eggs lower in fat and cholesterol, without sacrificing taste.

6   hard boiled eggs
1   tsp. sugar
1   tbsp. white vinegar
1   15-oz. can rinsed and drained garbanzos
2   tbsp. nonfat mayonnaise
2   tbsp. nonfat sour cream
2   tbsp. yellow mustard
¼   tsp. ground red pepper
2   tbsp. minced green onion
¼   tsp. ground clove
     paprika (optional)

Cucumbers

Avoid buying large cucumbers; they tend to be pithy. Select medium-sized, slender cukes for the best flavor and refrigerate until use. Don't store cucumbers near fruit in your refrigerator. Many fruits emit ethylene gas while ripening. The gas unpleasantly hardens cucumber seeds.

Mountain Hollyhock

1. Remove shells from eggs. Halve eggs lengthwise; remove and discard the yolks.
2. In small bowl, dissolve sugar in vinegar. In blender or food processor bowl, combine garbanzos, sugar mixture, mayonnaise, sour cream, mustard, pepper, onions and clove. Blend until smooth.
3. Fill fluted pastry bag with mixture and pipe into egg white halves (or use a teaspoon to fill halves). Sprinkle with paprika, if desired, and refrigerate until ready to eat.

Serves 12

Dean's Favorite Snack   *Dean and Julie Stayner*

Hot and cheesy and good.

    1   cup chopped olives
    ½   cup chopped green onions, including tops
    1½ cups grated sharp cheddar cheese
    ½   cup mayonnaise
    ½   tsp. salt
    ½   tsp. curry
    1   pkg. English muffins, sliced in half

1. Mix all ingredients except English muffins together. Spread on English muffins halves.
3. Place on ungreased cookie sheet and broil until cheese is bubbling, about 3 minutes. Cut each muffin half into quarters

Serves 12

Brandied Raisin Brie

Microwave preparation makes this impressive appetizer a breeze to prepare. Serve it with a selection of crackers or bread rounds.

    2   tbsp. brandy
    3   tbsp. golden raisins
    1   tbsp. currants or dark raisins
    1   8-oz. brie round or wedge
    2   tbsp. toasted walnuts, chopped

1. To toast walnuts, preheat oven to 350 degrees. Spread chopped nuts in a single layer on an ungreased baking sheet. Toast until aromatic and golden brown, about 3 minutes. Shake at 1½ minutes so nuts brown evenly, and to check color. Once nuts begin to color, they toast quickly. Don't let them burn! Remove pan from

oven and pour nuts onto a paper towel.

2. Place brandy, raisins and currants in a small microwave-safe bowl. Cover loosely with a paper towel and microwave until raisins absorb brandy, approximately 30 seconds to 1 minute
3. Place brie on a microwave-safe serving dish. Microwave until cheese is warmed and just begins to melt, about 30-60 seconds.
4. Top with brandy soaked fruit and toasted walnuts. Serve warm.

Serves 8

Chutney Curry Cheese Ball

An out-of-the-ordinary indulgence. Expect recipe requests.

12 ozs. cream cheese, chilled
 2 tbsp. sour cream
 2 tsp. curry powder
 ½ cup chopped green onions
 ½ cup currants or golden raisins
 ½ cup salted peanuts, chopped
     coconut
 ⅔ cup commercial fruit chutney (peach, mango, plum or apple are good)

1. Combine all ingredients except chutney together in a medium bowl and mix together with hands to form a ball or log. Roll in coconut and chill, covered, in refrigerator.
2. Just before serving, top with chutney. Serve with assorted crackers.

Serves 8-12

Toasted Walnut Bites

Great cocktail nibbles.

72 walnut halves
 5 oz. Gorgonzola cheese at room temperature
 3 tbsp. softened, unsalted butter

1. Preheat oven to 350 degrees. Spread walnut halves in a single layer on an ungreased baking sheet. Toast until aromatic and golden brown, about 5-7 minutes. Shake at 3 minutes so nuts brown evenly, and to check color. Once nuts begin to color, they toast quickly. Don't let them burn! Remove pan from oven and pour nuts onto a baking sheet to cool completely.

Bulk Cheese

Bulk cheese keeps longer when it's wrapped in a paper towel dampened with vinegar and placed in a sealed plastic bag. The vinegar inhibits mold growth. Remoisten the paper towel as needed, typically every few days.

Miller Homestead

2. In a small bowl, use a wooden spoon to blend cheese and butter.
3. Use a knife to spread a generous dab of the cheese mixture on a walnut half. Top with another half to form a sandwich.
4. Refrigerate walnut bites for 10 minutes to firm the cheese. Serve cool.

Yield: 36 bites

Peppered Pecans

Utterly addicting.

½ cup sugar
1 tbsp. kosher salt
1½ tbsp. freshly ground black pepper
1 qol. pecan halves

1. In a small bowl, mix the sugar, salt and pepper together and set aside.
2. Heat a cast iron skill over medium high heat until it is hot enough to vaporize water. Pour pecans into skillet and shake for 1 minute to release the nuts' oil. Lightly toast until the nuts are aromatic, about 3 minutes, stirring often with wooden spoon so the pecans toast evenly.
3. Pour in half of the sugar mixture, shaking the skillet constantly. When sugar starts to caramelize and melt, add the rest of the sugar mixture. Continue shaking an additional 2 minutes.
4. Remove skillet from heat and pour nuts onto a baking sheet. Separate halves and let cool. Store in an airtight, covered container.

Yield: 2 cups

Roasted Eggplant Spread   *Sherrie Jern*

Really, really good.

1 medium eggplant, peeled
2 red bell peppers, seeded
1 red onion, peeled
2 garlic cloves, minced
3 tbsp. good olive oil
1½ tsp. kosher salt
½ tsp. freshly ground black pepper
1 tbsp. tomato paste

70

1. Preheat oven to 400 degrees.
2. Cut the eggplant, bell peppers and onion into 1-inch cubes. Toss in a large bowl with the garlic, olive oil, salt and pepper.
3. Spread mixture on an ungreased baking sheet.
4. Roast for 45 minutes, or until the vegetables are lightly browned and soft, tossing once during cooking. Cool slightly.
5. Place the vegetables in a food processor or blender fitted with a steel blade, add the tomato paste, and pulse 3 or 4 times to blend. Adjust salt and pepper to taste. Serve on toasted bread rounds, with pita crisps, or with raw vegetable sticks.

Serves 6 to 8

Artichoke-Green Chile Dip   *Jayne Ottman*

The addition of green chiles to this classic dip adds zing and flavor.

    2   jars artichoke hearts, drained and finely chopped
    2   4-oz. cans diced green chiles
    1   cup mayonnaise
    1   cup freshly grated Parmesan cheese

1. Preheat oven to 350 degrees.
2. Combine ingredients in small ovenproof casserole and mix well to blend. Bake for 20 minutes or until hot and bubbly. Serve warm with Triscuits® or other crisp crackers

Yield: 2½ cups

First Newspaper

The Jackson Hole Courier was the first newspaper published in the valley. Publisher Douglas Rodebeck, financed by Roy Van Vleck, rolled the inaugural issue off the press on January 28, 1909.

Jackson Hole Courier Building.

Bobcat kitten

Bobcat young are born in a litter of 1-7 kittens in April or May. They wean at two months, but remain with their mother for up to five months, traveling with her as they hunt for small rodents, beaver, skunk and ground-nesting birds. Bobcats utilize any available shelter instead of establishing a permanent den. While more tolerant of human presence than the elusive mountain lion, this shy cat is not often seen.

Cheesy Onion Dip

Margie Reimers

1 cup Swiss cheese, grated
1 cup mayonnaise
1 cup Vidalia, Walla Walla or other sweet onions, coarsely chopped

1. Preheat oven to 350 degrees.
2. Combine ingredients and pour into one-quart ovenproof casserole. Bake for 30 minutes, or until hot and bubbly and lightly browned. Good spread on crackers or slices of rye bread.

Yield: 3 cups

Blue Cheese Dip

A cool dip for chicken wings, chili chips and other spicy appetizers.

¾ cup light sour cream
1 tbsp. finely diced red onion
1 tbsp. skim milk
½ cup crumbled blue cheese
¼ tsp. garlic salt
⅛ tsp. stone ground mustard
    paprika

1. Combine all ingredients in blender and blend until smooth and creamy, about a minute.
2. Pour dip into serving bowl and lightly sprinkle with paprika. Cover and chill in refrigerator to blend flavors.

Yield: Approx. 1½ cups

Hot Pecan Dip

Sherri McFarland

½ cup chopped pecans
2 tsp. butter, melted
¼ tsp. salt
1 8-oz pkg. softened cream cheese
½ cup sour cream
2 tsp. milk
1 3-oz. pkg. dried beef, chopped fine
¼ cup chopped green pepper
1 small onion, finely chopped
½ tsp. garlic salt
¼ tsp. pepper

1. Preheat oven to 350 degrees. Place butter and salt in a small bowl. Add pecans and toss to coat. Spread on an ungreased baking sheet and toast until golden, 3-5 minutes. Watch carefully: nuts burn easily. Shake nuts onto paper towels to cool and drain excess butter. Increase oven temperature to 375 degrees.
2. Combine remaining ingredients and beat until well blended. Put in buttered baking dish and top with pecans. Bake for 20 minutes, or until hot and bubbly. Serve warm with crackers.

Yield: Approx. 2 cups

Roasted Red Pepper and Cream Cheese Dip

Sherrie Jern

Roasted red pepper fans will go wild over this dip.

1	large red bell pepper, roasted, or ⅓ jar of roasted red bell peppers (drained)
2	cloves garlic, cut up
1	3-oz. pkg. cream cheese, at room temperature
¼	cup plain nonfat yogurt or sour cream
¼	tsp. dried oregano, crumbled
¼	tsp. dried basil, crumbled
¼	tsp. paprika
¼	tsp. salt
2	drops Tabasco sauce

1. Preheat broiler.
2. Roast red pepper. (Note: Skip this step if using jarred peppers.) Cut pepper in half lengthwise and remove stem, seeds and ribs. Place skin side up in a pie plate. Broil 4-inches from heat, turning to expose all sides of the skin, until evenly charred and blackened, 10-15 minutes. Transfer to a paper bag and close the top. Let stand until cool, 10-15 minutes. Remove pepper from bag and peel off skin. Cut pepper into large pieces.
3. Place roasted pepper pieces and all remaining ingredients in food processor and blender. Process until smooth.
4. Transfer to a small bowl, cover, and refrigerate. Serve chilled with crackers, bread or raw vegetable sticks.

Yield: Approx. 1 cup

Bell Peppers

Take advantage of bell peppers on sale, even if you don't plan on using them while fresh. Seed and chop the peppers and store in a freezer bag. Next time a recipe calls for chopped bell pepper, you'll have what you need in the freezer.

Teater Studio

This rustic log cabin, which today houses a custom jewelry store, was built c. 1940 as a studio/showroom for artist Archie Teater. Teater painted hundreds of paintings of Grand Teton National Park and Jackson Hole over a career of two plus decades. He was a well-known fixture near the town square, where he would set up a palette and paint plein air.

Best-Ever Guacamole

Sherrie Jern

True to its name.

4   ripe Haas avocados
3   tbsp. freshly squeezed lemon juice (1 lemon)
8   dashes Tabasco sauce
1   small red onion, diced small (½ cup)
1   large garlic clove, minced
1   tsp. kosher salt
1   tsp. freshly ground black pepper
1   medium tomato, seeded and diced small

1.   Halve avocados and remove the pits. Scoop the flesh into a large bowl and add the lemon juice, Tabasco, onion, garlic, salt and pepper. Stir to blend.
2.   Slice through the avocados in the bowl with a knife until the flesh is diced. Add the tomatoes and mix. Adjust seasonings to taste.

Serves 8

Eight Layer Fiesta Dip

Emily Duggan
submitted by Erika Muschaweck

2   15-oz. cans refried beans
2   avocados, chopped
1   4-oz. can diced green chiles
1   cup mayonnaise
1   cup sour cream
1   env. taco seasoning
1   cup grated cheddar cheese
1   cup Monterey Jack cheese
1   bunch green onions, tops included
2   tomatoes, deseeded and chopped
1   4-oz. can chopped or sliced black olives

1.   In a small bowl, mix together the mayonnaise, sour cream and taco seasoning until well blended. Set aside.
2.   In a 9x13-inch serving dish or pan, layer the above ingredients in the following order: refried beans, avocado, chiles, mayonnaise mixture, cheddar cheese, Monterey Jack cheese, onions, tomatoes and black olives. Serve with corn or tortilla chips.

Serves 8-10

Pita Crisps with Tuna Tapenade

The combination of ingredients in this adapted recipe, showcased in *First* magazine, is a winner.

      4   8-in. pita breads
    2½   tbsp. chopped parsley, divided
      1   tbsp. olive oil
      1   clove garlic, minced
      1   3¼-oz. can solid white tuna packed in water, drained
      1   7-oz. jar roasted red peppers, drained and chopped
      1   cup Kalamata olives, pitted and chopped fine
      2   tbsp. mayonnaise
      1   tbsp. capers
      1   tsp. grated lemon peel
          salt and pepper to taste

1. In a small bowl, mix together the tuna, roasted red peppers, olives, mayonnaise, capers, lemon peel and 2 tbsp. of parsley until tuna is broken up and ingredients are well blended. Salt and pepper to taste. Transfer mix to serving dish and set aside.
2. Heat oven broiler. Place pita bread on rack in broiler pan and brush top with olive oil. Sprinkle ½ tbsp. of the parsley and the minced garlic on the bread. Broil on a rack in the top third of the oven for approximately 2 minutes, or until lightly browned. Watch carefully so bread doesn't burn. Remove from oven. Cut into 1-inch strips with pizza cut or bread knife. Serve warm or cold with tuna tapenade.

Serves 8

Town of Moran

In 1927, Ben Sheffield, an early guide and pioneer in northern Jackson Hole, owned 343 acres and all the buildings in the small tourist town of Moran. The town officially began with establishment of a post office in 1902, but didn't grow significantly until 1916 when hastily constructed cabins were built to house workers constructing Jackson Lake Dam. The dam, ironically, sealed the fate of the town. Its concrete face blocked views of the mountains and placed the town below its face, causing tourism to dip. Sheffield sold the acreage, Teton Lodge and 107 other structures that comprised the town to the Snake River Land Company in 1928 for $106, 425. The last building from the former town "beneath the dam" was removed in July of 1957.

Town of Moran, 1924.

Veggie Pizza Bites

Colorful, crunchy and fun.

  1   8-oz. can refrigerated crescent rolls
  1   8-oz. pkg. of cream cheese, softened
  ⅓   cup low-fat or regular mayonnaise
  1   tsp. dried dill weed
  1   tsp. dried, minced onion
  2½ cups raw vegetables of your choice, chopped fine (broccoli, red and green pepper, cauliflower, onion and celery are good choices)
  ½   cup shredded carrot

1. Preheat oven to 400 degrees.
2. Spread crescent rolls on an ungreased 12-inch round pizza pan or a cookie sheet, pressing dough perforations closed with thumbs. Bake for 10 minutes or until lightly browned. Remove from oven and cool.
3. Place softened cream cheese, mayonnaise, dill and minced onion in a bowl and mix together with a wooden spoon until well blended and smooth. Spread mixture on cooled crust.
4. Evenly sprinkle chopped raw vegetables over cream cheese and top with shredded carrots. Gently press down to "set" vegetables. Refrigerate until serving time. Cut into brownie-sized squares or thin pizza wedges.

Serves 10-12

Smoked Salmon and Apple Quesadilla Wedges with Horseradish Creme

Divine. Served with a mixed green salad, this also makes an appealing lunch or light meal for 4.

Quesadillas
  8   ozs. thinly sliced smoked salmon, julienned
  1   small Granny Smith apple, cored and julienned
  8   ozs. Monterey Jack cheese, grated
  ¼   cup Asiago cheese
  1   tbsp. fresh dill, chopped
  3   tbsp. finely diced red onion
  1   tsp. fresh lime juice
  4   flour tortillas at room temperature
  2   tbsp. unsalted butter, melted

Hidden Falls

Truly hidden until you are almost upon it, pretty Hidden Falls plunges 200 feet. The falls thunder early season, when spring run-off turns Cascade Creek into a white torrent. The short trail to the falls is one of the most popular destinations in Grand Teton National Park.

Horseradish Creme

    2 tbsp. prepared horseradish
    2 tbsp. fresh chopped chives
    ½ cup sour cream
    ½ cup mayonnaise
    3 tbsp. heavy cream
    1 tbsp. fresh lemon juice
    1 tsp. salt

1. Whisk horseradish creme ingredients together in a mixing bowl. Transfer to a small serving dish and set aside.
2. In a large bowl, mix the salmon, apple, cheeses, dill, onion and lime juice together. Spread ¼ of the mixture over half of each tortilla. Fold tortillas over to form a half-circle.
4. Heat a large nonstick pan over medium heat. Brush one side of each tortilla with butter. Place buttered side down in heated pan. Cook 3-4 minutes, or until golden brown. Brush top with butter, turn over and cook another 3-4 minutes. Tortillas may be kept warm on a plate in a 200 degree oven until all are cooked.
6. Cut each tortilla into 3 triangles. Serve warm with horseradish creme.

Serves 12

Garlic Bagel Chips

Yum.

    2 2-oz. frozen unsplit plain bagels, thawed
    1 tbsp. butter
        butter-flavored cooking spray
    1 tsp. garlic powder

1. Preheat oven to 350 degrees.
2. Cut each bagel in half vertically. Place halves in food chute of food processor and slice. (For bigger chips, use a serrated knife to cut bagels in half horizontally. Cut each half in half again, being carefully not to cut your fingers.
3. Place butter and garlic powder in microwave-safe dish and microwave on high until melted, 15-30 seconds.
4. Lightly coat slices with cooking spray, then brush with melted garlic butter, placing each sprayed and buttered slice in a single layer on an ungreased baking sheet.
5. Bake until crisp, approximately 15 minutes. Remove from sheet and cool completely on wire rack before serving.

Serves 2

Removing garlic skin

To easily remove papery garlic skin, zap separated cloves placed on a paper towel in the microwave for 15 seconds. The skins will slip off easily.

Chili Chips

The secret to these wonderful, lip-smacking chips is slicing the potatoes extra thin. Temper the spiciness by serving them with frosty mugs
of ale, or the chilled blue cheese dip on page 72.

    2 large, unpeeled Idaho baking potatoes
    1 tbsp. olive oil
    1 tsp. ground chili powder
    ¼ tsp. black pepper
    ¼ tsp. salt
       cooking spray

1. Preheat oven to 450 degrees.
2. Cut potatoes in half crosswise. Use a professional mandolin to slice
   potato halves extra thin, or push each half through the chute of
   your food processor, cut side down, using a thin slicing disc.
3. Remove excess moisture by patting slices dry with a paper towel.
4. Add oil, chili powder, pepper and salt to a large, heavy-duty ziplock
   bag. Put potato slices in bag, seal and toss well to coat.
5. Coat two baking sheets with cooking spray. Place potato slices on
   sheets in a single layer.
6. Bake for 10-12 minutes, or until potatoes are crisp. Turn chips
   over and bake another 10-12 minutes, or until crisp. Serve warm.

Serves 4

Hauling mail over Teton Pass, 1912.

Mango White Bean Salsa

Mary Howley, R.D.

Mary is the owner of Beyond Broccoli, a nutrition counseling business. This is one of many yummy recipes she has developed for her "Lunch and Learn" classes.

 1 medium cucumber, peeled, seeded and cut into ½-inch dice
 ½ tsp. chiles, seeded and diced, or more to taste
 1 ripe mango, cut into chunks. (Mango may be mushy or stringy. This is okay.)
 1 small red bell pepper, seeded and diced
 2 tbsp. unsweetened, shredded coconut
 1 tbsp. fresh lemon juice
 1 tbsp. fresh lime juice
 2 tsp. unpacked brown sugar
 ½-1 garlic clove, minced or pressed, to taste
 1 cup cooked white beans
   salt and pepper to taste
   fresh chopped cilantro to taste (optional)
   pinch cayenne pepper (optional)

Teton Pass,
Winter of 1936.

1937 was the first year Teton Pass was kept open to traffic the entire winter. As evidenced by this photo, the job was a challenge for comparatively primitive snow removal equipment.

1. Combine everything except salt, pepper and optional ingredients in a bowl. Mix well to blend. Season to taste with salt, pepper, cilantro and cayenne pepper.
2. Cover bowl and let sit at room temperature at least 30 minutes to allow flavors to mingle. Or chill, covered, for up to 1 day before serving.

Serves 4

Peach Salsa

A superb accompaniment to fish or chicken.

 1 cup peeled, chopped peaches
 ¼ cup chopped red onions
 ¼ cup chopped yellow or green bell pepper
 1 tbsp. fresh lemon or lime juice
 2 tsp. chopped fresh cilantro, parsley, or basil
 1 tsp. sugar
   dash ground red pepper

1. Combine ingredients in a medium bowl. Stir to mix.
2. Cover and chill for up to 6 hours before serving.

Yield: 1½ cups

Cedar Waxwing

This crested bird with a wide yellow band at the tip of its tail is easy to identify. Occasional visitors to the valley, waxwings are most often seen in late summer and early fall when the chokecherries ripen. The birds gorge themselves on the sour berries. They are known to eat both wild and domesticated fruits as well as some insects.

Island Fruit Salsa

A perfect accompaniment to grilled meats or broiled fish. Try it with Marinated Flank Steak, page 172.

½ cup fresh pineapple, cut into ½-inch dice
½ cup ripe mango, cut into ½-inch dice
½ cup papaya, cut into ½-inch dice
½ cup Granny Smith apple, cut into ½-inch dice
¼ cup each green and red bell pepper, cut into ½-inch dice
2 tbsp. white wine vinegar
1 tbsp. fresh snipped cilantro
1 tbsp. plus 1 tsp. sugar
¼ tsp. crushed red pepper flakes

Mix ingredients together. Cover and chill up to 1 day before serving.

Note: Salsa is best mixed at least 1 hour before serving time to give flavors a chance to blend.

Serves 4

Creamy Roasted Red Pepper Salsa   *Marcia Kunstel*

As a co-owner of Flat Creek Ranch with husband, Joe Albright, Marcia frequently creates new recipes to tantalize guests. This is one of her successful results. Serve with crackers, bread or raw vegetables, or use as an accompaniment to grilled fish or chicken.

2 (small) garlic cloves
1 chopped scallion
½ inch tip of jalapeno pepper
½ cup roasted red pepper (peppers from a jar are fine)
2 tbsp. coarsely chopped sun dried tomatoes, softened in enough hot water to cover (reserve water).
1 tbsp. reserved tomato water
1 tbsp. half-and-half or cream
salt and pepper
red pepper flakes

1. Mince garlic, scallion, jalapeno and red pepper in a food processor or hand chopper. Place in a small bowl.
2. Add softened sun dried tomatoes and 1 tbsp. of the reserved tomato water. Stir to mix.
3. Add half-and-half. Stir to blend. Add more cream if salsa is too thick.

4. Sprinkle with salt, pepper and red pepper flakes to taste. Chill, covered, until ready to serve.

Serves 2

Black Bean and Corn Salsa

Great with chips and "south of the border" entrees.

Storing corn

Corn, beans, peas and other vegetables will lose sweetness as sugar in their tissues turns to starch. Store dry and un-washed in plastic bags in the refrigerator.

2   15-oz. cans black beans, rinsed and drained
1   cup frozen yellow corn kernels, defrosted and drained
1   cup frozen white shoepeg corn kernels, defrosted and drained
½   cup fresh cilantro, chopped
1   jalapeno, deseeded, stem removed and minced
1   large tomato, deseeded and chopped
2   cloves garlic, minced
1   large sweet onion (Bermuda, Florida, Maui, Vidalia), chopped
3   green onions, thinly sliced, tops included
1   tsp. chili powder
1   tbsp. ground cumin
3   tbsp. lime juice
¼   tsp. ground black pepper
    dash cayenne pepper, salt to taste

1. Thoroughly, but gently, mix everything together. Refrigerate at least 4 hours and up to 2 days to allow flavors to blend.
2. Bring to room temperature before serving with tortilla chips.

Yield: Approximately 4 cups

Fresh Tomato Salsa

Good and easy. You may never buy commercial salsa again.

4   large plum tomatoes
¼   cup chopped green onions, tops included
¼   cup chopped cilantro
1   tbsp. fresh oregano
2   cloves garlic, minced
1   tsp. minced jalapeno pepper
1   tbsp. olive oil
2   tsp. lime juice
    salt and freshly ground pepper, to taste

1. Cut tomatoes in half lengthwise and remove seeds. Cut the halves into ¼-inch dice and place in a medium bowl. Add the remaining

ingredients. Let sit, loosely covered, at room temperature for 20 minutes to blend flavors. May be refrigerated for up to 4 hours.
2. Serve with chips or as an accompaniment to grilled chicken or beef.

Yield: Approx. 2 cups

Pico de Gallo

(Pronounced "guyo.") This is the stuff that makes fajitas taste *so-o-o* good. Pico de Gallo is great with tortilla chips and just about any southwestern or Mexican dish. It's addicting! Abuelitos Restaurant in Jackson serves a great version, but alas, the recipe is a trade secret. We give you ours.

4   ripe plum tomatoes, seeded, pulp removed, finely chopped
1   small white onion, finely chopped
2   large cloves garlic, finely minced
⅔   cup cucumber, peeled, seeded and finely diced
5   peeled radishes, finely diced
2   tbsp. minced cilantro leaves
3-4 fresh serrano chiles, seeded and very finely chopped
    (Note: always wear rubber gloves when working with hot peppers.)
1   tbsp. white wine vinegar
1   tbsp. fresh lime juice
    salt and pepper to taste

1. Place tomatoes, onion, garlic, cucumber, radishes, cilantro, chiles and vinegar in a bowl. Sprinkle lime juice over all and gently mix. Add salt and pepper.
2. Chill, covered, for at least 1 hour. Pico de Gallo should be served the same day it is made.

Serves 6

South side of the Jackson Town Square, 1930s.

Marilyn's Pesto

Marilyn Quinn

Professional Jackson Hole gardener Marilyn Quinn uses her precious crop of basil to make this flavorsome pesto. The recipe is used with permission from her book, *Peak Bloom: Honest Advice for Mountain & Northern Gardeners.*

2 cups fresh basil
½ cup fresh parsley leaves, chopped
½ cup olive oil
2 garlic cloves, coarsely chopped
1 tsp. salt
½ cup freshly grated Parmesan cheese

1. Puree the basil, parsley, oil, garlic and salt in a blender or food processor to a coarse texture.
2. Place mixture in bowl and stir in Parmesan cheese
3. Toss with warm pasta of choice. Leftover pesto may be stored in the refrigerator. Pour a thin layer of olive oil on top to keep moist.

Serves 6

Red Pepper Almond Pesto

Sloane Andrews

A zesty sauce that compliments Mexican or Southwestern dishes such as quesadillas and enchiladas. It's also great with tortilla chips.

2 red bell peppers, cored, seeded and chopped
2 shallots or green onions (white section only), chopped
4 cloves garlic, minced
¼ cup blanched almonds, toasted
4 tbsp. fresh grated Parmesan cheese
¼ cup olive oil

1. Preheat oven to 350 degrees. Spread almonds in a single layer on a baking sheet and place on a rack in the middle of the oven. Toast until aromatic and brown, about 3-5 minutes. Watch carefully so they don't burn.
2. Mince peppers, shallots, toasted almonds and garlic in a blender or food processor. Add oil and cheese. Blend.

Serves 4-6

Wort Hotel

In September of 1941, Jess and John Wort opened the Wort Hotel, then described as the first modern hotel in the valley. The elegant hotel, listed on the National Register of Historic Places, was overhauled after a major fire in 1980. The Worts were among the valley's earliest settlers, moving to Jackson Hole from Nebraska in 1893.

Red-naped Sapsucker

This common avian valley resident derives its name from feeding on the soft inner bark and sap of trees. Its red head is bordered with black, and its chest sports a black breast patch. Male adults are close to 9-inches in length. Females are somewhat smaller.

Zesty Hamburger Relish

Chef Karen Norby

Uncommonly good.

2	ripe tomatoes, peeled and seeded
¼	head green cabbage, cored
2	small green peppers, seeds removed
2	onions, peeled and cut into wedges
1	quart white vinegar
1¼	cups sugar
2	tsp. Dijon mustard
1	tsp. celery seeds
1	tsp. ground cloves
1	tsp. cinnamon
½	tbsp. tumeric

1. Place tomatoes, cabbage, peppers and onions in a food processor or blender and pulse until roughly chopped.
2. Combine remaining ingredients in a large saucepan and bring to a boil. Add chopped vegetables and return to a boil, then reduce heat to a simmer. Cook uncovered until thick, roughly 1 hour.

Yield: 1 quart. Relish keeps in refrigerator about 3 weeks.

Salads & Dressings

Camp on Goosewing Creek, 1887

Storing Nuts

Store your nuts in the
freezer. They last longer
and crack more easily.

Red Onion, Pear and Feta Salad with Caramelized Pecans
Alyssa McCormack

"This salad rocks. Bring it to a potluck and people will be talking about it for months to come."

Salad
- 1 bunch greenleaf lettuce or bag of gourmet salad mix
- 1 small red onion, peeled and slivered
- 1 medium pear, thinly sliced
- 1 cup feta, blue or Gorgonzola cheese, crumbled

Caramelized pecans
- ½ cup sugar
- 1 cup pecan halves

1. Caramelize pecans first. Melt sugar over low heat in nonstick pan until liquefied, about 5 minutes. Stir frequently, watching closely so the sugar doesn't burn. When the sugar has liquefied, add pecans and stir until nuts are evenly coated. Remove nuts from heat and spread them in a single layer on a sheet of wax paper to cool.
2. Toss salad ingredients together and top with cooled pecans.
3. Lightly dress with a slightly sweet vinaigrette when ready to serve. (Briana's Blush® is ideal).

Serves 6

Minted Caesar Salad
Margie Reimers

This delicious, unusual rendition of the classic Caesar salad is a creation of the chefs at Candless restaurant in San Francisco.

Salad
- 1 head of romaine lettuce, washed, dried and torn into pieces
- ¼ cup chopped fresh mint
- 8 slices of bacon, fried crisp and crumbled
- ½ cup fresh grated Parmesan cheese
  croutons

Dressing
- 1 coddled egg, whipped
- ⅔ cup olive oil
  juice of 2½ lemons
  large pinch of oregano
- 1 tsp. salt

1. Coddle egg. Bring egg to room temperature. Fill a small saucepan

with enough water to cover the egg and bring to a boil. Place egg on a tablespoon and lower into the boiling water. Turn off the burner, cover the saucepan and let sit for one minute. Remove from water and shell immediately into bowl. Egg will still be very runny. Whip.
2. Add remaining dressing ingredients to whipped egg. Whisk together until well blended, then set aside.
3. Mix salad ingredients together. Pour dressing over salad and toss. Top with fresh ground pepper.

Serves 6

Mandarin Orange Salad with Sugared Almonds
Eva Marie Watson

Salad
- ¼ cup sliced almonds
- 1 tbsp. sugar
- ½ head of iceberg lettuce
- ½ bag fresh spinach, stems removed
- ¾ cup celery, chopped
- 2 green onions, thinly sliced with tops
- 1 11-oz. can mandarin orange segments, well drained

Dressing
- ¼ cup salad oil
- 2 tsp. vinegar
- 2 tbsp. sugar
-   dash ground black pepper
- ½ tsp. salt
-   dash of Tabasco sauce
- 1 tbsp. fresh parsley, chopped

1. In a small bowl, combine dressing ingredients and whisk to thoroughly blend. Refrigerate to cool.
2. Place sliced almonds and sugar in a nonstick skillet over low heat. Stir occasionally until sugar is melted and almonds are coated, about 7-9 minutes. Remove from heat and spread, separated, on baking sheet to cool.
3. Rinse and dry lettuce and spinach. Tear into bite-sized pieces and place in salad bowl. Add celery, green onions and mandarin oranges. Toss to mix.
4. Pour chilled dressing over salad and toss to coat. Sprinkle almonds on top and lightly toss again. Serve immediately.

Serves 4-6

Pika

This small relative of the rabbit family is under 8 inches long and weighs less than 9 oz. Its high-pitched squeak gives away its presence in rockslide areas, where it both lives and forages for plants, grasses and sedges. Pikas build their grass-lined nests under rock ledges. Their young are born after a 30-day gestation and open their eyes when they are 10 days old. They are weaned by the end of the first month.

Elizabeth McCabe's Spinach Salad   *Liz McCabe*

So many people asked Liz McCabe for her recipe that she "went public" and had *Jackson Hole Guide* food columnist Carole Anderson Travis (Henikoff) include it in the November 26, 1980, "Cooking with Carole" column.

    1   pkg. or up to 1 lb. fresh spinach
    1   can water chestnuts, drained and sliced
    ½   cup bean sprouts
    6   slices bacon, fried crisp and crumbled
    ¼   cup sesame seeds

Salad dressing
    1   cup salad oil
    ¼   cup balsamic vinegar
    ¼   cup vinegar
    ½   cup sugar
    ⅓   cup catsup
    2   tbsp. Worcestershire sauce
    ½   tsp. garlic powder
         salt and pepper to taste

1. Place well-washed and dried spinach in bowl. Top with water chestnuts, bean sprouts, bacon and sesame seeds. Set aside.
2. Mix salad dressing ingredients in separate container. Pour desired amount over salad and toss. (Remaining dressing will keep, covered, up to 10 days.) Serve immediately.

Serves 6 generously

Joe Pfeifer Homestead in GTNP.

Guissy's Salad

Eva Watson

Eva was given this great mixed greens salad recipe from an Italian woman who became a good friend when the Watson family lived in Italy.

Lettuce

Don't chop lettuce with a steel blade. The steel causes the edges to wilt and brown quicker. Tear by hand or use a plastic knife.

1   small bunch romaine lettuce
1   small bunch red leaf lettuce
1   small bunch radicchio lettuce
1   bunch green onions, thinly sliced, tops included
1   avocado, peeled, pit removed, and thinly sliced

Salad Dressing
½   cup extra-virgin olive oil
3   tbsp. red wine vinegar
    pinch of salt
2   cloves garlic, crushed
1½ tbsp. sugar
½   tbsp. dark French mustard

1. Rinse and dry lettuces. Tear into bite-sized pieces and place in salad bowl. Add onions and avocado. Toss to mix.
2. In a small bowl, combine dressing ingredients. Whisk to blend. Pour dressing over salad, toss and serve immediately.

Serves 6-8

Cinema Salad

Frank Londy

"An entire restaurant chain was built on this recipe. It's a great salad."

½   head of iceberg lettuce
6   romaine lettuce leaves, torn into pieces
3   ozs. diced red pimento
½   cup sliced red onions
½   cup quartered artichoke hearts

Dressing
2   ozs. salad oil
1½ ozs. of red wine vinegar
1   oz. freshly grated Parmesan cheese
    pinch of salt and pepper

1. Combine dressing ingredients in a small, lidded jar or cruet and shake vigorously to blend.
2. Toss salad ingredients together in salad bowl. Pour dressing over salad and toss again to coat. Serve immediately.

Serves 4

Summer Salad

Christy Walton

Refreshing! (And great to eat year-round.)

2   pink or white grapefruit, peeled, one-half per person
1   small white onion, finely diced.
½ -1   cup Queso fresco, panela, or other mild fresh cheese, crumbled
      extra-virgin olive oil
      sea salt to taste

1. Remove membrane from peeled grapefruit and slice into ¾-inch thick "wheels."
2. Place grapefruit wheels on individual salad plates, mound onion on fruit, crumble cheese upon onion, drizzle olive oil over all and sprinkle with sea salt.

Serves 4

Insalata Capricciosa

An Italian classic, best prepared in mid- to late summer when tomatoes and basil are at their peak.

4   oz. fresh mozzarella
2   large tomatoes
8   large fresh basil leaves, shredded
1   tbsp. extra-virgin olive oil
3   tbsp. white balsamic vinegar
1   tsp. garlic, minced
⅛   tsp. sugar
¼   tsp. dry mustard
      coarse salt and freshly ground pepper to taste

1. In a small bowl, combine the oil, vinegar, garlic, sugar and mustard. Whisk to blend; set aside.
2. Slice mozzarella into rounds ⅛ to ¼-inch thick. Slice tomatoes ¼-inch thick.
3. On a large platter or individual plates, arrange alternate slices of cheese and tomato.
4. Spoon dressing over salad, salt and pepper to taste, and garnish with shredded basil. Serve immediately.

Serves 4

Avocado and Tomato Salad

Linda Bourett

"I serve this all the time with Mexican food. People love it."

- 6 slices of bacon
- 3 tbsp. vegetable or salad oil
- 1 tbsp. vinegar
- ½ tsp. salt
- ⅛ tsp. pepper
- 3 drops of red pepper sauce
- 2 medium avocados, peeled and cubed
- 2 medium tomatoes, cut into ½-inch dice
- 1 small, chopped onion
  salad greens

1. Fry the bacon crisp and crumble it.
2. Mix oil, vinegar, salt, pepper and red pepper sauce and pour over avocadoes. Toss.
3. Stir in bacon, tomatoes and onions. Mix well. Cover and refrigerate 2 hours. Just before serving, place on salad greens with a slotted spoon.

Serves 4-6

Distinctly Different Slaw

Judy Eddy

Distinctly delicious.

- 1 pkg. ramen noodles
- 1 pkg. coleslaw
- 1 cup toasted sliced almonds
- ¾ cup sliced green onions, with tops
- ½ cup sunflower seeds
- ⅓ cup salad oil
- ⅓ cup sugar
- ⅓ cup white vinegar

1. Break ramen into small pieces. Put seasoning packet aside.
2. In large bowl, stir together ramen, slaw, almonds, green onions and sunflower seeds; set aside.
3. In glass jar or cruet, combine oil, sugar, vinegar and seasoning packet from noodles. Cover and shake to dissolve sugar. Pour mixture over salad; toss to coat. Serve immediately, or cover and chill in the refrigerator for up to 4 hours.

Serves 6

Mule Deer Fawn

Does give birth to one to three fawns in late May or early June following a gestation of about seven months. Young are born with light spots, thought by some biologists to replicate the pattern of sun and shadow in the forest to aid in camouflaging them from predators. The spots are visible until the fawns molt, typically in August. Fawns are weaned from their mother when they are four or five months old.

Citrus Broccoli Slaw

This colorful, sweet-and-sour salad nicely complements grilled fish and meats.

¼	cup sugar
2	tbsp. apple cider vinegar
2	tbsp. fresh snipped parsley
1	tbsp. extra-virgin olive oil
½	cup fresh squeezed orange juice
1	tbsp. grated orange peel
1	16-oz. pkg. broccoli slaw

1. Put broccoli slaw in a large serving bowl. Set aside.
2. In a separate, smaller bowl, whisk the sugar, vinegar, parsley, oil, orange juice and orange peel together until well blended. Pour over broccoli slaw and toss to coat. Chill, covered, until served. Toss again before serving.

Serves 4.

Mango Curry Tuna Salad

The addition of mango chutney and curry elevates pedestrian tuna to "special guest" status!

1	6½-oz. can solid white tuna, drained and finely flaked
2	green onions, finely sliced, green tops included
¼	cup celery, chopped
¼	cup water chestnuts, thinly sliced
¼	cup slivered almonds
¼	cup light mayonnaise
¼	cup purchased mango chutney or canned mango slices, chopped
1	tsp. curry powder
	salt and white pepper to taste

1. In a medium-sized bowl, combine tuna, green onions, celery, water chestnuts, almonds and mango chutney. Mix well.
2. In a separate small bowl, whisk together mayonnaise and curry until well blended. Pour over tuna mixture and stir to incorporate. Season with salt and pepper to taste. Chill covered for 1 hour to blend flavors. Serve on plates lined with green leaf lettuce.

Serves 4

Walnut Chicken Salad

A scrumptious affair that will bring people back for seconds. Adapted from *Cooking Light* magazine.

- ¼ cup plus 2 tbsp. walnuts, chopped and toasted
- 2 tsp. low-sodium soy sauce
  vegetable cooking spray
- 1½ lbs. skinless, boneless chicken breasts
- 3 cups cooked couscous, prepared without salt or fat
- ½ cup carrot, coarsely shredded
- ⅓ cup green onion, sliced with tops
- 2 tbsp. shallots, minced
- 3 tbsp. rice wine vinegar
- 2 tbsp. water
- 1½ tsp. walnut oil
- 2 tsp. brown sugar
- 1 tsp. grated lemon rind
- 1 tsp. ginger root, peeled and grated
- ¼ tsp. salt
- ¼ tsp. pepper
- 2 cloves garlic, minced
- 7½ cups loosely packed fresh spinach, sliced into thin strips

1. Preheat oven to 350 degrees. Sprinkle chopped walnuts on a single layer on an ungreased baking sheet, and place sheet in the middle of the oven. Toast for approximately 5 minutes, or until aromatic and brown. Check at 3 minutes for doneness and to turn nuts for even browning. Watch carefully to prevent burning: once nuts begin to change color, they brown very quickly. Remove from oven and spread nuts on a single layer on paper towels to cool.
2. Coat a large, nonstick skillet with cooking spray and place over medium heat until hot, about 3-4 minutes. Add chicken. Cook approximately 6 minutes on each side, or until middle of breast is no longer pink and juices run clear.
3. Cut cooked chicken into bite-sized pieces and place them in a large bowl. Add couscous, carrot and green onions. Stir to combine, then set aside.
4. In a small bowl, combine the soy sauce, shallot, rice wine vinegar, water, walnut oil, brown sugar, lemon rind, gingerroot, salt, pepper and garlic. Whisk until well blended. Add mixture to chicken and couscous. Stir well to evenly distribute.
5. Place 1¼ cups spinach on six individual serving plates. Place a cup of the chicken/couscous mixture on top, then sprinkle with toasted walnuts.

Serves 6

William Owen, 1934

The official first ascent of the Grand Teton occurred on August 11, 1898, when William O. "Billy" Owen, Frank Spalding, Frank Petersen and John Shive scaled the peak via what came to be known as the Owen-Spalding route. Spalding is credited with both finding and leading most of the route.

Main lodge of the new
Elbo Ranch, c. 1949

Santa Fe Grilled Chicken Salad with Honey Lime Vinaigrette

Nicola Esdorn
Submitted by Erika Muschaweck

Daughter Nicola Esdron passed this on to Erika after preparing it during a cooking course in Rye, N.Y. It is superb.

Chicken and marinade
- 2 boneless, skinless chicken breasts
- 2 limes, juiced and zested (only green part)
- ½ cup vegetable oil
- 1 tbsp. cilantro, chopped
- 1 tsp. jalapeno pepper, minced
- 1 tsp. garlic chopped
- ½ tsp. chili powder
- 1 tsp. Dijon mustard

Salad
- 2 ears fresh corn, cooked, cooled and cleaned from cob, or ¾ cup canned corn, cooked and drained
- 1 cup black beans, cooked until soft and cooled (soak overnight, drain, cook in fresh water about 1½ hours.)
- ½ cup shredded cheddar cheese
- 4 corn tortillas, julienned and deep fried until crisp (try to find yellow, red or blue tortillas)
- 4 plum tomatoes, sliced
- ¼ bunch fresh cilantro leaves
- 1 avocado, cut into quarters and sliced
- ½ pound mixed lettuces

1. Combine the marinade ingredients in a stainless steel bowl and mix thoroughly. Add chicken breasts and marinate for 1 hour.
2. Make the Honey Lime Vinaigrette, following instructions on the next page.
3. Preheat your grill or sauté pan over medium high heat. When hot, grill the marinated chicken breasts for approximately 3-5 minutes on each side, or until juices run clear when pricked by a fork. Remove from grill and let cool for 5 minutes while you assemble the salad components.
4. Mix the cilantro with the lettuces. Place this mixture on a platter. Arrange the corn, black beans, cheese, tomatoes, and avocado around the perimeter of the platter. Slice the chicken breasts "on the bias" and fan out over the salad. Garnish with the crisp tortillas and drizzle with the Honey Lime Vinaigrette.

94

Honey Lime Vinaigrette

2 limes, juiced and zested
½ cup rice wine vinegar or white balsamic vinegar
3 tbsp. honey
1 tsp. Kosher salt
⅛ tsp. ground white pepper
1 tsp. Dijon mustard
1½ cups blended oil (¾ cup vegetable oil, ¾ cup olive oil)
1 tbsp. chives, chopped

1. In a blender or food processor, combine lime juice, lime zest, Dijon mustard, rice wine vinegar, honey, salt and pepper. Pulse to blend ingredients.
2. On a low speed setting, slowly add oil until vinaigrette is slightly thickened and thoroughly mixed.
3. Add the chopped chives and pulse just enough to disperse the chives. Refrigerate, covered, until ready to use.

Serves 4

Elbo Ranch Gate, c. 1949.

Elbo Ranch

In the mid-1930s, Paul Petzoldt and Gustav Koven formed a partnership to run the Ramshorn Dude Ranch. They hired the Woodward brothers to build the main lodge building in 1937. Shortly afterwards, Petzoldt and Koven dissolved their partnership. After going through a series of owners, the guest operation was eventually sold to the National Park Service for $68,000 in 1956. Two years later, the park issued a concession permit to Katie Starratt to run the dude ranch. Starratt had managed the Old Elbo Ranch, which the park was dismantling, since the late 1940s. She renamed the Ramshorn the Elbo Ranch and successfully ran the operation until her death in 1974. The park then granted a special use permit to Grand Teton Environmental EducationCenter to operate Teton Science School at the ranch.

Elk Bugling

Elk mate by dominance. They begin to gather their harem in late August/early September, bugling to attract females and let smaller bucks know they are staking out their territory. Their mournful, piercing cry is often heard at dawn and dusk, when the animals are most active.

Curried Chicken Salad

Jolene Loos

Wonderful served on a bed of crisp lettuce. Pair with oven-fresh rolls for a light summer dinner.

Salad Ingredients

    4 whole, cooked and cubed chicken breasts
  ½ cup sliced water chestnuts
  ½ cup chopped pecans
  ½ cup seedless green or red grapes
  ¼ cup chopped celery
  1 tsp. minced candied ginger

Dressing

  ¾ cup mayonnaise
  2 tbsp. white wine vinegar
  1 tbsp. soy sauce
  2 tsp. minced onion
  ½ tsp. curry powder

1. Mix salad ingredients together and set aside.
2. In a separate bowl, combine dressing ingredients, stirring well to blend. Pour dressing over salad and gently mix. Refrigerate, covered, at least two hours before serving to blend flavors.

Serves 6.

Chinese Vegetable Salad with Honey Sesame Dressing

Therese Metherell, R.D.

Therese loves the Chinese salad at the Betty Rock Cafe in Jackson. It inspired her to develop a similar version without the added oil. She shared her wonderful result with *Jackson Hole News* readers in her December 8, 1999, "Sound Bites" column.

Salad ingredients

  1 large cucumber, peeled, halved lengthwise and cut into thin crescents
  ½ head green cabbage, thinly sliced
  1 orange, peeled, halved and thinly sliced
  ¼ cup thinly sliced red onion
  ¾ cup chow mein noodles
  2 tbsp. sesame seeds
  ¼ cup fresh, chopped cilantro

Honey Sesame Dressing

½ cup rice vinegar
⅓ cup honey
1 tbsp. tamari or soy sauce
1 tbsp. fresh grated ginger root
1 tbsp. dark sesame oil

1. Place dressing ingredients together in a small bowl and whisk to blend.
2. Combine salad ingredients in large bowl and stir to mix.
3. Pour dressing over salad. Toss to mix and serve immediately.

Serves 6.

Mixed Greens with Pickled Beets, Pineapple and Feta
Anne Band

Anne was introduced to this unusually tasty salad when she worked at Cafe Christine.

9 cups mixed greens of choice, rinsed and torn into pieces
chilled julienned pickled beets
pineapple tidbits, drained
feta cheese, crumbled
freshly ground black pepper, to taste
vinaigrette dressing

1. Place greens in salad bowl.
2. Top with beets, pineapple tidbits, feta and black pepper. Gently toss to mix. Dress with a simple vinaigrette. Serve immediately.

Serves 6

Feeding Elk

Widespread concern over elk wintering in Jackson Hole began during the severe winter of 1908-09, when thousands of elk were starving in the valley. Townspeople, with help from the state of Wyoming, bought hay to help the animals make it through the harsh season. The following winter was no better. Through the tireless crusading efforts of local rancher Stephen Leek and his powerful photographs, the federal government established a 1,000-acre U.S. Biological Survey Elk Refuge. Today's National Elk Refuge is the direct descendant of the original refuge. It encompasses nearly 25,000 acres. Over 7,000 elk are fed every winter.

Feeding elk, 1920

Glenn Exum, c. 1948

On July 15, 1931, 18-year-old Glenn Exum made the first ascent of the south ridge of the Grand Teton that now bears his name. Glenn and Paul Petzoldt guided together at Petzoldt's American School of Mountaineering in Grand Teton National Park until 1956, when Glenn took over the business and renamed it the Exum School of Mountaineering. The charismatic Exum was diagnosed with cancer in 1976, yet managed to complete a 50th anniversary ascent of Exum Ridge in August of 1981. Exum died peacefully at his home in Littleton, Colorado, on March 17, 2000, with his beloved wife Beth at his side.

Cucumber and Yogurt Salad   *Susie Rauch*

This cool, delicious salad is a staple throughout the Middle East. It nicely balances curried dishes and other spicy food.

> 1   large or 2 small cucumbers, peeled and cut into ½-inch dice
>   salt
> 2-3   cloves garlic, crushed
> 1½   cups plain yogurt
>   white pepper
> 3   tbsp. fresh mint, chopped fine, or 1 tbsp. dried, crushed mint
>   dried mint for garnish

1. Place diced cucumber in colander, sprinkle with salt and drain for 30 minutes.
2. Place yogurt in a bowl.
3. Crush garlic with a pinch of salt in a small bowl. Mix 3 tbsp. of the yogurt with the garlic, then add garlic mixture to remaining yogurt and mix well. Salt and pepper to taste.
4. Add mint to the yogurt mixture.
5. Place drained cucumbers in serving bowl. Pour yogurt mixture over them and stir to mix. Garnish with dried mint, if desired.

Serves 4

Frozen Lemon-Blue Cheese Salad with Marinated Artichoke Hearts   *Dave Bloom*

This unique, tasty recipe is adapted from a 1969 cookbook. An oldie, but goodie!

> 1   pint lemon sherbet, softened
> 3   tbsp. blue cheese, crumbled into small bits
> 1   jar marinated artichoke hearts, drained and cut into quarters
> 4   cups greenleaf, Boston or bibb lettuce

1. Mix blue cheese into softened sherbet.
2. Pour into 8-inch square baking pan, cover, and freeze until firm, about 3 hours.
3. Remove sherbet from freezer. Place lettuce onto individual serving plates. Scoop sherbet on top of lettuce, and top with quartered artichoke hearts. Serve immediately.

Serves 4

Crunchy Broccoli Salad

Kay Loos

The crunch, flavor and color of this salad nicely complements grilled meats.

Salad ingredients
- 2 heads of broccoli, chopped
- 1 cup green onions, finely cut, tops included
- 8 slices of bacon, cooked crisp, drained and crumbled
- ½ cup raisins
- ½ cup unsalted sunflower seeds

Dressing
- 1 cup low-fat mayonnaise
- ⅓ cup sugar
- 2 tbsp. vinegar

1. Combine all but dressing ingredients in a salad bowl.
2. Whisk dressing ingredients together in small bowl. Pour over the broccoli mixture and toss to mix. Refrigerate at least one hour before serving to blend flavors. Serve cold.

Serve 6-8

Bean and Seashell Pasta Salad

Judy Eddy

This chilled salad combines seashell pasta with beans, herbs and vegetables. It's a great side dish with lunch or dinner but it can also stand on its own as a main course.

- 2 tbsp. olive oil
- 2 tbsp. wine vinegar
- ½ tsp. each of salt and pepper
- 3 cloves garlic, minced
- 2 15-oz. cans cannelloni beans, drained and rinsed
- 1 15-oz. can black beans, drained and rinsed
- 2 tomatoes, chopped
- 1 medium red onion, chopped
- 2 cups seashell pasta, cooked al dente

1. In a cruet or jar with a cover, combine oil, vinegar, salt, pepper and garlic; shake well.
2. In a salad bowl, combine remaining ingredients; pour dressing over and toss. Chill several hours.

Serves 12

Choosing Broccoli

Thick stems, wilted leaves and open or yellowish buds indicate that broccoli is past its peak. Look for closed buds and a fresh, green color. Refrigerate until use, preferably as soon as possible to retain high vitamin A and C content.

Summer Pasta Salad

Martha MacEachern

The secret to this fail-proof, great salad—which can be customized to taste—is its fabulous dressing. A sure-fire hit.

Dressing

1½	tsp. salt
½	tsp. dry mustard
¼	cup sour cream
1	cup oil
2	tsp. sugar
¼	tsp. pepper
¼	cup plus 2 tbsp. red wine vinegar
1	clove garlic, minced
1	tsp. parsley
1	pkg. pasta of choice

Add any combination/amount of:
   cherry tomatoes, capers, green or green onions, broccoli, carrots, cucumber, shrimp, cooked chicken, shredded cheese, etc.

1. Cook 12 pasta servings according to package directions, drain and refrigerate to cool completely before assembling.
2. Add selected vegetables/seafood/meats to cooled pasta.
3. In mixing bowl, combine dressing ingredients. Pour on salad and toss. Keep chilled until ready to serve.

Serves 12

Southwestern Bean Salad

Judy Eddy

Colorful and tasty, this bold salad perks up a summer picnic.

2	cups cilantro, chopped
1½	cups cooked corn
1	15-oz. can black beans, rinsed
2	cups cooked rice
1	cup diced red pepper
½	cup chopped red onion
½	cup olive oil
2	tbsp. vinegar

1. Combine ingredients in mixing bowl and stir to mix. Keep chilled until ready to serve.

Serves 12

Cold Dilled Peas

Bette Caesar

Bette was served cold dilled peas while visiting friends in Canada, and promptly requested the recipe. It's delicious, and only takes 10 minutes to prepare and stick in the frig.

- 2 cups fresh or frozen tiny peas
- ½ cup sour cream
- 1 tsp. each of dill weed and chopped chives
  salt and pepper to taste
- ½-1 tsp. curry powder
- 2 tsp. lemon juice

1. Cook and drain peas according to directions. Place in serving bowl and set aside
2. In a medium bowl, combine remaining ingredients, stirring well to blend. Carefully fold into peas. Chill, covered, at least one hour to blend flavors. Garnish with additional dill or chives.

Serves 4

Chapel of the Transfiguration

The Chapel of the Transfiguration in Grand Teton National Park was erected the summer of 1925, primarily to service guests at nearby dude ranches. The building is made of lodgepole pine cut from nearby Timbered Island. The pews are constructed of quaking aspen. Jack Dornan and Ellen Jones were the first couple to be married in the now popular wedding site, tying the knot on October 11, 1927.

Chapel of the Transfiguration, late 1920s.

Raspberry Poppy Seed Salad Dressing

Delectable on a salad of spinach, red onion, mandarin oranges and sunflower seeds.

Black Bear in Yellowstone, 1934

This common resident of the Rocky Mountains stands about three-and-a-half feet high at the shoulder and typically caps out at under 600 pounds. Away from humans, the bulk of a black bear's diet consists of plant matter, though it will opportunistically eat carrion, insects and honey. Around humans, it eagerly seeks out garbage and handouts. Black bears were once common along Yellowstone's roads—where delighted tourists fed the begging bears—and at park dumps, where people routinely gathered to watch the bears. With feeding bears outlawed and closure of the park dumps in the late 1960s, black bear sightings have become comparatively rare.

1	tbsp. grated onion
¾	cup sugar
1	tsp. dry mustard
1	tsp. salt
⅓	cup raspberry vinegar
1	cup vegetable oil
1½	tsp. poppy seeds

1. Combine onion, sugar, mustard, salt and raspberry vinegar in blender. Whirl for 15 seconds. Slowly add vegetable oil and poppy seeds. Turn blender on and off to mix.
2. Store in a covered container in the refrigerator. Shake well before pouring.

Honey French Dressing   *Martha Hansen*

This is one of the former First Lady of Wyoming's favorite dressings. Martha shared the recipe in a 1965 State of Wyoming publication titled *Cooking in Wyoming: 1890-1965*. It is particularly good with a salad of grapefruit segments and avocado slices.

⅔	cup sugar
1	tsp. dry mustard
1	tsp. paprika
1	tsp. celery seed
¼	tsp. salt
⅓	cup honey
5	tbsp. vinegar
4	tbsp. fresh lemon juice
1¼	cups salad oil

1. Combine all ingredients in a lidded jar and shake vigorously until blended.
2. Store in a covered container in the refrigerator for up to 1 week. Reshake before using. If used for a mixed garden salad, add 1 tbsp. of snipped fresh parsley or 1 tsp. of dried parsley flakes and 1 tsp. of green onion flakes.

Honey Dressing

Jayne Ottman

This sweet dressing is excellent drizzled over fresh fruit salad.

⅔ cup sugar
2 cups honey
5 tbsp. vinegar
¼ tsp. salt
1 cup oil
1 tsp. dry mustard
1 tsp. paprika
1 tsp. celery seed
1 tsp. onion juice

1. Combine all ingredients in a blender and blend for 2-5 minutes.
2. Store in a covered container in the refrigerator. Dressing should be stirred to remix ingredients before using.

Gorgonzola Walnut Dressing

Anne Whiting Richardson

Use to dress a simple green salad. This is especially good over romaine or spinach.

¼ cup raspberry or red wine vinegar
½ cup olive oil
1 medium clove garlic, coarsely chopped
2 ozs. Gorgonzola cheese
¼ cup walnuts
    pinch of salt
    pepper to taste
    pinch of sugar

1. In a blender or food processor fitted with a metal blade, blend vinegar, oil and garlic for 15 seconds.
2. Add Gorgonzola cheese, salt, pepper, walnuts and sugar. Blend another 15 seconds or until walnuts are chopped, but not pureed. They should remain slightly chunky. Store dressing, covered, in the refrigerator no longer than 4 days.

Measuring Honey

When measuring honey, molasses, syrup or other sticky liquids, use a cooking spray or oil the measuring spoon or cup first so the honey et al will slide off easily.

Oil in Dressings

Cut down on the oil content of any salad dressing by substituting up to a third of the oil with wine, vegetable or defatted chicken broth, vegetable or tomato juice, or hot water. Whisk the substituted ingredient into the dressing after the other ingredients are combined.

Lime Salad Dressing

Judy Eddy

This is a great, zesty low-fat dressing. It is light and bright, and will get you excited for warm weather. Serve on fresh green salad.

    ¼   cup nonfat yogurt
    6   tbsp. fresh squeezed lime juice
    2   tsp. grated lime peel
    2   tsp. prepared horseradish
    2   tsp. Dijon mustard
    2   tbsp. white wine vinegar
        freshly ground black pepper to taste

1. Combine ingredients into a bowl and beat with a whisk to blend.
2. Store in a covered container in the refrigerator. Dressing should be stirred to remix ingredients before using.

Peppery Parmesan Dressing

An excellent, low-fat alternative to ranch dressing.

    ⅓   cup low-fat cottage cheese
    ¼   cup Parmesan cheese, freshly grated
    2   tbsp. non-fat or low-fat plain yogurt
    1   tsp. lemon juice
    1   tsp. vinegar
        pinch of tarragon
    ¼   tsp. garlic, finely minced
    ¼   tsp. freshly ground black pepper

1. Put all ingredients in a blender and purée until smooth consistency is attained, about 1 minute. If too thick for personal preference, blend in a little non-fat milk.
2. Refrigerate, covered, up to 2 days. Whisk or stir before serving.

Basic Vinaigrette

    1   cup olive oil
    ⅓   cup balsamic or white wine vinegar
    1   tbsp. sugar
    ½   tsp. dried oregano
    ¼   tsp. crushed red pepper flakes
    1½ tsp. salt
    1   clove garlic, crushed

1. Combine all ingredients in a blender or in a bowl with a wire whisk.
2. Refrigerator in a covered container. Shake well before using.

Balsamic Orange Salad Dressing   *Marcia Kunstel*

Marcia's creation is delightfully different. Try it on a salad of green leaf lettuce, sliced red onion and avocado slices.

> 1 clove garlic
> 1 shallot, thinly sliced
> 1 tsp. coarsely grated orange rind
> 1 tbsp. coarsely chopped parsley
> ⅓ cup fresh orange juice
> 2 tbsp. good balsamic vinegar
> ½ - ¾ cup canola oil

1. Mix all ingredients except canola oil in a blender or food processor until well blended.
2. Slowly add canola oil to incorporate with other ingredients. Amount is a matter of personal preference. Salt and pepper to taste.

Maple Vinaigrette

Simple to make and oh, so good. A version of this vinaigrette drew crowds at the Sugarfoot Café in Jackson. Serve over green salad, or drizzle over grilled meat and fish.

> ¼ cup balsamic vinegar
> ½ cup pure maple syrup
> 1 tbsp. lemon juice
> 1 cup extra-virgin olive oil
> ½ tsp. dried basil
> 1 tsp. dry mustard
> 1 clove garlic, minced
> ¼ tsp. black pepper, or to taste
> 1 tsp. salt

1. In a medium-sized bowl, combine the basil and mustard, stirring to blend. Whisk in the vinegar, maple syrup, lemon juice and garlic.
2. Slowly pour the olive oil into the syrup mixture, constantly whisking until the oil is incorporated. Whisk in salt and pepper.
3. Refrigerate in a covered container for up to 2 weeks. Whisk or shake before serving.

Paul Petzoldt, 1934

In 1924, 16-year-old Paul Petzoldt made his first ascent of the Grand Teton. Seven years later, he started the first guide concession in Grand National Teton Park, an operation he ran with partner Glenn Exum until leaving the business in 1956. Petzoldt went on to found the National Outdoor Leadership School, an international operation headquartered in Lander, Wyoming, and the Wilderness Education Association. A famed, colorful mountaineer, Petzoldt was a member of the first American expedition to K2 in the Himalayas. He died on October 6, 1999, after a lengthy illness.

Vinaigrette Ratio
and Substitutions

The classic ratio for a
vinaigrette is 3 parts oil to
1 part vinegar, lemon
juice, etc. Wine is acidic
and can be substituted
for all or part of the vinegar or lemon juice. If you
substitute yogurt for sour
cream in a dressing, use
a little less vinegar to
compensate for the yo-
gurt's natural acidity.

Cranberry Maple Vinaigrette

A tasty variation of maple vinaigrette. Toss with a salad of mixed greens, dried cranberries and toasted pine nuts.

     ¼   cup salad oil
     3   tbsp. cranberry juice
     1   tbsp. pure maple syrup
         salt and freshly ground pepper, to taste

1. Whisk oil, cranberry juice and syrup together until incorporated. Add salt and pepper to taste.
2. Refrigerate in a covered container for up to 2 days. Shake or whisk before serving.

Herb Croutons

So easy. So good. You may never buy packaged croutons again.

     6   ½-inch thick slices French bread
     2   tbsp. butter
     2   tbsp. extra-virigin olive oil
     1   clove garlic, finely minced
     ¼   tsp. each oregano, thyme, basil and crumbled rosemary

1. Preheat oven to 300 degrees.
2. Cut crust from bread and dice into ½-inch cubes.
2. In a large skillet, heat butter and olive oil over medium heat, stir-ring with a wooden spoon to combine. When mixture is hot but not smoking, stir in the garlic and herbs. Add bread cubes and stir to coat.
3. Place coated bread cubes in a single layer on a rimmed, ungreased baking sheet. Bake on a middle rack in the oven until crisp and slightly browned, about 30 minutes.
4. Store in a covered container in a cool place for up to 1 week. Croutons may be frozen.

Yield: Approx. 2 cups (8 servings)

Sides

Putting up Ice, 1940s.

Elk Calf

Within an hour of birth, an elk calf will stand and nurse. The single calves are born in late May/ early June. The cow and calf rejoin the herd within two to four weeks. Calves grow quickly and are weaned from their mother by fall.

Scalloped Leeks and Potatoes

Therese Metherell, R.D.

A creamy vegetable dish that is surprisingly low in fat and rich in vitamins A and C. Serve with ham or roasted meats, or as a vegetarian entrée.

- ¼ cup vegetable or chicken broth
- 4 cups sliced leeks, white and pale green parts only
  butter-flavored cooking spray
- 2 cups evaporated skim milk
- 3 large garlic cloves, mashed
- 4 lbs. unpeeled russet potatoes, rinsed, dried and thinly sliced
- 1 cup low-fat, grated cheddar cheese
- ¼ cup fat-free Parmesan cheese, freshly grated

1. Preheat oven to 375 degrees.
2. Mix the evaporated milk and minced garlic together. Seat aside.
3. In a heavy skillet, warm broth over medium heat. Add leeks and cover skillet. Cook until leeks are tender, stirring occasionally, about 5 minutes. Remove cover and cook an additional 3 minutes, or until liquid evaporates.
4. Coat a 13x9-inch baking dish with the butter-flavored cooking spray. Place half of the sliced potatoes in the dish and cover with half of the leeks. Sprinkle with half of the cheddar cheese, then pour half of the evaporated milk/garlic mixture on top. Repeat layers and top with the grated Parmesan cheese.
5. Bake for one hour and 15 minutes, or until the casserole is bubbly and the top is golden brown. Let stand 15 minutes before serving to allow the casserole to set up. Note: This dish can be assembled in advance and refrigerated, covered. Allow to sit at room temperature for 1 hour before baking.

Serves 8

Mashed Potatoes with Garlic

Turns bland into "Wow!" Also keeps vampires away.

- 5 lbs. baking potatoes
- 1 cup garlic cloves, peeled
- ¾ cup whipping cream or whole milk
- 3 tbsp. butter
  salt and white pepper to taste

1. Peel and wash potatoes, then cut into quarters. Place in a 6-quart

pan and add water until potatoes are completely covered. Bring water to a boil, then cover and reduce heat to simmer. Cook until potatoes are fork tender, about 20 minutes.

2. While the potatoes are cooking, combine the garlic, cream or milk and butter in a small saucepan over low heat. Cover and bring to a simmer, stirring occasionally, for 10 minutes or until garlic is fork tender. Pour mixture into a blender and puree until smooth.

3. Five minutes before potatoes are done cooking, preheat oven to 400 degrees.

4. Drain potatoes well, then dry in preheated oven for 5 minutes. Return to cooking pan. Pour in the garlic puree and beat with a mixer until smooth and creamy. Season with salt and pepper to taste.

Serves 8-10 generously

Mashed Potatoes

For light and fluffy mashed potatoes, use the water they cooked in instead of milk. Drain potatoes, saving the liquid. Incorporate the liquid back into the potatoes a little at a time as you mash or whip them.

Roasted New Potatoes   *Chef Holly Herrick*

Holly shared her "absolute favorite potato recipe" with *Jackson Hole Guide* readers in her April 8, 1998, cooking column. It was given to her by a fellow culinary student, who learned it while apprenticing at the Hotel Crillon in Paris. Holly thinks it is simple to make, fabulous and can be served with anything, any time of the year. We agree.

   24   red-skinned new potatoes, of equal size
   ¼   cup good-quality olive oil
   ⅛   cup coarse salt (coarse salt is key)
       fresh rosemary or thyme sprigs
       cloves from 1 whole head of garlic, peeled

1. Preheat oven to 425 degrees.
2. Scrub potatoes and pierce with fork. Dry thoroughly.
3. Place in a single layer in a large baking dish. Drizzle oil and salt over potatoes. Toss to coat.
4. Add rosemary or thyme and garlic, and place dish on a rack in the middle of the oven.
5. Bake 40 minutes or until potatoes are soft, occasionally tossing to recoat. Serve immediately.

Serves 4-6

Place an apple in a bag
of potatoes and close.
The potatoes will keep
close to eight weeks
without sprouting or
wrinkling. Spuds should
be stored in a cool, dry
place.

Golden Parmesan Potatoes   *Thelma Hamby*

Thelma shared this recipe in *Teton Temptations*, a Teton County Extension Homemakers' cookbook, in the 1970s. It's worth repeating.

    6   large russet potatoes
    ¼   cup flour
    ¼   cup freshly grated Parmesan cheese
    ¾   tsp. salt
    ⅛   tsp. pepper
    ⅓   cup butter
        fresh parsley

1. Preheat oven to 375 degrees. Place the butter in a 13x9-inch baking pan and put pan into the oven until butter is melted. Remove the pan and set aside.
2. Combine flour, Parmesan cheese, salt and pepper in a large sturdy plastic or brown paper bag.
3. Pare potatoes and cut into eighths. Moisten the wedges with water, then place them in the bag with the dry ingredients. Shake to coat. Place wedges in single layer in the buttered pan.
4. Bake for approximately one hour or until golden brown, turning once.
5. Sprinkle with fresh parsley just prior to serving.

Serves 6-8

Spicy Oven Fries

Zingy fries with a fraction of the fat.

    1½ lbs. russet potatoes, peeled and cut into French fry-thin strips
    1   tbsp. vegetable oil
    1½ tsp. chili powder
    ½   tsp. salt
    ½   tsp. dried oregano
    ¼   tsp. garlic powder
    ¼   tsp. cumin

1. Preheat oven to 450 degrees.
2. Combine ingredients in a large bowl and toss well to coat potatoes. Arrange on a single layer on a baking sheet(s).
3. Place sheet(s) on racks in the center of the oven and bake until fries are golden brown and crisp, about 35 minutes.

Serves 4

Sweet Potato Fries

Therese Metherell, R.D.

These are addicting.

        2   lb. sweet potatoes, cut like ½-inch thick French fries
        2   tsp. olive oil
        ½   tsp. paprika
        ¼   tsp. salt
        ⅛   tsp. black pepper
        1   tbsp. balsamic vinegar
            cooking spray

1. Preheat oven to 450 degrees. Coat baking sheet with cooking spray.
2. Toss sweet potato wedges with olive oil, paprika, salt and pepper. Place potatoes on a single layer on baking sheet and bake until golden brown and tender, about 25 minutes, turning several times. Remove from oven, sprinkle with vinegar and toss to coat.

Serve 4-6

Sweet Potatoes and Pears with Streusel Topping

Sherrie Jern

Sherrie adapted this fantastic recipe from a cooking magazine. It has become a family Thanksgiving tradition.

        5   lbs. sweet potatoes
        6   tbsp. butter, at room temperature
        6   large pears, peeled, cored and sliced
        ¾   cup pear nectar
    Streusel topping:
        ¼   cup light brown sugar
        ½   tsp. each of cinnamon and cardamom

1. Preheat oven at 400 degrees.
2. Scrub sweet potatoes and prick with fork. Bake until tender, about 40 minutes. Remove from oven and reduce heat to 350 degrees.
3. Cool, peel and mash sweet potatoes in a large bowl.
4. Mash pears in separate bowl.
5. Add butter, pear nectar and mashed pears to mashed potatoes. Whip with blender until mixture is smooth. Pour into a lightly oiled casserole dish.
6. Mix streusel ingredients together and sprinkle on top. Bake in 350 degree oven for 30 minutes. Serve warm.

Serves 6-8

Teton Glacier

Teton Glacier is the largest of the 12 active, re-entrant glaciers in Grand Teton National Park. With record temperatures the last decade widely attributed to global warming, the glacier has receded since it was photographed in 1929 by Harrison Crandall.

Peeling Sweet
Potatoes

Sweet potatoes are more
nutritious if cooked in
their skins. To easily peel
boiled sweet potatoes,
drain off the hot water
and immediately plunge
the potatoes into cold
water. The skins will slip
right off.

Brandied Sweet Potatoes

Sunny Howell
Submitted by Erika Muschaweck

Simply superb.

4 medium sweet potatoes
⅔ cup brown sugar, firmly packed
¼ cup water
2 tbsp. butter
¼ cup cognac

1. Wash the sweet potatoes, but do not peel. Boil covered in water
   until barely soft, about 15 minutes. Drain, cool, and peel. Slice into
   a greased casserole.
2. Preheat oven to moderate (350 degrees)
3. Bring to a boil the brown sugar, water and butter. Add cognac and
   pour mix over potatoes.
4. Bake uncovered for 30 minutes, basting several times with the syrup
   in the casserole.

Serves 4

Acorn Squash with Apples

Scrumptious. Serve with pork or turkey, or as a vegetarian main course.

2 small acorn squash
½ cup melted butter, divided
¼ cup brown sugar
2 cups chopped Granny Smith or other tart apples
2 tsp. grated orange peel
¼ cup raisins
⅛ tsp. nutmeg
⅛ tsp. cinnamon

112

1. Preheat oven to 350 degrees.
2. Halve squash with a sharp knife and remove seeds.
3. Place 4 halves in a baking pan, cut sides down, and bake 40 minutes.
4. Meanwhile, shortly before removing the squash, mix together ¼ cup of the melted butter and the brown sugar in a small bowl. In a separate bowl, combine ¼ cup melted butter, the chopped apples, orange peel, raisins, nutmeg and cinnamon. Stir to blend.
5. Remove squash from oven and turn the halves so the cut side is up. Prick surface of squash with a fork, then brush the cut surface with the butter/brown sugar mixture, pouring any extra mixture into the halves. Fill each half with equal amount of the apple mixture.
6. Place filled squash halves in oven and bake an additional 30 minutes, or until apples are tender.

Serves 4

Butternut Squash Purée with Pomegranates and Scallions

Chef Holly Herrick

Holly shared her favorite holiday recipes with *Jackson Hole Guide* readers a number of years ago. This dish is simple yet spectacular. What could be better? It can be make ahead, and reheated in a saucepan over low heat.

1	large butternut squash
1-2	tbsp. butter
¼	cup sour cream
¼	cup whole milk
	pinch ground ginger
	salt and fresh ground pepper to taste
	seeds from ½ pomegranate
2	scallions, finely sliced

1. Whisk together sour cream and milk until smooth. Set aside.
2. Split squash in half, remove seeds and fibers, and cut off rind. Cut into small pieces. Steam until tender in a small amount of water.
3. Place squash and butter in food processor or blender. Process until smooth. With machine running, slowly add sour cream mixture to make a smooth, creamy purée. Season to taste with salt and pepper. Garnish with pomegranate seeds and scallions. (To remove pomegranate seeds, cut in half and gently pull out seeds. Discard white pulp.)

Serves 6

Diplomacy at the Lake

An historic diplomatic meeting occurred at Jackson Lake in September of 1989. U.S. Secretary of State James Baker and Soviet Foreign Minister Eduard Shevardnadze held high-level talks at Jackson Lake Lodge. Baker chose Grand Teton National Park to display the wonderful preserved land and heritage of the US. The table used in the talks is on display in the upper lobby of the lodge.

Selecting squash

Winter squash is mature when you cannot pierce the skin with your thumbnail. If the squash has a soft skin, it means the squash is old and past its peak.

Whipped Citrus Winter Squash

Therese Metherell, R.D.

Colorful and tasty, this side dish is an alternative to mashed potatoes.

  1 12-oz. pkg. frozen winter squash
 ½ cup fresh-squeezed orange juice
 ½ tsp. dried thyme
  1 tsp. honey
  2 tsp. light, whipped butter
  1 tsp. grated orange peel
     salt and pepper to taste

1. Place squash, orange juice and thyme in a medium saucepan. Bring to a simmer over medium heat. Cover and cook until squash is thawed and heated through, about 15 minutes.
2. Uncover and cook until squash has thickened to desired consistency. Stir in honey, butter, orange peel, salt and pepper to taste. Serve when honey and butter are melted.

Serves 4

Zingy Herbed Squash

With the help of your microwave, this flavorful dish could not be easier or quicker to prepare. It capitalizes on summer's bounty of fresh squash, tomatoes and herbs. A perfect side dish to summer suppers!

  ¼ cup butter
  1 clove garlic, minced
  1 tbsp. fresh snipped oregano
1½ tsp. fresh snipped basil
 ½ tsp. salt
 ⅛ tsp. pepper
  2 medium zucchini, sliced thin
  1 medium yellow squash, sliced thin
  1 large tomato, cut into 8 wedges

1. Place garlic and butter in a microwave safe 2-quart dish and microwave on high until butter melts, about 45 seconds.
2. Add all other ingredients except tomato. Toss to coat. Microwave on high for 8-10 minutes or until squash is tender.
3. Remove from microwave and stir in tomato wedges. Cover. Let stand 2 minutes before serving.

Serves 4

Savannah Red Rice

Lokey Lytjen

"Sandy is my best friend from high school and is married to my oldest brother. She passes along her favorite recipes to me, particularly those that are quick and easy. This is Sandy's version of a Low Country classic, Savannah Red Rice. Naturally, it is one of my favorite dishes. If y'all come to my house for supper and I don't serve Sandy's lasagna (page 190), I'll probably dish up this wonderful southern treat with ham or boiled shrimp."

Olaus Murie

> 3-5   strips of bacon (turkey bacon okay)
> 1   cup chopped bell pepper
> 1   cup chopped onion
> 2   small cans tomato sauce
> 2   cups cooked long-grain rice
>   salt
>   Worcestershire sauce (optional)
>   Tabasco (optional)

1. Fry bacon in large pan until crisp. Remove.
2. Sauté onion and bell pepper in bacon drippings over medium heat until onions are soft and translucent. Add tomato sauce and crumbled bacon. Heat mixture to boiling over medium heat, then reduce heat to simmer. Add salt, Worcestershire sauce and Tabasco to taste. Stir.
4. Add cooked rice to tomato mixture. Simmer for about 30 minutes, stirring often so rice doesn't stick to the bottom of the frying pan. Periodically add water to mixture, if needed, to keep rice moist (this is key).
5. Remove from heat. Serve immediately. If desired, sprinkle with fresh grated Parmesan cheese and sage.

Serves 4

In 1927, the U.S. Bureau of Biological Survey hired biologist Olaus Murie to comprehensively investigate the Jackson Hole elk herd. His studies resulted in the publication of "The Elk of North America." In 1945, Murie resigned from the survey to become director of the Wilderness Society. He conducted many meetings from the Muries cabin in Moose. During his tenure, Olaus and Mardy spearheaded the crusade to set aside the 9 million-acre Arctic National Wildlife Refuge. When Olaus died on October 21, 1963, he was widely recognized as one of America's foremost preservationists and conservation leaders.

Apricot-Cashew Couscous

Judy Eddy

Excellent with roasted chicken or fish.

> 2   cups couscous
> 1   cup chopped raw cashews
> 1   cup diced dried apricots

1. Prepare couscous, following directions on box.
2. Mix in cashews and apricots. Serve immediately.

Serves 6

Toasted Pecan Pilaf

A great accompaniment to a variety of meats, this toothsome dish also shines as a main course. Pair it with cooked spinach and curried fruit (recipe on page 127).

8 tbsp. butter, divided
1 cup chopped pecans
½ cup onion, chopped
2 cups uncooked long grain rice
4 cups chicken broth
½ tsp. salt
¼ tsp. thyme
⅛ tsp. pepper
2 tbsp. fresh snipped parsley

1. Melt 3 tbsp. butter in a large skillet over medium heat. Add pecans and sauté until nuts are lightly browned, about 10 minutes. Place pecans on a plate, cover and set aside.
2. Melt the remaining butter in the same skillet. Add chopped onion and sauté until tender, about 3 minutes. Add rice and stir with a wooden spoon to thoroughly coat the grains with butter. Stir in chicken broth, salt, thyme and pepper.
3. Cover with a tight fitting lid, lower heat and simmer for 20 minutes or until rice is cooked and liquid is absorbed.

Ranger stuck in the mud.

116

4. Remove skillet from heat and stir in nuts and fresh parsley. Serve immediately.

Serves 8 as a side dish, 4 as a main course

Wild Rice Supreme

A tasty dish worthy of the holidays.

1	cup wild rice, uncooked
4	cups water
1	tsp. butter
1½	tsp. salt, divided
½	cup brown rice, uncooked
8	strips of bacon, cut into ½-inch pieces
1	lb. fresh mushrooms, sliced
1	large onion, chopped
1	medium green pepper, chopped
1	medium red pepper, chopped
1	celery rib, sliced thin
1	14½-oz. can beef or vegetable broth
2	tbsp. cornstarch
½	cup cold water
½	cup slivered almonds, toasted

1. Combine wild rice, water, butter and ½ tsp. of salt in a large saucepan and bring to a boil over medium heat. Reduce heat to simmer, cover, and cook for 40 minutes. Stir in brown rice. Cover and cook until rice is tender, about 30 minutes.
2. While rice is cooking, cook turkey bacon in a large skillet until crisp. Drain bacon on paper towels. Drain grease from skillet. Return 2 tbsp. of bacon drippings to the pan; discard the excess.
3. Sauté the mushrooms, onion, peppers and celery in the bacon drippings, stirring occasionally, until vegetables are tender. Stir in the broth and remaining salt. Bring to a boil.
4. While the mushroom mixture is heating, whisk cornstarch and cold water together until smooth. Pour into boiling mushroom mixture. Cook, stirring constantly, until mixture is thick and bubbly, about 2 minutes. Stir in toasted almonds and bacon. Remove from heat.
5. Preheat oven to 350 degrees. Grease a 13x9-inch baking pan.
5. Drain rice. Add mushroom mixture and stir to blend. Pour into prepared baking dish. Cover and bake 25 minutes. Remove cover and bake until heated through, about 10 minutes.

Serves 10-12

Cinema Arrives

The first movie house in Jackson Hole was started by Fred Lovejoy and Stephen Leek. Films were shown in the International Order of Odd Fellows Hall. The first film rolled on March 21, 1919.

Barley Yields

One pound of uncooked
barley yields 2 1/8 cups,
or three pounds cooked
barley.

Steamed Brown Rice and Barley

Mary Howley. R.D.

Interesting, nutty taste. This grain dish is a favorite in Mary's "Beyond Broccoli Lunch and Learn" classes. It is chock full of minerals and vitamins E and B. Enjoy!

- ¼ cup pearl barley
- ¾ cup brown rice
- 2¼ cups water
- ½ tsp. salt (optional)
- 1 tsp. butter (optional)

1. Combine all ingredients in a 3-quart saucepan. Stir to mix, then bring to a boil over medium high heat.
2. Cover with a tight-fitting lid, reduce heat to simmer, and cook 45 minutes. (Note: Barley sometimes requires more water. Check mixture after 30 minutes to make sure there is still liquid in the pan.)
3. Remove from heat and let stand, covered, for 10 minutes.

Yield: 3 cups (4-6 servings)

Booktrader Barley

Dean and Julie Staynor

Dean's favorite cold weather meal.

- 1 lb. mushrooms, sliced
- ⅔ cup butter
- 2 cups pearl barley
- 3 cans Campbell's® onion soup (undiluted)
- 1 can water

1. Preheat oven to 350 degrees.
2. In a large skillet over medium heat, lightly sauté mushrooms in butter. Add pearl barley and brown.
3. When barley is slightly browned (be careful not to burn!) add undiluted soup and water and heat until boiling. Remove from heat and pour into a large casserole dish.
4. Bake uncovered for 1 hour.

Serves 6-8

118

Company Cabbage

Marion Dolge

Unusually good.

- ¼ cup water
- 1 tsp. instant beef bouillon granules
- 5 cups coarsely shredded or sliced green cabbage
- ½ cup chopped onion
- ½ tsp. salt
- 1 cup coarsely shredded carrots
- ¼ tsp. pepper
- 2 tbsp. butter, melted
- ⅓ cup chopped pecans
- 1 tsp. prepared mustard
- paprika

1. In a large saucepan, heat bouillon over medium heat in ¼ cup water until granules are dissolved.
2. Add cabbage, carrots, onion, salt and pepper and toss to mix. Cook, covered, over medium heat, until cabbage is tender, stirring occasionally during the 5-10 minute cooking time. Remove from heat and drain off any excess liquid.
3. Combine the melted butter, pecans and mustard. Pour over vegetables. Toss to mix and sprinkle with paprika. Serve warm.

Serves 6-8

Baked Tomatoes with Herbs

Pair with grilled meats or broiled fish.

- 2 large, firm tomatoes
- ½ tsp. sugar
- ¼ tsp. each of salt and onion powder
- ⅛ tsp. each of dried basil, dried oregano and pepper
- ½ cup bread crumbs
- 2 tbsp. Parmesan cheese, freshly grated

1. Preheat oven to 350 degrees.
2. Cut tomatoes in half and gently scoop out seedy portion of pulp. Place in a shallow baking dish, cut sides up
3. Combine remaining ingredients and evenly spoon over tomatoes.
4. Bake 20 to 30 minutes, or until tomatoes are tender.

Serves 4

Storing Tomatoes

Don't refrigerate under-ripe tomatoes purchased at the local market. Store them stem-side down in a basket or bowl on your kitchen counter or table and they will continue to ripen, improving their flavor and texture. Refrigerate after desired ripeness is reached and use as soon as possible.

Frozen Spinach

To remove excess mois-
ture from frozen spinach,
hold it over the sink and
squeeze it with your
hands. Place the squeez-
ed spinach in a double
layer of paper towel,
bring up the edges and
twist the topknot until all
the liquid is expelled. If
you want the liquid from
the spinach for soups,
etc., squeeze over a
bowl.

Spinach and Bacon Stuffed Tomatoes

Popeye would approve—and so will you! Serve with roast beef, grilled
meats or simple pasta dishes.

1   10-oz. pkg. frozen chopped spinach
1   tbsp. vinegar
½   cup onion, chopped
4   strips bacon or turkey bacon, fried crisp and crumbled
4   medium firm-ripe tomatoes
    prepared mustard
1   3-oz. pkg. cream cheese, softened
1   tsp. salt
¼   tsp. pepper
¼   tsp. nutmeg
2   tbsp. freshly grated Parmesan cheese
¼   cup dried bread crumbs

1.   Add onion, vinegar and spinach to a saucepan and cook according
     to directions on the spinach package. Drain well. Put spinach mix-
     ture, cream cheese, salt, pepper and nutmeg in a blender and pulse
     until well blended. Set aside.
2.   Preheat oven to 350 degrees.
3.   Cut off top quarter of tomatoes and gently scoop out pulp to form
     a tomato shell. Lightly brush inside with prepared mustard. Stand
     tomatoes up in a 9-inch square baking pan or other small casse-
     role dish and sprinkle an equal amount of bacon in the bottom of
     each tomato. Fill with spinach mixture.
4.   Bake in the middle of the oven for 20 minutes, or until tomatoes
     are tender. Serve hot.

Serves 4

Spinach Gratin

The addition of cheese, dill and nutmeg turns ordinary spinach into an
extraordinary side dish. Great with roast beef, turkey or baked fish.

1   cup white onion, finely chopped
½   cup feta cheese, crumbled
½   cup Edam cheese, grated
¼   cup blue cheese, crumbled
2   tbsp. fresh dill, chopped
¼   tsp. ground nutmeg
2   tbsp. fresh bread crumbs
1   egg yolk

3 tbsp. olive oil
2 10-oz. pkgs. fresh baby spinach, rinsed and dried
2 tbsp. Parmesan cheese, freshly grated
   butter-flavored cooking spray

1. Preheat oven to 350 degrees. Lightly coat a gratin pan or 11x7-inch baking dish with cooking spray. Set aside.
2. In a small bowl, combine the onion, feta, Edam, blue cheese, dill, nutmeg, bread crumbs, egg yolk and nutmeg, stirring to blend. Set aside.
3. In a large stockpot or Dutch oven, heat olive oil over medium-high heat. Place spinach in pot and sauté 3 minutes. Transfer to strainer and drain, shaking to remove as much liquid as possible.
4. Place spinach in prepared baking dish (the layer will be thin). Spread onion mixture on top, then sprinkle with Parmesan. Bake on a rack in the middle of the oven for 20 minutes, then remove pan.
5. Adjust oven rack so dish will sit about 6-inches from the broiler and turn broiler on, waiting several minutes for the broiler to heat up. Return spinach to oven and place on adjusted rack. Broil until the Parmesan cheese is golden brown on top. This will take 2 minutes or less. Watch carefully so the cheese doesn't blacken. Serve warm or hot.

Serves 4

Teton County was created in 1921, with the town of Jackson designated the county seat. Jackson and other towns in the valley were formerly part of Lincoln County, with the county seat in distant Kemmerer. Kelly went head-to-head with Jackson to be named county seat—and lost by only a narrow margin. The hamlet's 402 voting supporters fell just short of Jackson's 424 yea votes.

An adventurous motorist hitches up to a horse team to cross the Snake River.

Sherried Onions

A nice side to grilled steak or roast beef.

    ¼   cup butter
    5   medium yellow onions, sliced thin
    ½   tsp. sugar
    ½   tsp. salt
    ½   tsp. freshly ground pepper
    ½   cup sherry
    ¼   cup freshly grated Parmesan cheese
    ⅛   tsp. of nutmeg

1. Melt butter in a large skillet over medium heat. Add onions, sugar, salt and pepper. Cook, stirring often, until onions are soft, about 7-8 minutes.
2. Add sherry and increase heat to high. Cook an additional 3 minutes, stirring constantly.
3. Transfer onions to warm serving dish. Sprinkle evenly with first Parmesan cheese then nutmeg. Serve immediately.

Serves 4

Roasted Red Onions

This delightful side dish is adapted from a recipe created by the California Culinary Academy. It is a great accompaniment to roasted meats, chicken and pasta. Although easy to prepare, over two hours is needed to marinade and bake the onions, so plan ahead.

    3   medium red onions
    1   clove garlic, minced
    ¼   cup balsamic vinegar, divided
    ¼   cup olive oil
    ⅛   tsp. each of salt and freshly ground black pepper

1. Slice onions in half lengthwise. Peel papery skin off onion.
2. In a 13x9-inch baking pan, mix garlic with 2 tbsp. of the vinegar, oil, salt and pepper Add onions and gently toss to coat. Marinate at room temperature for 1 hour, occasionally brushing marinade on the onions.
3. Preheat oven to 350 degrees. Bake onions in marinade for 1 hour and 15 minutes, or until a knife inserted into the center of an onion meets no resistance. Remove onions from oven and place on a serving dish. Sprinkle with remaining vinegar. Serve immediately.

Serves 6

Caramelized Onions

A superb accompaniment to grilled or roast meat, caramelized onions also add flavor and punch to sandwiches. They can be served immediately, or refrigerated in a covered container for up to a week.

    2   tbsp. butter (no substitutes!)
    2   large yellow onions, sliced in thin rings

1. In a large skillet, melt butter over medium-low heat. Add sliced onions and stir to coat. Cover skillet and cook over medium-high heat, without stirring, for 15 minutes.
2. Uncover skillet and continue cooking, stirring occasionally, for about 30 minutes or until the onions are soft and the color of light brown sugar. Serve immediately or store.

Serves 4

No Tear Onions

For no more tears when cutting onions, simply place them in the freezer for 15 minutes before cutting or slicing them.

Roasted Carrots and Parsnips

The color and flavor of this winter root vegetable side dish may steal the show. Serve with roasted meat, poultry or pasta dishes.

    1   lb. carrots
    1   lb. parsnips
    8   cloves garlic
    2   tbsp. butter, melted
    1   tbsp. extra-virgin olive oil
    ½   tsp. salt
    ¼   tsp. black pepper
    2   tsp. fresh tarragon, chopped
    2   tsp. fresh parsley, snipped

1. Preheat oven to 425 degrees.
2. While oven is heating, peel and cut carrots into 1-inch pieces. Peel and cut parsnips into 2-inch pieces and peel garlic cloves.
3. Place carrots, parsnips, garlic, melted butter and olive oil in roasting pan and lightly toss to coat vegetables. Sprinkle with salt, pepper and herbs.
4. Place in oven and roast until vegetables are tender, approximately 1 hour. Stir occasionally for even roasting.

Serves 6-8

123

Corn Pudding

People *love* this. Serve with spicy Mexican dishes, roast beef, ham or grilled chicken.

    4   eggs
    ½   cup flour
    3   tsp. sugar
    1   tsp. salt
    4   cups whole milk
    4   tbsp. butter, melted
    3   cups fresh corn kernels
        (if using frozen kernels, decrease milk to 3½ cups.)

1. Preheat oven to 375 degrees. Grease a 3-quart casserole dish. Set aside.
2. In a large mixing bowl, beat eggs with a mixer. Add flour, sugar and salt. Stir well to blend. Mix in corn and melted butter. Stir. Add corn and stir until well blended.
3. Pour mixture into prepared dish and place on lower rack of oven. Bake for 15 minutes. Stir. Bake 10 more minutes and stir again. Move casserole to top rack and continue baking until a toothpick inserted in the center comes out clean and the top is just beginning to brown, about 25 minutes.

Serve 8-10

Fresh Green Bean and Mushroom Casserole

This is not your mother's high fat, high sodium canned green bean, canned mushroom soup and canned French-fried onion casserole. Updated with fresh ingredients, this flavorful version of a classic is just plain good.

    2   lbs. green beans, washed and trimmed
    ½   large white onion, finely diced
    1   10-oz. pkg. fresh mushrooms, cleaned and halved
    2   tbsp. butter
    1   tbsp. flour
    ½   cup low-fat sour cream
    ½   cup low-fat ricotta cheese
    ¼   tsp. salt
    ¼   tsp. white pepper
    4   oz. cheddar cheese, shredded

1. Preheat oven to 350 degrees. Grease a 2-quart casserole and set aside.
2. Place green beans in large saucepan filled with enough water to cover the beans. Bring to a boil, and boil for 5 minutes. Remove from heat, place beans in a colander, and rinse with cold water to stop cooking. Set aside.
3. Place a large skillet over medium-high heat. Melt butter, than add onion and mushrooms. Sauté for 8 minutes. Stir in flour and cook for an additional minute.
4. Remove skillet from heat. Stir in sour cream, ricotta cheese, salt, pepper, beans and cheddar cheese.
5. Pour mixture into prepared casserole and bake 30-35 minutes, or until hot and bubbly.

Serves 6-8

Old Settler Beans

Brooks Lake Lodge

These sweet baked beans are great as a main course or served with ham or barbecued ribs. They are a big hit at outdoor cookouts, potlucks, and on camping trips.

½ pound hamburger
½ pound chopped bacon
1 medium onion, chopped
1 16-oz. can pork & beans
1 can kidney beans
1 can butter beans
⅓ cup brown sugar
⅓ cup granulated sugar
¼ cup barbecue sauce
¼ cup ketchup
½ tsp. chili powder
1 tbsp. prepared mustard

1. Preheat oven to 350 degrees.
2. Brown hamburger, bacon and onion. Drain.
3. Drain the liquid from the butter and the kidney beans and add to meat mixture. Stir in the undrained can of pork and beans.
4. Mix sugars, BBQ sauce, ketchup, chili powder, mustard and small amount of ground pepper. Add to meat and bean mixture. Mix well and pour into sprayed 13x9-inch pan. Bake for 1 hour. Serve hot.

Serves: 8

First LDS Church in Jackson Hole

The first Latter Day Saints Church was constructed of brick in 1905 by Parker and Mullens, at a cost of $3,000. Most of the money was donated by the 14 Mormon families then living in the valley. The church was the first brick building in Jackson Hole. Parker and Mullens operated a lime kiln in what is now west Jackson.

Teton Trail Ride Beans

Joyce Rudd

The Rudds operated Teton Trail Rides in Grand Teton National Park from 1950-1993. When guests on their steak rides asked for a less expensive dinner, they were served this hearty alternative. Try it for your next large gathering!

1 #10 can (or small cans to equal approx. 74 ozs.) red kidney beans, drained (reserve liquid)
2 #303 cans tomatoes, chopped (or small cans to equal approx. 66 ozs.)
2½ lbs. hamburger
1 lb. bacon, cooked crisp, drained, and cut into small pieces
1 large onion, chopped
1 green pepper, diced
6-8 garlic cloves, minced
2 cans mushrooms, chopped
1 can mushroom soup
2 tbsp. vinegar
2 tbsp. mustard
1 cup brown sugar
1 cup dark molasses
1 cup barbecue sauce
chili powder, cumin, cayenne pepper and oregano to taste

1. In a large stockpot, brown hamburger over medium high heat. Drain off excess grease and set hamburger aside.
2. In the same stockpot, sauté onions and green peppers until onions are soft and translucent.
3. Add hamburger and remaining ingredients. Lower heat and simmer for approximately 2½ hours. Add reserved bean juice as necessary to adjust consistency of bean mixture. (The Rudds preferred theirs thick.)

Serves 25

Canoeing Jenny Lake, 1924

Curried Fruit

Lokey Lytjen

"This recipe dates to c. 1830. It is from a Low Country South Carolina plantation. My mother found it years ago in the *Geechee Cookbook.*" Serve fruit warm with ham, pork, chicken or game.

- 1 large can peach halves
- 1 large can pineapple slices
- 1 large can pear halves
- Maraschino cherries
- ⅓ cup butter
- ½ cup light brown sugar, packed
- 1 tsp. curry powder

1. Preheat oven to 325 degrees.
2. Drain fruit well and arrange in a large, shallow casserole dish. Dot with cherries. Melt butter. Add brown sugar and curry to melted butter and mix well. Spoon butter mixture over fruit.
3. Bake uncovered for one hour. This is better if baked the day before and reheated, so the flavors blend.

Serves 8

Baked Apples and Butternut Squash

A fragrant, colorful side dish. Great with pork or ham.

- 1 medium butternut squash, peeled, seeded and cut into 1-inch chunks
- 3 Granny Smith or other tart apples, cored, peeled and thinly sliced
- 1 tbsp. fresh lemon juice
- ¾ tsp. cinnamon
- 1 tbsp. brown sugar
- ½ cup apple juice

1. Preheat oven to 350 degrees.
2. Combine squash and apples with lemon juice and cinnamon. Place in a 1-quart casserole and sprinkle evenly with brown sugar. Pour apple juice over mixture and cover casserole.
3. Bake for 1 hour, or until squash is fork tender.

Serves 6

First Bank

Jackson State Bank was the first financial institution in the valley. It opened its doors in 1914 with $10,000 in capital and Robert E. Miller at the helm. His sharp business practices earned him the nickname "Old Twelve Percent." Miller ran the bank for 21 years. He was succeeded in 1935 by Felix Buchenroth.

In 1888, only 18 people lived in Jackson Hole—17 men and Millie, the Native American wife of John Carnes. With the arrival of several Mormon families the following year, the population swelled to 64.

Scalloped Oysters

Jackie Lynes

Scalloped oysters have been a holiday tradition in Jackie's home as long as she can remember.

  2 ½-pint jars of oysters, chopped
    Saltine crackers
    whole milk
    butter
    salt and pepper to taste

1. Preheat oven to 350 degrees.
2. Grease a two-quart casserole dish with butter. Crush enough saltine crackers to cover the bottom of your dish 1-inch thick. Cover crackers with a layer of chopped oysters. Cover oysters with a layer of crackers. Continue alternating until dish is full, ending with oysters on top.
3. Pour milk over the mixture until it just reaches the top layer of oysters. Salt and pepper to taste and dot with butter.
4. Bake for 1 hour, or until mixture is hot and bubbly and top is slightly browned.

Serves 8

Town of Jackson, before 1920. The I.O.O.F. building was located on the southwest corner of the park. The brick building across the street was used by the Jackson State Bank and later as a drinking parlor before being torn down to make room for the Ford garage. Snow King Mtn. is in the background.

Oyster Dressing

Judy Chalfant

If you like oysters, you'll relish this recipe. It's a Chalfant family holiday tradition.

- 3 loaves bread, cut in sugar-cube size cubes (approx. 8 cups)
- 1 cup butter
- 2 8-oz. cans oysters, drained and chopped
- ¾ cup onion, finely chopped
- 1½ cups celery, chopped with leaves
- 2 tsp. salt
- 1½ tsp. dried sage leaves, crumbled
- 1 tsp. dried thyme leaves

1. Melt butter in large skillet over medium heat. Add celery, onions and oysters and sauté until vegetables are tender. Stir in 2 cups of the bread cubes. Place mixture into a large, deep bowl.
2. Add remaining bread pieces and seasonings, toss to blend. Stuff turkey just before roasting. Extra dressing may be covered with foil and heated in a 350 degree oven until warm, about 20 minutes.

Yield: Enough dressing for a 12-lb. turkey.

Toasted Walnut Cranberry Stuffing

The ultimate stuffing. This mouth-watering, flavorful recipe is adapted from Julia Rosso's *The New Basics Cookbook*. Even people who aren't stuffing fans love this. Don't limit it to turkey—this makes a great side for beef or pork tenderloin, too.

- 2 tbsp. vegetable oil
- 3 cups chopped celery, with leaves
- 2 cups chopped onion
- 1 lb. bulk pork sausage
- 2 Granny Smith or other tart apples, cut into ½-inch cubes
- 1 cup chopped walnuts
- 1 cup cherry flavored Craisins®
- 6 cups dry bread cubes
- ½ tsp. salt
- ¾ black pepper
- 1 tsp. dried thyme leaves
- 1 tsp. dried, crumbled sage leaves
- ½ cup cooking sherry
- ½ cup white cooking wine
- 1 cup canned chicken broth

Removing Stuffing

To easily remove stuffing from the turkey, line the inside of the turkey cavity with cheesecloth before stuffing the bird. When the turkey is done, pull out the cheesecloth. Dressing will come out intact without digging or scraping with a spoon.

Feeding a
Yellowstone Black
Bear, 1923

Before scientists recognized the dangers of feeding wildlife to both the animals and people, feeding bears in Yellowstone was common. Here, University of Chicago Botany Professor George Fuller offers a tidbit to a black bear. It is now illegal to feed any wildlife in the park.

1. Preheat oven to 350 degrees.
2. Spread chopped walnuts in a single layer on an ungreased baking sheet. Place on a rack in the middle of a preheated oven. Shake after 1½ minutes to evenly brown. Check in another 1½ minutes for doneness. If not browned, shake again and put baking sheet back in the oven. Watch closely so they don't burn: once nuts begin to brown, they toast quickly! Remove from oven and place in a small bowl. Set aside.
3. Heat oil in a large skillet over low heat until hot but not smoking. Add celery and onions and sauté until tender but not browned, 8-10 minutes. Transfer to large bowl.
2. In the small skillet, add the sausage. Break into small pieces with a spoon and cook until lightly browned, about 10 minutes. Add to vegetables in bowl.
3. Stir in the chopped apple, toasted walnuts and Craisins® until mixture is well blended. Add bread cubes, salt, pepper, thyme and sage. Toss to blend.
4. Mix together sherry, white wine and chicken broth. Pour over stuffing mixture and toss until well blended.
5. Stuff turkey just before roasting. For excess stuffing, or for preparing stuffing as a side dish, place in a preheated 325 degree oven in a loosely covered casserole dish and bake for approximately 45 minutes, or until heated through.

Yield: Enough stuffing for an 18-lb. turkey. Serves 12-16.

Soups & Sandwiches

Attempting to pack Skyrocket

White Gazpacho with Crab, Avocado and Tomato

Snake River Grill

A spectacular cold soup with a wonderful balance of flavors. Serves four as a main course, six as a first course.

1   cucumber, peeled, seeded and diced
1   cup seedless green grapes
2   cloves peeled garlic
2   thick slices day-old French baguette, torn into small pieces
2   cups cold water
2   tbsp. sherry
1   tbsp. lemon juice
1/4   cup toasted almonds
2   tbsp. olive oil
1/4   tsp. cayenne pepper
     salt to taste
     crab meat
     avocado, sliced just before serving
     tomato, seeded and diced

1. In a small nonstick skillet over medium heat, lightly toast almonds until golden brown, about 6-7 minutes, stirring occasionally for even browning. Remove pan from heat.
2. Combine all ingredients except crab, avocado and tomato in large bowl. Pour half of mixture into a blender and puree until smooth and slightly thickened. Pour pureed mixture into a large empty bowl and process the remaining mixture in a second batch. Mix batches together.
3. Strain mixture through a large hole, mesh strainer. Chill, covered, at least one hour before serving.
4. Pour soup into bowls. Garnish with crab meat, avocado and to-mato.

Serves 4-6

Patty's Cold Avocado Soup

Christy Walton

Cascade Canyon

4 ripe avocados
2 ice cube trays of frozen chicken broth (2 14-oz. cans)
1/4 cup roughly chopped cilantro
3-4 green onions coarsely chopped
salt to taste
salmon or red lumpfish caviar, cilantro leaves to garnish

1. In blender or food processor, process first four ingredients, in two separate batches, until smooth.
2. Slowly stir in cold water until consistency is creamy but still thick (typically ½ to 1 cup). Salt to taste.
3. Ladle soup in bowls. Garnish with 3 salmon eggs or ½ spoon caviar and cilantro leaf. Serve as first course or as light lunch with a tomato stuffed with crab salad.

Serves 4

Chilled Cucumber Soup

Judy Eddy

This refreshing soup is perfect for a hot summer night when you don't want a big meal. Allow at least one hour to chill the soup.

1 onion, chopped
2 tbsp. olive oil
2 peeled, seeded and diced cucumbers
1½ cups vegetable stock
1 tbsp. heavy or whipping cream
salt and pepper to taste
fresh mint

1. Heat oil in stock pot or large skillet over medium-high heat. Add chopped onion and sauté until soft and translucent, stirring occasionally.
2. Add cucumber and sauté until soft.
3. Remove from heat and spoon mixture into a blender or food processor. Blend until smooth.
4. Return blended mixture to pot or skillet and add vegetable stock and cream. Cook 5 minutes over medium heat, stirring frequently, until soup is hot but not boiling. Remove from stove, transfer to serving bowl and let cool at room temperature for 15-20 minutes. Cover and place in refrigerator at least one hour before serving to chill. Garnish with fresh mint, if desired.

Serves 4

Potato Soup with Asparagus

Pat Opler

A superb, hearty soup. Pat included this recipe in her famed *At Home on the Range* cookbook, and graciously granted permission to include it in this publication.

    5 medium-sized Idaho potatoes, pared and quartered
    2 large onions, chopped
    2 lbs. fresh asparagus, washed and chopped or 2 10-oz. pkgs.
       frozen asparagus spears, thawed and drained.
    1 tbsp. curry powder
    2 quarts chicken stock
    1 pint heavy cream
       salt and pepper to taste

1. Combine potatoes, onions, asparagus, curry and chicken stock. Stir together. Bring to a boil over medium heat, then reduce heat and simmer 30-40 minutes. Remove pan from heat.
2. Remove asparagus. Cut off 2-inch tips and reserve. Chop asparagus bottoms and add to soup.
3. Puree soup in batches in a food processor or blender.
4. Return soup to pan, stir in cream and return to a simmer over low heat.
5. Serve hot or cold. Garnish with reserved asparagus tips.

Serves 8

Carrot Tarragon Soup

Judy Eddy

The distinctive flavor of tarragon and appealing color of cooked carrots combine to make this simple soup a standout.

    4½ cups water
     4 cups chopped carrots
     2 cloves chopped garlic
    ½ cup chopped, fresh tarragon
     1 tbsp. balsamic vinegar
    ½ tsp. salt

1. Bring the water, carrots, garlic, and tarragon to a boil, then reduce heat and simmer, covered, for 10 minutes.
2. In a food processor or blender, blend mixture in several batches until smooth, then return it to the soup pot.
3. Add the vinegar and salt to the soup. Bring to a boil, stirring constantly to prevent sticking. Remove from heat and serve.

Serves 4

134

Ginger Carrot Bisque

Erika Muschaweck

Erika clipped this recipe from a cooking magazine some years ago. It has been a family favorite ever since.

¼ cup plus 2 tbsp. unsalted butter
2 lbs. carrots, peeled and thinly sliced
2 large onions, chopped
1 tbsp. minced, peeled fresh ginger
2 tsp. grated orange peel
½ tsp. ground coriander
5 cups chicken stock or canned broth
1 cup half-and-half
½ cup minced parsley

1. Melt butter in large, heavy saucepan over medium heat. Add carrots and onions. Cover saucepan and cook until vegetables begin to soften, stirring occasionally, about 15 minutes.
2. Mix in ginger, orange peel and coriander. Add 2 cups stock. Reduce heat to medium low. Cover pan and simmer soup until carrots are very tender, about 30 minutes.
3. Puree soup in batches in processor or blender. Return to pan.
4. Add remaining 3 cups stock and half-and half to soup and cook over medium heat, stirring frequently, until warm. Season with salt and pepper. Ladle into bowls and sprinkle with parsley before serving. Soup can be prepared a day ahead. Cover and refrigerate, then heat over medium heat until warm.

Serves 10

Elk Ranch

The Elk Ranch was one of the largest working ranches in Jackson Hole when the Ferrin family sold it to the Snake River Land Company in 1929. The company paid $114,662 for 3,629 acres of land and improvements. It fenced its new holdings and continued to raise hay. In the 1940s, the property was leased for cattle ranching in support of the war effort. Today, the property is leased by the National Park Service for grazing. Frame buildings and a concrete spring house remain on the site.

A building on the Elk Ranch today.

135

Winter Snows

According to measurements taken by the Jackson Hole Mountain Resort, the average winter snowfall in Jackson Hole over the past 30 years has been 402 inches.

Squash Soup

Judy Eddy

Delicious! Use of pre-cooked, frozen squash reduces preparation time.

¼	cup butter
1	onion, chopped
2	12-oz. pkgs. frozen cooked squash, thawed
½	tsp. salt
½	tsp. freshly ground black pepper
½	tsp. crushed red pepper
1½	cups vegetable broth or soup stock

1. Place onion and butter in a large saucepan over medium heat. Stir occasionally until butter melts. Add salt and peppers and cook another 20-30 minutes over medium heat to caramelize the onions, stirring occasionally.
2. Add the thawed squash and soup stock. Cook over medium heat, stirring occasionally, until the soup is heated through but not boiling. Reduce heat and simmer about 30 minutes, or until mixture reduces to a thick consistency. Serve hot.

Serves 4.

Pumpkin Curry Soup

Becky Woods

Be prepared for recipe requests if you serve this soup. It is adapted from a grand prize winning entry submitted to a cooking magazine.

1	lb. fresh mushrooms, cleaned and sliced
1	cup chopped onion
4	tbsp. butter
4	tbsp. flour
1	tsp. curry powder
6	cups vegetable broth
1	28-oz. can pumpkin pie filling
2	12-oz. cans evaporated milk
1	tsp. salt
½	tsp. pepper
	fresh chives for garnish, optional

1. In a large kettle or stock pot, melt butter over high heat. Add mushrooms and onion and sauté, stirring frequently, until tender, about 5 minutes. Mix in flour and curry powder, stirring until well blended.
2. Reduce heat to medium and gradually pour in vegetable broth, stirring to blend. Bring mixture to a boil, then stir for 2 minutes or until the mixture has thickened.

3. Add pumpkin, milk, salt and pepper, stirring to blend. Heat through.
4. Ladle into warm bowls and garnish with snipped fresh chives, if desired. Serve warm.

Serves 12.

Roasted Eggplant and Red Bell Pepper Soup

A richly colored, flavorful soup worthy of the time it takes to prepare.

3 large Japanese eggplant (or 1 very large regular)
2 sweet red peppers
1 large onion, sliced
4 cloves garlic, crushed
1 quart chicken stock
1 bunch fresh basil
   salt and pepper
   extra virgin olive oil
   fresh basil, chopped

1. Preheat oven to 400 degrees.
2. Wash eggplant and split lengthwise in halves (quarters if using 1 large regular eggplant). Place in one layer in large baking dish, season with salt and pepper and sprinkle with olive oil to taste. Roast, uncovered, for 45 minutes or until eggplant is tender and golden brown. Place roasted eggplant, including skin, in blender or food processor and puree until smooth. Set mixture aside.
3. Cut red peppers in half, seed, and place in pan cut side down under broiler. Broil until skins are scorched on all sides. Remove scorched peppers from oven and place in sealed plastic bag for 10 minutes to soften skin. Remove charred peel and puree flesh in food processor until smooth. Pour into bowl and set aside.
4. Heat 1 tbsp. olive oil in a large, heavy skillet. Sauté onion and garlic over high heat until tender. Reduce heat to low, cover, and cook mixture for 5 minutes. Add roasted eggplant puree and chicken stock to onion-garlic mixture and cook over low heat for 15 minutes to heat mixture through and blend flavors.
5. Puree mixture in blender or food processor until smooth, then strain into a large bowl and season to taste with salt and pepper. Ladle soup into individual serving bowls. Spoon roasted pepper puree into the center of the soup and gently swirl to mix. Sprinkle with chopped basil. Serve hot.

Serves 6

Selecting Esggplant

Overripe eggplant loses its shine. Look for eggplant that is shiny, plump and heavy, and avoid ones that are bruised or scarred in any way. The stem and cap of the eggplant should be mold-free and appear fresh. Eggplant may be stored, refrigerated, for up to two days.

Striped Skunk

Baby skunk are born in April or May in litters of 2-10, with an average size of five per litter. Blind and helpless at birth, their eyes and ears don't open until they are 3-4 weeks old. Skunk can spray their noxious scent almost 20 feet.

Roasted Vidalia Soup

Chef Holly Herrick

A wonderful springtime treat, when sweet vidalias are at their peak. Holly shared her superb recipe with *Jackson Hole Guide* readers in 1999.

3 large Vidalia onions, cut in wedges
2 tbsp. olive oil
5 cloves garlic, mashed
1 cup dry sherry
5 cups chicken broth
1 bay leaf
   salt and pepper to taste
2 sprigs fresh thyme for garnish
   plain yogurt and ground peanuts for garnish

1. Preheat oven to 425 degrees.
2. Place onions and olive oil in a large roasting pan and toss to coat. Roast for 40 minutes.
3. Add mashed garlic cloves and roast an additional 20 minutes.
4. Add sherry and roast until evaporated.
5. Add remaining ingredients, except garnish items, and roast for 20 minutes
6. Puree soup in small batches in a food processor until slightly chunky.
7. Pour batches into a soup pan and reheat over stove burner until hot. Ladle into bowls and top with a dollop of plain yogurt, a sprinkling of ground peanuts and a sprig of fresh thyme, if desired.

Serves 4-6

Creamed Tomato Soup with Cognac

Dave Bloom

This is one of Dave's favorite soups, included in Anna Thomas' classic *The Vegetarian Epicure* cookbook. Publisher Alfred A. Knopf graciously granted permission to include it in this publication.

3   lb. ripe red tomatoes (15-16 medium tomatoes)
1   large onion
3   ozs. butter
1   tsp. sweet basil leaves, crushed
1   pint heavy cream
1   tsp. brown sugar
4-5 tbsp. cognac
     salt and pepper to taste

1. Scald tomatoes in hot water and slip them out of their skins.
2. Chop the skinned tomatoes and place in a bowl. Use a spoon or ricer to pound them into a coarse pulp. Set aside.
3. Peel and finely chop the onion.
4. In a large soup pot, melt butter over medium heat until it just begins to turn brown. Add the onions and stir to coat, then add the tomatoes and sweet basil leaves. Lower heat and let mixture simmer, uncovered, for 30 minutes.
5. Remove mixture from heat and press through large mesh sieve. Discard any remaining onion or seed pulp. Return mixture to low heat to heat through. Do not allow to boil.
6. In another pan, heat the cream and brown sugar until hot. Do not allow it to boil, or the cream will curdle.
7. Stirring quickly with a wire whisk, pour the heated cream into the tomato mixture. Add the cognac and season to taste with salt and pepper. Serve hot with a warm loaf of homemade French bread or thin slices of buttered pumpernickel.

Serves 6

Tomato Basil Soup   *Margie Reimers*

No one will guess this easy-to-make soup is made from canned soup and chicken broth. It is so good it is a staple for Margie's entertaining Mississippi mavens when they invite the "girls" to lunch.

Basil

Refrigerate fresh basil, wrapped in barely damp paper towels inside a plastic bag, for up to 4 days. Basil loses much of its flavor in long-cooking dishes, so add minced fresh basil just before serving.

1 lb. can crushed tomatoes
2 10-oz. cans Campbell's® tomato soup
2 14-oz. cans chicken broth
1 tbsp. dried basil
3 green onions, chopped, green tops included
1 tbsp. butter
  salt and pepper to taste

1. In a soup pot over high heat, sauté chopped green onions in butter until tender, about 3-5 minutes.
2. Lower heat to medium and add remaining ingredients. Heat through, stirring occasionally. Salt and pepper to taste. Ladle into bowls and garnish with a dollop of sour cream and a sprig of fresh dill, if desired.

Serves 6-8

Cauliflower will remain
snowy white as it cooks
if you add 2 tablespoons
lemon juice or white vin-
egar to the cooking wa-
ter.

Cauliflower Soup

Anne Whiting Richardson

Anne garnered this recipe from a friend. It is a satisfying, creamy alternative to standard vegetable soups.

1	2 lb. head of cauliflower
1½	cups chicken stock or broth
1	cup half-and-half or light cream
½	cup heavy cream
¾	tsp. salt
	white pepper to taste
6	tbsp. butter, softened and cut into bits
	sun dried tomatoes and Italian parsley for garnish (optional)

1. In a large soup pot or kettle, bring 1-quart of salted water to a boil.
2. While the water is heating up, remove outer leaves and core from cauliflower, rinse head and break into flowerets.
3. Put flowerets into boiling water and boil until tender, about 15 minutes. Drain. Puree cauliflower in blender or food processor and return to the kettle. Add chicken stock or broth and bring mixture to a boil over medium heat, stirring occasionally.
4. Add the half-and-half, heavy cream, salt and white pepper and heat thoroughly but do not boil. Swirl in the softened butter. Ladle soup into heat bowls and garnish with sun dried tomatoes and Italian parsley, if desired.

Serves 6

Black Bean Soup

Anne Whiting Richardson

Good enough for company. You'll make this several times a season!

1	lb. dried black beans
3	tbsp. olive oil
1	tbsp. minced garlic
1	large onion, diced
4	stalks celery, chopped (optional)
6½	cups chicken stock or broth
1	ham bone
1	bay leaf
½	red bell pepper, diced
1	tbsp. cumin
½	tsp. cayenne pepper
	salt and pepper to taste
1	tbsp. each brown sugar and lemon juice
⅓	cup sherry
4	tbsp. chopped fresh parsley

½ cup sour cream
¼ cup chopped scallions

1. Soak beans overnight and drain, or quick prepare per instructions on bean package.
2. In a soup pot, heat the olive oil and sauté garlic, onions and celery until vegetables are transparent.
3. Add the stock, ham bone, beans and bay leaf and simmer for 1 hour. Add red pepper, cumin, cayenne, salt, pepper, brown sugar, lemon juice and sherry and simmer for 20 minutes.
4. Remove the ham bone. Puree about a quarter of the soup in a blender or food processor and mix it back in, or use a stick blender and puree soup until desired thickness is reached.
5. Chop the meat from the ham bone and add it to the soup. Add chopped parsley. Serve soup hot, garnished with a dollop of sour cream and a sprinkling of chopped scallions.

Serves 6

Bean Me Up Soup

Therese Metherell, R.D.

A hot, hearty meal for cold, wintry days.

1 tsp. olive oil
1 cup red bell pepper, chopped
1 cup celery, chopped
1 cup onion, chopped
1 cup carrots, chopped
1 clove garlic, minced
1 jalapeno pepper, seeded and minced
3 cups low-fat vegetable broth
1 cup tomato sauce
2 cups canned black beans, drained and rinsed
2 cups pinto beans, drained and rinsed
2 tbsp. fresh cilantro
1 tbsp. each fresh lemon juice and brown sugar
1 tsp. each chili powder, ground cumin and soy sauce
½ tsp. black pepper
    low-fat sour cream for garnish

1. Heat oil in nonstick skillet and sauté vegetables until softened.
2. Add all other ingredients except sour cream. Bring to boil, then simmer for 10 minutes or until vegetables are tender. For a thicker, creamy soup, blend half of the soup in batches until smooth. Return blended batches to pot and reheat soup.
3. Ladle into bowls and garnish with a dollop of sour cream.

Serves 8-10

Golden-Mantled Ground Squirrel

This charming little rodent's striped back often leads people to believe it is the much smaller chipmunk. Its size (11-13 inches long verses a chipmunk's total length of 7-9 inches) and stripes set it apart. While all chipmunks have stripes running through their cheeks, the stripes on this squirrel stop at the back of the neck. Golden-mantled ground squirrels, named for the rich, honey-chestnut color of their head and shoulders, dine on green vegetation, berries, insects and carrion. In the fall, conifer seeds are an important component of their diet.

Mink

This active but not often seen member of the weasel family typically burrows close to water, occasionally taking over a muskrat or beaver burrow. Mink are accomplished swimmers, with the ability to dive several yards underwater in pursuit of fish. Waterfowl, frogs, snakes and small mammals round out the diet of this resolute hunter.

Kale and Bean Soup

This yummy soup showcases kale, a tasty, underused member of the cabbage family. Good and good for you!

6	cups fresh kale, julienned and tightly packed
1	cup chopped yellow onion
1	tsp. garlic powder
1	tsp. onion powder
3	16-oz. cans red kidney beans, undrained
2	14½-oz. cans sodium-free whole tomatoes, chopped (reserve juice)
1	15-oz. can garbanzo beans, undrained
1	14½-oz. can sodium-free, low-fat chicken broth

1. Combine all ingredients, including bean and tomato juices, in a large Dutch oven or stock pot. Bring to a boil over medium heat.
2. Reduce heat to low, cover and simmer for 1 hour. Serve hot.

Serves 10-12

Simple Lentil Soup

Alisan Peters

Alisan copied down this healthy recipe while watching "Bodies by Jake." The addition of ginger and molasses turn simple lentil soup into something extraordinary. Serve it with crusty bread and a nice bottle of chianti.

1	16-oz. pkg. of lentils
6	cups water
2	tbsp. olive oil
1	large carrots, chopped
2	ribs of celery, chopped
1	large onion, chopped
1-2	cloves of garlic, minced
1	1-inch chunk of ginger, peeled and minced
1	tbsp. oregano
1	tbsp. basil
1	tsp. tarragon
1	tsp. pepper
1	28-oz. can crushed tomatoes, undrained
1¾	cups water
1	tbsp. chicken or vegetable bouillon
2	tbsp. molasses
1	tbsp. cider vinegar

1. Sort and wash lentils carefully. Place in soup or stock pot and cover with 6 cups of water. Bring to a boil, then reduce heat, cover and simmer.
2. While lentils are simmering, heat olive oil in a large skillet and sauté the carrots, celery, garlic and onion. When the onion is soft and translucent, add the oregano, basil, tarragon and pepper.
3. Continue sautéing, stirring frequently, until the vegetables are tender. Add sautéed vegetables, tomatoes, 1¾ cups water and bouillon to lentils.
4. When mixture has returned to a simmer, add ginger, molasses and cider vinegar. Simmer another 20 minutes, or until lentils are tender. Serve hot.

Serves 8

Linda's Southwestern Chicken Vegetable Soup

Linda Nousianen

Use of pre-cooked, seasoned chicken makes this tasty soup a snap to prepare.

3	green onions, sliced
1	tbsp. olive oil
1	garlic clove, minced
1	cup thinly sliced carrots
3¾	cups chicken stock or broth
1½	cups broccoli, chopped bite-size
1½	cups cauliflower, chopped bite-size
¼	sweet red pepper, diced
½	tbsp. thyme
1	pkg. Louis Rich Carving Board Southwestern Chicken Breast Strips, cut into bite-size pieces
	salt and pepper to taste

1. In a large skillet over high heat, sauté onions, garlic, red pepper and carrots in olive oil until onions are soft. Add chicken broth and bring to boil. Reduce heat, cover, and simmer 5 minutes.
2. Increase heat to high and add broccoli, cauliflower, thyme and black pepper to broth mixture. Cook, stirring occasionally, until mixture returns to a full boil.
3. Reduce heat and simmer until broccoli and cauliflower just start to get tender, then add chicken strips. Continue cooking until chicken is heated. Do not overcook vegetables. Salt to taste.

Serves 2-3

Chicken and Avocado Soup

Linda Kaess

A superb, main-dish soup that is quick and easy to prepare. Need we say more?

7	cups chicken stock or broth
½	cup onion, chopped
½	cup celery, chopped
1	clove garlic, minced
1	tsp. pepper
¾	cup couscous or orzo
2	boned and skinned chicken breast halves
3	tbsp. fresh lemon juice
1	tbsp. fresh parsley, chopped
¼	cup fresh cilantro leaves, tightly packed
1	large ripe but firm avocado, peeled and thinly sliced just before serving.

1. Place broth, onion, celery, garlic and pepper in a large pan over high heat. Bring to a boil, stirring occasionally. Add pasta and chicken breasts and return to a boil.
2. Reduce heat to low, cover and simmer for about 5 minutes, or until the thickest part of the chicken breast is white (cut with a knife to test doneness). Lift out breasts and place on cutting board. Let stand.

Hatchet Motel, 1957.

3. Simmer soup, uncovered, until pasta is tender, about 2 more minutes. Reduce burner heat to lowest setting and cover pan to keep soup warm.
4. Tear slightly cooled chicken into large shreds and return to soup. Stir in lemon juice, parsley and cilantro.
5. Ladle into four bowls and top with slices of avocado. Serve with warm slices of crusty bread.

Serves 4

Chicken Corn Chowder *Lisbeth Beise*

Lisbeth serves this excellent chowder at her annual Christmas cookie exchange luncheon. Her recipe is adapted from the famed *Silver Palate* cookbook.

3½	cups frozen corn kernels, thawed
1	cup chicken stock or broth
¼	cup butter, softened
2	cups milk
1	garlic clove, minced
1	tsp. oregano
1	tbsp. canned chiles, diced
1	whole cooked boneless chicken breast, chopped
1	cup tomatoes, seeded and diced
	salt and pepper to taste
1	cup shredded Monterey Jack or munster cheese
	variety of tortilla chips (black bean and blue corn are good), broken into bite-size pieces
2	tbsp. fresh parsley, minced

1. Puree corn kernels and chicken stock or broth in a food processor or blender until just slightly chunky.
2. Pour corn mixture into a large, 3-quart soup pan. Add butter. Simmer for five minutes, stirring frequently to prevent corn mixture from sticking to the pan.
3. Stir in milk, garlic, oregano, salt and pepper. Bring mixture to a boil, then reduce heat to low and add chiles. Simmer for five minutes.
4. While the chiles are simmering, divide the diced chicken and tomatoes into 6 soup bowls.
5. Ladle chowder into the soup bowls. Top with shredded cheese, minced parsley and tortilla pieces and serve.

Serves 6

Canned Broth

When using canned broth as a soup base, be sure to double-check if it is ready-to-serve or condensed, which requires added water or milk. If you don't dilute condensed broth, your soup will be too salty to eat. Store canned broth in the refrigerator so fat in the broth congeals on the surface. Spoon or lift it off the top before using.

Mulligatawny Soup

Lemon rind, curry, tart apples and coconut milk flavor this piquant Indian soup.

      ½   cup diced onion
      1   medium carrot, diced
      2   ribs celery, diced
      ¼   cup butter
   1½   tbsp. flour
      2   tsp. curry powder
      4   cups chicken broth or stock
      1   bay leaf
      ¼   cup diced, tart apples
      ½   cup cooked rice
      ½   cup diced cooked chicken
      1   tsp. salt
      ¼   tsp. pepper
      ⅛   tsp. thyme
      ½   tsp. grated lemon rind
      ½   cup hot coconut milk

1. Cook rice according to package directions and set aside.
2. In a large skillet over medium-high heat, sauté the onion, carrot and celery in butter, being careful not to let the vegetables brown.
3. Stir in flour and curry powder. Cook, stirring constantly, for 3 minutes. Add chicken broth and bay leaf and heat to boiling, then reduce heat to low and simmer 15 minutes.
4. Add chopped apple, rice, chicken, salt, pepper, thyme and lemon rind. Simmer an additional 15 minutes.
6. While mixture is simmering, heat coconut milk in a small saucepan until hot but not boiling. Keep warm. Immediately before serving, stir hot coconut milk into soup.

Serves 4

Cabbage and Beef Soup

Huff House Inn Bed and Breakfast

"Soup freezes well in serving size portions—if any is left. This is yummy!"

      1   lb. lean ground beef
      ½   tsp. garlic salt
      ¼   tsp. garlic powder

146

¼ tsp. pepper
2 stalks celery, chopped
½ medium head of cabbage, chopped
1 16-oz. can red kidney beans, undrained
1 28-oz. can diced tomatoes
1 28-oz. can water
4 beef bouillon cubes

1. Brown beef in deep skillet or stockpot; drain off excess fat.
2. Add remaining ingredients and bring to a full boil over medium heat, stirring occasionally. Reduce heat and simmer covered for 1 hour. Serve warm.

Serves 8

Spicy Beef Stew

Raisins, molasses and ginger flavor this fantastic stew.

3 lbs. lean, boneless chuck roast, trimmed of fat.
3 tbsp. flour
1 tbsp. olive oil
2 14½-oz. cans sodium-free whole tomatoes, chopped. Reserve juice.
3 medium yellow onions, cut into wedges then sliced vertically (about 3 cups)
1¼ tsp. pepper
1 tsp. salt
2 cups water
⅓ cup molasses
⅓ cup white vinegar
2½ cups carrot, peeled and thinly sliced
½ cup raisins
½ tsp. ground ginger

1. In a stock pot or large Dutch oven, heat olive oil over medium high heat. Dredge beef in flour and place in pot. Brown beef on all sides.
2. Add tomatoes, reserved tomato juice, onion, pepper and salt. In a medium bowl, combine the water, molasses and vinegar, stirring to blend. Add mixture to beef mixture and stir.
3. Cover, reduce heat to low and simmer for 75-90 minutes, or until the beef is tender. Add carrots, raisins and ginger; stir to blend. Cover and simmer until carrots are tender, about 30 minutes.
4. Remove beef from pan. Cut into bite-size pieces, then shred pieces with two forks. Return shredded beef to pan, stir and heat through. Spoon stew into bowls.

Serves 6-8

Burrowing Owl

This uncommon visitor to Jackson Hole historically bred in Yellowstone National Park; it has recently been observed nesting in the valley. Burrowing owls prefer open grasslands and semi-arid shrublands. They are named for their custom of using abandoned ground squirrel, hare and badger burrows to nest, using their talons to enlarge the burrow to depths of seven feet. They eat mostly ground insects, but will also opportunistically consume small rodents, reptiles and birds.

Icy Pine Needles

Green Chile Stew

Sue McGuire

Sue created this recipe while living in New Mexico after experimenting with several versions given to her by neighbors. The "heat" can be adjusted according to the amount and type of green chile used. See her notes below.

2   lbs. boneless sirloin pork roast, trimmed of fat and cut into 1-inch chunks
¼   cup vegetable oil
1   medium yellow onion, peeled and chopped
4   medium white-skinned potatoes, peeled and chopped
2   cloves garlic, minced
2   cups chicken stock or broth
3   cups water
1½   tsp. Mexican oregano leaves
     green chile to taste*

1.   In a large soup pot over medium heat, heat vegetable oil until hot. Increase heat to medium-high and add pork, onion, potato and garlic. Cook, stirring frequently, until the meat and vegetables are lightly browned, about 5 minutes.
2.   Add the chicken broth and water. Stir to release any browned bits that have stuck to the pan. Add green chiles and bring stew to a boil.
4.   While stew is being brought to a boil, toast the oregano by putting it in a small frying pan over low heat. Gently shake the pan to keep the oregano from burning. It will take on a slightly browned color and have a distinctive toasted smell after a couple of minutes; add to the stew.
5.   Lower the heat and simmer until the potatoes and meat are cooked through, about 20 minutes. If desired, thicken by ladling out ¼ cup of the stew broth. Add 2 tbsp. flour to this and stir to create a paste with a smooth consistency. Add this paste slowly to the stew, stirring constantly. Boil gently until it reaches the thickness you want.

Serves 6

*A word about green chile:
The easiest thing is to buy the cans or jars of diced green chile. These are usually labeled mild to hot so you have a general idea of what you're getting. You can also make your own by roasting fresh Anaheim, Poblano or Ancho chiles. Put the chiles under your broiler or on a charcoal grill until the skin cracks and blackens. Let sit at room temperature until cool, then peel off the charred skin. The heat of these chiles depends on the varieties' genetics

and on the conditions where they are grown. Well-watered chiles are milder than those grown under water stress. It isn't always easy to know what you're getting (mild to hot) when you buy chiles fresh, but the flavor is better. You can always put some into the stew while it cooks, then provide additional as a condiment for anyone who wants to liven up their own serving.

Rockin' Moroccan Stew   *Therese Metherell, R.D.*

Simply the best vegetarian stew around.

- 2   tsp. olive oil
- 1   cup chopped yellow onions
- 1   cup chopped green pepper
- 1   cup diced celery, including leaves
- 1   clove garlic, minced
- 3   cups vegetable broth
- 3   cups unpeeled, cubed sweet potatoes
- 1   14-oz. can tomatoes
- 1   14-oz. can chickpeas (garbanzo beans), drained and rinsed
     juice of one lemon
- 2   tsp. grated gingerroot
- 1   tsp. cumin
- 1   tsp. curry
- 1   tsp. ground coriander
- 1   tsp. chili powder
- 1   tsp. black pepper
- 1   cup raisins
- 2   tbsp. peanut butter
- 2   tbsp. fresh, chopped cilantro

Browning Stew Ingredients

Browning meats and vegetables gives stew a richer flavor. Add 1 tsp. sugar to the oil or fat and heat, stirring often, until the oil/fat is hot. Brown meat and vegetables before proceeding with recipe directions. The sugar caramelizes, enhancing color and flavor with negligible sweetness.

1. Heat olive oil in a nonstick heavy, large kettle. Over medium-high heat, sauté onions, celery, green pepper and garlic. Cook and stir until vegetables begin to soften, about 5 minutes.
2. Add all remaining ingredients except raisins, peanut butter and cilantro. Bring to a boil, then reduce heat and simmer covered for 20 minutes.
3. Stir in raisins, peanut butter and cilantro. Mix well, then simmer for another 5 minutes to blend flavors. Serve hot.

Serves 8

Add freshness to leftover
soup by stirring in 1- 2
tablespoons of chopped,
fresh herbs just before
serving. The same
amount of wine, sherry
or Madeira also adds
zest to leftover soup.
Add spirits before you
reheat.

Seafood Stew with Tomatoes and Basil

Savory and satisfying.

¼	cup olive oil
1¼	cups chopped onion
2	tbsp. chopped garlic
4	tsp. dried oregano
1½	tsp. fennel seeds
2½	cups crushed tomatoes with added puree
2½	cups bottled clam juice
1	cup dry white wine
2	6½-oz. cans chopped clams, drained, liquid reserved
1	lb. uncooked large shrimp, peeled, deveined
1	6-oz. can crabmeat, drained
½	cup chopped fresh basil
	cayenne pepper

1. Heat olive oil in heavy large pot over medium heat. Add onion, garlic, oregano and fennel seeds and sauté until onion is tender, about 8 minutes.
2. Add tomatoes, clam juice, white wine and liquid reserved from clams. Increase heat and boil until slightly thickened, about 15 minutes.
3. Add clams, shrimp and crabmeat. Reduce heat and simmer 2 minutes. Mix in fresh basil and simmer until shrimp are just opaque in center, about 2 minutes longer. Season stew to taste with cayenne, salt and pepper.

Bookbinder's Light Fish Chowder

This is one of the favorite dishes at the popular Bookbinder's Restaurant in Philadelphia.

3	slices turkey bacon, coarsely chopped
	vegetable cooking spray
2	tsp. butter
1	cup chopped onion
2	cloves garlic, minced
1¼	cups reduced sodium chicken broth
1¼	lbs. red potatoes, peeled and chopped (about 3 cups)
¼	cup flour
2	cups 2% low-fat milk
¾	tsp. salt
¼	tsp. pepper
1	lb. group, haddock or other firm white fish, cut into 1-inch chunks

1. Cook bacon over medium heat until crisp in a large Dutch oven coated with cooking spray. Remove and set aside.
2. Melt butter in the Dutch oven, then add onion and garlic. Cook, stirring constantly until tender, about 5 minutes. Stir in chicken broth, potatoes and bacon. Bring to a boil, then reduce heat to low, cover, and simmer for 20 minutes or until potatoes are tender.
3. Place half of the potato mixture into a blender and process until smooth, scraping down the sides if necessary. Stir into remaining potato mixture.
4. In a separate medium-sized bowl, whisk flour and milk together until well blended. Stir into potato mixture.
5. Increase heat to medium and cook, stirring often, until chowder thickens. Stir in salt, pepper and fish. Cover and cook for 5 minutes or until fish flakes easily when pierced with a fork. Serve hot.

Serves 6-8

Spicy Fish and Pumpkin Stew

Anne Whiting Richardson

True to its name, this tasty dish is spicy! If your palate prefers milder fare, reduce the amount of jalapeno peppers

2	medium yellow onions, sliced
4	cloves garlic, minced
2 or 3	jalapeno peppers, chopped
1	tbsp. ground coriander
1	tsp. ground cumin
1	tsp. mace
1	tsp. allspice
1	tsp. black pepper
½	tsp. nutmeg
¼	cup olive oil
3	tbsp. unsalted butter
1½	cups chicken broth
1	cup fresh pumpkin, medium dice (squash is OK)
2	cups tomatoes, peeled, seeded and chopped
1	lb. snapper, tuna or halibut, medium diced
1	red pepper, seeded and chopped
¼	cup cilantro, chopped
	juice from 2 limes
	salt and pepper to taste

1. In a large skillet, heat olive oil and butter until hot. Add onions, garlic, jalapeno peppers and spices and cook until onions are soft.

2. Increase heat to high and add the chicken broth. Cook until on-
    ions are translucent, about 3 minutes.
3. Add the pumpkin and tomatoes and reduce heat to low. Cook,
    covered, over low heat until pumpkin is tender but not mushy,
    about 15 minutes.
4. Add the fish, red pepper and cilantro and increase heat to me-
    dium. Cook until fish is tender and cooked all the way through. Do
    not overcook the fish. Add the lime juice and season with salt and
    pepper. Serve with rice if desired.

Serves 6

Turkey Sausage Stew

4	garlic cloves, coarsely chopped
1	medium onion, diced in ½-inch pieces
2	tbsp. vegetable oil
2	jalapeno peppers, finely chopped (optional)
½	lb. Italian-style turkey sausage
½	lb. skinless boneless chicken breast, diced in ½-inch pieces
1	cup diced carrots
1	15-oz. can navy beans, undrained
1	15-oz. can kidney beans, undrained
2	15-oz. cans diced tomatoes, undrained
1	cup water
2	bouillon cubes
2	cups frozen corn kernels
	chopped cilantro to taste
	salt and pepper to taste

Forest rangers collecting botany specimens, 1914.

152

1. Sauté the onion, garlic and jalapeno pepper (if used) in a large stockpot over medium-high heat until the onion is translucent, about 3 minutes.
2. Crumble in the sausage and add the chicken and sauté for 5 minutes. Add carrots, water and bouillon cubes and reduce heat to medium. Heat until bouillon cubes are dissolved, stirring occasionally.
3. Add beans, tomatoes, cilantro and corn. Season with salt and pepper to taste. Heat thoroughly. Serve hot with thick slices of homemade wheat bread.

Serves 6

White Chicken Chili

Easy. Quick. Delicious. This recipe was an award winner in a chili cooking contest. You may never eat the red stuff again.

Uinta Ground Squirrel

Locally known as "chiselers" for their propensity to eat flower and vegetable gardens, Uinta ground squirrels feed on leafed plants and grasses. They live in colonies underground, digging complex burrow that end in nesting chambers. Males begin hibernating as early as mid-July.

1	lb. boneless, skinless chicken breast halves cut into ½-inch dice (approximately 2 cups)
1	yellow onion, chopped
1½	tsp. garlic powder
1	tbsp. vegetable oil
2	15½-oz. cans great northern beans, drained and rinsed under cold water
1	14½-oz. can low-fat chicken broth
2	4-oz. cans mild green chiles, chopped
1	tsp. salt
1	tsp. cumin
1	tsp. oregano
½	tsp. white pepper
¼	tsp. cayenne pepper
1	cup light sour cream
½	cup whipping cream

1. Heat oil over high heat in the bottom of a large skillet or stock pot. Add diced chicken, onion and garlic powder and sauté until chicken is cooked through, about 5 minutes.
2. Reduce heat to medium. Add beans, broth, chilies, salt, cumin, oregano and peppers. Stir to blend. Bring mixture to a boil, stirring occasionally, then reduce heat and simmer uncovered for 30 minutes.
3. Remove chili from heat and stir in sour cream and whipping cream. Ladle into bowls and garnish with 2 cherry tomato halves and a sprig of parsley, if desired.

Serves 6

Flat Creek Ranch

In 1898, alleged horse and cattle rustler Cal Carrington squats on a hidden Valley at the head of Flat Creek—the perfect place for corralling stolen stock. By March 1901, he builds the first cabin on what would become Flat Creek Ranch. When the law catches up with his partners in crime, Carrington "turns respectable," working as a forest ranger and the first foreman of the Bar BC Ranch. There, he meets Countess Cissy Patterson in 1916 and the two begin a long friendship. Carrington sells the ranch to Patterson in February, 1923 for $5,000. Through a succession of heirs, the ranch is how owned by Joe Albright and Marcia Kunstel. After extensive renovations, they reopened Flat Creek in 2001 for new generations to enjoy.

Flat Creek Ranch
Grilled Curried Chicken Sandwiches

Marcia Kunstel

"This is one of my concoctions that works especially well on a cloudy or rainy day when you've been spending time outdoors. It's a Flat Creek Ranch favorite."

Rub mixture

2	tbsp. curry powder
¼	tsp. cayenne pepper
⅛	tsp. ground mace
	salt and pepper to taste

Sauce

½	cup plain yogurt (nonfat works fine)
½	cup mayonnaise
2	medium garlic cloves, pressed or minced
1	tbsp. curry powder
½	tsp. ground cumin
¼	tsp. ground coriander
¼	tsp. cinnamon
	salt and pepper to taste
	(If this is too highly seasoned for you, dilute it with more yogurt and mayo.)

Sandwich makings

8	skinless, boneless chicken breasts
8	Soft sandwich buns
	lettuce and sliced tomato

1. Combine the sauce ingredients in a small bowl and set aside.
2. In a separate small bowl, blend the rub mixture ingredients and rub the mixture onto the chicken pieces an hour or so before grilling.
3. Grill breasts over medium heat approximately 5 minutes per side, or until chicken is no longer pink when pierced with a fork. Remove chicken from grill.
4. Spread buns generously with curried sauce, add a leaf of lettuce and slice of tomato and top with a grilled chicken breast.

Serves 8

154

Roast Beef Sandwiches with Roasted Red Onion on Sourdough bread

These delicious sandwiches are adapted from a recipe printed in *Bon Appétit* magazine.

3 large red onions (about 2½ pounds), each cut vertically into 8 wedges and peeled
7 tbsp. extra-virgin olive oil, divided
¼ cup balsamic vinegar
   salt and pepper to taste
1 cup light mayonnaise
¼ cup fresh basil, chopped
1½ tbsp. lemon juice, preferably fresh
2 tsp. grated lemon peel
1 lb. roast beef, sliced thin
2 cups red leaf lettuce, washed and torn into bread-sized pieces
12 slices sourdough bread

1. Preheat oven to 425 degrees. Line large rimmed baking sheet with foil and set aside.
2. Place red onions, 5 tbsp. olive oil and vinegar in a large bowl, sprinkle with salt and pepper and gently toss to coat the onions. Arrange onions in a single layer on prepared baking sheet. Bake until onions are tender and brown at the edges, about 40 minutes. Remove from oven and set aside to cool.
3. In a small bowl, mix the mayonnaise, basil, lemon juice, lemon peel and 2 tbsp. olive oil together. (Note: Onions and mayonnaise can be prepared up to 2 days ahead. Cover separately and store in refrigerator.)
4. Spread mayonnaise over bread. Top with roast beef, onions and lettuce. Cover with top halves of bread.

Makes 6 sandwiches

Onion Odor

To get rid of the odor on your hands after peeling onions, rub your fingers on a stainless steel sink or spoon—no need to buy the pricey stainless steel soap-shaped bars sold in mail-order catalogs.

Billy Bierer and the
Gros Ventre Slide

"Uncle" Billy Bierer, a trapper and prospector, wandered into Jackson Hole with partner Albert Nelson to test his prospecting luck in the valley. Both men ended up staying. Bierer built a cabin at Slide Lake in the Gros Ventre. He predicted that one day Sheep Mountain above his homestead would slide, after hearing water moving underground when he placed his ear to the slope. Health problems led him to sell his ranch to Guil Huff and move to Pennsylvania to live with his daughter. He died in 1923, unaware that his prediction would come true on June 23, 1925, when 50 million cubic yards of rock and dirt on the north end of Sheep Mountain slid over a mile and a half down to the Gros Ventre River and up the other side in under three minutes.

Baked Eggplant, Roasted Red Peppers, Tomatoes and Cucumber in Pita

These fantastic stuffed pockets are a complete meal.

Sauce
- 1 cup nonfat plain yogurt
- ½ cup light mayonnaise
- ⅓ cup packed fresh basil leaves, thinly sliced
- 1 large garlic clove, finely minced or pressed
- 1 7-oz. jar roasted red peppers, drained and chopped
- salt and pepper to taste

Sandwiches
- Nonstick vegetable oil spray
- ¼ cup olive oil
- ¼ cup balsamic vinegar
- 1½ tbsp. dried oregano
- 2 eggs
- 2 tablespoons water
- ¼ cup bread crumbs
- ½ cup flour
- 1 medium eggplant (about 1¼ pounds), unpeeled, cut crosswise into ¼-inch thick slices
- 6 pita bread rounds
- 4 plum or roma tomatoes, sliced
- 1 cucumber, peeled and cut diagonally into ¼-inch slices
- 1 7-oz. jar roasted red pepper, drained and cut into strips

1. In a medium bowl, whisk together the sauce ingredients until well blended. Salt and pepper to taste. Cover and refrigerate.
2. Preheat oven to 425 degrees. Coat two large, rimmed baking sheets with vegetable oil spray and set aside.
3. In a small bowl, whisk olive oil, vinegar and oregano together until well blended. Season to taste with salt and pepper. Set aside.
4. In a medium bowl, whisk the eggs and water together to blend.
5. Place bread crumbs in a shallow dish. Place flour in a separate shallow dish.
6. Lightly dust each eggplant slice with flour. Dip slices into egg mixture then into the bread crumbs. Coat well. Place breaded slices on prepared baking sheets. Drizzle with olive oil and vinegar mixture. Let stand 15 minutes, then place sheets in preheated oven and bake 30-35 minutes or until tender, turning occasionally to brown both sides. Remove from oven and place sheets on wire racks. Cool eggplant on the baking sheets for 15 minutes. Cut each pita in half and stuff halves equally with an eggplant slice, tomatoes, cucumber and red pepper strips. Drizzle with sauce and serve.

Serves 6

156

Mango Turkey Wraps with Curry Mayonnaise

A great wrap!

- 2 tsp. curry powder
- ½ cup light mayonnaise
- 2 tsp. lemon juice
- 4 large flour tortillas
- 8 ozs. smoked turkey, thinly sliced
- 4 cups romaine lettuce, thinly sliced
- 2 cups English cucumber, peeled, seeded and thinly sliced
- 1 ripe mango, peeled, pitted and chopped or 1 cup canned mango, well-drained and chopped
- ½ cup fresh cilantro leaves
- ½ ripe avocado, peeled and thinly sliced

1. In a small, heavy skillet over low heat, heat curry, stirring constantly, for 2 minutes. Remove from heat and place in small bowl. Add mayonnaise and lemon juice and whisk until well blended. Salt and pepper to taste.
2. Spread each flour tortilla with 2 tbsp. of curry mayonnaise. Divide turkey equally on top of the tortillas and top each tortilla with lettuce, cucumber, mango cilantro. Top with avocado slices. Fold in top and bottom of each tortilla and roll up like a burrito to enclose the filling. Cut wraps in half and serve. If not eating immediately, wrap turkey rolls tightly in plastic wrap and refrigerate for up to four hours.

Makes 4 servings

Gros Ventre Flood

The experts said the earthen dam created by the Gros ventre slide would hold. They were wrong. On May 18, 1927, the dam breached, releasing water backed up into Lower Slide Lake by the blocked Gros Ventre River. A wall of water inundated Kelly, destroying property in its wake and killing six people. The flood literally washed the town away. The general store, gone. The hotel, gone. The blacksmith shop, livery stable, auto garage and homes—all gone. Only the Episcopal church and school were left standing.

The Huff House, floating in newly-created Lower Slide Lake after the Gros Ventre slide dammed the Gros Ventre River.

Lower Falls

At 308 feet, the Lower
Falls of the Yellowstone
River are more than
twice as high as Niag-
ara. Water spilling over
the lip off the falls varies
from 5,000 gallons a
second in autumn to
63,500 gallons a second
at peak run-off in late
spring/early summer.

Grilled Turkey, Cheddar and Cranberry Sandwiches

8   slices sourdough bread
6   tbsp. whole berry cranberry sauce
2   cups grated cheddar cheese
8   ozs. roasted turkey breast, thinly sliced
1   tbsp. butter, softened

1. Divide and spread cranberry sauce equally on 4 slices of bread. Top each slice with ¼ of the grated cheddar cheese, then cover each with ¼ of the roasted turkey. Top each sandwich with a piece of bread and lightly butter the top of the sandwich.
2. Place sandwiches, butter side down, in a skillet over medium heat to grill. While the bottom is grilling, butter the top slice of bread. Grill bottom until the bread is golden and crisp, about 4 minutes. Carefully turn sandwiches with a spatula and grill until the second side is done, about 3 minutes more. Serve warm.

Serves 4

Entrees

Checking the Range, 1917

Wolf track

Wolf tracks are considerably bigger than coyote tracks. They typically measure 4-inches wide and 5-inches in height. Male wolves in North America weigh between 80-110 pounds. Coyotes usually weigh between 20-50 pounds. The heaviest documented wolf in North America tipped the scales at 175 pounds.

Southwestern Grilled Chicken

Erin Dann

Fantastic flavor for very little effort—perfect for summer entertaining. Erin serves this fish with her beer batter biscuits (see page 39), corn on the cob and a garden salad.

8-10	split chicken breasts, boned and skinless
2	medium tomatoes, chopped
2	cups chopped onion
½	cup red bell pepper
4	cloves garlic (optional)
¼	cup fresh cilantro leaves, packed
⅔	cups soy sauce
6	tbsp. fresh lime juice
1½	tsp. black pepper

1. Place everything but the chicken in a blender and blend for 30 seconds.
2. Pour over chicken breasts placed in a heavy-duty ziplock bag, squeeze out excess air, seal and marinate in refrigerator for 4-5 hours.
3. Grill marinated breasts over medium heat, basting with marinade as you grill. Discard any marinade not used in grilling.

Serves 8

Key Lime Chicken

Lisa O. Robertson

Sweet, tangy and delicious.

1	cup key lime juice
2	tsp. honey
⅔	cup water
2	tsp. salt
½	tsp. pepper
8	chicken pieces

1. Place all ingredients except chicken in blender. Cover and process until ingredients are combined.
2. Place chicken in a pan and pour marinade over it, turning chicken pieces to coat. Marinate covered in refrigerator for 1-6 hours, turning chicken pieces occasionally.
3. Preheat oven to 325 degrees.
4. Remove chicken from refrigerator. Drain and reserve marinade. Place chicken pieces in a baking dish large enough for chicken to be in a single layer. Brush with reserved marinade and place pan on a rack in the middle of the oven. Bake until chicken is cooked

through and juices run clear, about 1 hour 25 minutes. Baste with reserved marinade every 20 minutes. Throw out any marinade not used in cooking.

Serves 4

Ricotta Parmesan Stuffed Chicken with Apricot Sauce

Jayne Ottman

Company spectacular—but why wait for company?!

6 halved/boned chicken breasts, skin attached
1 cup ricotta cheese
1 cup freshly grated Parmesan cheese
1 egg, beaten
2 tbsp. butter
¼ cup finely chopped walnuts
1 tbsp. parsley
¼ tsp. nutmeg
⅛ tsp. pepper

1. Cut one side of skin on top of the chicken breasts, leaving one side still attached. This creates a flap for the stuffing. Set chicken breasts aside.
2. Combine the cheeses, egg, walnuts, parsley, nutmeg and pepper. Stir well to blend.
3. Preheat oven to 350 degrees.
4. Spoon stuffing mixture between the flesh and skin of the chicken breasts. Secure with toothpicks. Lightly brush with melted butter and place in baking pan large enough to hold breasts in a single layer. Bake uncovered for 40-45 minutes. Approximately 10 minutes before chicken is done, prepare the apricot sauce.
5. Place cooked chicken on a serving platter and spoon sauce over chicken. Garnish platter with whole apricots and sprigs of parsley.

Apricot Sauce

⅓ cup chicken broth
⅓ cup apricot nectar
2 tbsp. cornstarch
6 whole dried apricots, for garnish

In a saucepan, combine all but the whole apricots and cook over medium heat until bubbly, approximately 5 minutes, then 2 minutes more. Simmer to keep warm until ready to spoon over chicken.

Serves 6

Gray Wolf

Wolves were reintroduced in Yellowstone National Park in 1995. Wolf bones discovered in Lamar Cave in the park verify that wolves inhabited the present park 1,000 years ago. They were eliminated from the park by the 1930s, following a national policy of killing wolves and other predators. The reintroduced wolf population is thriving, and has become a major draw for park visitors. Several packs have relocated in Jackson Hole.

Chicken with Hazelnuts and Mushrooms

Pat Opler

Teton Reflection

Infused with the wonderful flavor and texture of hazelnuts, this spectacular dish is worthy of royalty. Remember to prepare your crème fraîche a day in advance. This recipe is from Pat's *At Home on the Range* cookbook. She graciously granted permission to include it in this publication.

- 3 tbsp. unsalted butter
- 6 tbsp. walnut oil
- 3-4 lbs. chicken breasts, skinned and blotted dry
- ¼ lb. thickly sliced bacon, cut into ¼-inch strips
- 1 medium onion, finely chopped
- ¾ lb. domestic mushrooms, trimmed and quartered
- 5 shallots, finely chopped
- 1 clove garlic, finely minced
- ½ oz. dried porcini (or other wild variety) mushroom pieces, hydrated and coarsely chopped
- ½ lb. hazelnuts, blanched, skins removed, and coarsely chopped
- 2 sprigs fresh thyme
- 3 sprigs fresh parsley
- ¼ cup good-quality port
- ¾ cup crème fraîche
  salt and pepper to taste

1. Melt butter and oil together in large skillet over medium heat until bubbly. Add chicken and brown lightly on both sides. Remove from pan to drain.
2. In the same skillet, brown bacon pieces with onion until the bacon is crisp. Remove bacon and onion pieces to drain.
3. Pour off all but 3 tablespoons of fat from the skillet and sauté quartered mushrooms with shallot and garlic until golden.
4. Add the chopped, hydrated wild mushrooms, hazelnut pieces, herbs and brandy to the skillet. Stir. Heat the mixture and flambé it to remove alcohol.
5. Add port, chicken and bacon to skillet. Cover and cook over medium heat about 30 minutes or until chicken is cooked through.
6. When chicken is cooked, remove it with the bacon, hazelnuts and mushrooms to a heated serving platter. Keep warm.
7. Add crème fraîche to skillet liquids and stir until creamy and thickened. Salt and pepper to taste. Pour sauce over chicken and serve.

Serves 6-8

To blanch hazelnuts (or other nuts):

Spread on a cookie sheet and roast in a 350 degree oven for 10-15 minutes. Rub the nuts inside a towel or brown bag to loosen skins. If some skins don't come off, further roasting won't help. Use them as they are.

Crème fraîche

Make at least 24 hours before serving. Crème fraîche may be used as is, whipped to serve on desserts, or added to hot soups and sauces without curdling.

    1   cup whipping cream
    1   tbsp. buttermilk, sour cream or yogurt (Pat likes buttermilk)

1. Thoroughly mix ingredients, pour into a clean container and cover tightly.
2. Allow to sit at room temperature undisturbed for 24-36 hours, or until visibly thickened. (To accelerate this process, heat whipping cream until just tepid and proceed as above. The mixture will visibly thicken within 12-13 hours.)
3. Refrigerate tightly covered (it will continue to thicken as it chills) and use as desired. If tightly sealed, crème fraîche can be stored in a refrigerator for up to two weeks.

First Airplane

The first airplane landed in Jackson on August 19, 1920. H.H. Barker and his mechanic, I.G. Winton, flew over Teton Pass from Blackfoot, Idaho, and landed at the Jackson Hole rodeo grounds during the annual Frontier Days celebration. The 120-mile trip took a reported 75 minutes. During a two-day period, the pair offered fairgoers—many whom had never seen an airplane—a ride in the sky. Fifty-nine people took them up on their offer.

First airplane to fly into Jackson Hole, 1920.

For incredibly moist chicken breasts, submerge breasts in buttermilk, cover and refrigerate 3-4 hours before cooking. Whole chickens are juiciest when cooked at a low to moderate temperature that retains the fowl's fat and moisture content.

Chicken Marsala

Linda Drumm

Former Jackson resident Linda Drumm developed this recipe after a restaurant in New Jersey refused to share its version. After tinkering with ingredients for over two years, she finally "cracked the code." Her version has won local, regional and national awards. It was printed in *Teton Views* in 1998. *Teton Views* is a weekly paper distributed free throughout the valley; it routinely features recipes from local residents. For information on subscribing, see the acknowledgments section.

2	lbs. boneless chicken breasts
2	tbsp. flour
1	cup fresh mushrooms, sliced
2	tsp. crushed garlic
4	tbsp. butter
4	tbsp. olive oil
1	can Campbell's® beef broth
½	cup sweet marsala wine
1	cup heavy cream
¼	tsp. salt
¼	tsp. pepper

1. In a large skillet or frying pan, heat butter and olive oil over medium heat. Dredge chicken breasts in flour and sauté in skillet until breasts are lightly browned, about 5 minutes. Add garlic, mushrooms, salt and pepper. Cook, stirring occasionally, until mushrooms are tender.
2. Add broth and simmer until broth is reduced by half, about 10 minutes. Add wine and cook an additional 5 minutes.
3. Remove chicken to ovenproof serving platter and place in warm oven.
4. Reduce broth mixture until thickened, about 5 minutes, stirring occasionally. Remove from heat.
5. Remove chicken from oven and pour broth over chicken breasts. Serve immediately with a side of spaghetti, egg noodles or rice.

Serves 6-8

Parmesan Dijon Chicken

Pat Siegel

Pat says this recipe is a favorite in the Siegel home because it is "fast enough for everyday and good enough for company!"

¾	cup Italian bread crumbs
1	cup freshly grated Parmesan cheese
⅓	cup melted butter
⅔	cup Dijon mustard

3   tbsp. dry white wine
8   boned chicken breasts

1. Preheat oven to 500 degrees.
2. While your oven is heating up, combine mustard and wine in one bowl, and the bread crumbs, Parmesan cheese and melted butter in another.
3. Grease or spray a baking pan(s) large enough to hold the chicken breasts.
4. Dip the breasts into the mustard and wine mixture, then the crumb mixture and place in pan(s). Bake until chicken is cooked through, about 15 minutes.

Serves 8

Jackson Fun Fact

John Colter, a member of the Lewis and Clark expedition, is usually credited as the first white man to visit Jackson Hole. Trapper William Sublette named the valley, formerly known as Jackson's Hole, after his partner, David E. Jackson. Jackson reportedly spent the winter of 1829 at Jackson Lake.

Chicken Teriyaki

The Spice Merchants

Great flavor. If you can't find mirin and Japanese soy sauce in the Asian section of your supermarket, you may order them from The Spice Merchants. See the acknowledgments section for information.

4   chicken thighs, boned
    oil for pan frying
½   cup teriyaki sauce (recipe below)
    cooked rice
Teriyaki sauce
7   tbsp. sake
7   tbsp. mirin
7   tbsp. Japanese soy sauce
1   tbsp. sugar

1. Mix teriyaki ingredients together in a saucepan and bring to a boil over medium heat. Cook until the sugar is dissolved. Refrigerate if you are not going to use it right away.
2. Pierce the skin of the chicken with a fork to allow the sauce to penetrate. Heat a little oil in a frying pan over medium heat until oil is hot but not smoking. Add the pierced chicken, skin side down. Fry until the skin is well browned. Turn the chicken pieces over, reduce the heat and cook, covered, for about 10 minutes or until chicken is cooked through. Remove from the pan.
3. Pour ½ cup of the prepared teriyaki sauce into the pan juices and bring to a boil, stirring constantly. Return the chicken to the skillet. Continue cooking and turning the chicken until the sauce is reduced and the pieces are well coated, about 3 minutes.
4. Remove the chicken to a cutting board and cut into strips ½-inch wide. Serve at once over prepared rice.

Serves 4

Chicken with Lime Butter

Paul Bruun

When Paul penned his "Exit Eating" column for the *Jackson Hole News*, he shared several National Chicken Cooking Contest recipe winners with readers. This is one of them.

6 split chicken breasts, boned and skinned
½ tsp. salt
½ tsp. pepper
⅓ cup vegetable oil
1 lime, juiced
8 tbsp. butter
½ tsp. fresh chives, minced
½ tsp. dried dill weed

1. Sprinkle chicken on both sides with salt and pepper.
2. Heat a large skillet over medium temperature until hot, add oil and sauté chicken until lightly brown, about 4 minutes. Turn chicken breasts, cover skillet and reduce heat to low. Cook an additional 10 minutes or until fork can be inserted in chicken with ease. Remove chicken from skillet, place on serving platter and keep warm. Drain and discard oil in skillet.
3. Pour lime juice into same skillet and cook over low heat until juice begins to bubble. Add butter. Stir constantly until butter becomes opaque and forms a thickened sauce. Stir in chives and dill weed. Remove sauce from heat and spoon over chicken.

Serves 6

Kelly Post Office, circa 1940.

Baked Chicken Reuben

Paul Bruun

Ditto preceding comment!

4   split chicken breasts, skinned and boned
¼   tsp. salt
⅛   tsp. pepper
1   16-oz. can sauerkraut, hand drained of excess liquid
4-6   thin slices of Swiss cheese
1¼   cups bottled Thousand Island dressing
1   tsp. fresh chopped parsley

1. Preheat oven to 325 degrees.
2. Place chicken in a single layer in a greased 13 x 9-inch baking pan. Sprinkle with salt and pepper. Spread sauerkraut over chicken and top with cheese slices. Pour salad dressing evenly over cheese slices.
3. Cover with foil and bake for 1½ hours or until juices run clear when breasts are pricked with a fork. Remove from oven and sprinkle with chopped parsley. Serve hot.

Serves 4

Chicken and Walnuts

A classic.

4½   cups skinned and boned chicken breasts, cut into ¾-inch cubes
3   tsp. cornstarch
½   tsp. garlic powder
½   tsp. each of salt and pepper
1   tbsp. white wine
½   cup soy sauce
¾   cup brown sugar, lightly packed
½   cup walnut halves and pieces
⅓   cup vegetable oil
      cooked rice

1. In a medium-sized bowl, mix everything except oil together and let sit, covered, at room temperature for 30 minutes to 1 hour.
2. Put oil in wok or skillet and heat over medium-high heat until hot. Add chicken mixture and stir fry until chicken is firm and cooked through, about 5 minutes. Test for doneness. Serve immediately over hot rice.

Serves 6

County land
Ownership

Only three percent of Teton County's 3.8 million acres is under private ownership. Ninety-seven percent of the county is under state ownership or federal management, including Grand Teton National Park, Bridger-Teton National Forest and the National Elk Refuge.

Pork loin and chops are
lean cuts of meat that will
be dry and flavorless if
cooked too long. The
USDA recommends that
pork prepared at home
be cooked to an internal
temperature of 160-165
degrees to destroy trichi-
nae bacteria. Because
cooked pork removed
from the oven continues
to cook, remove the pork
when a meat thermom-
eter inserted into the
thickest part of the meat
reaches 150 degrees.
Loosely cover the pork
with foil and let sit at
room temperature for 10
minutes. It will cook an-
other 10 degrees, to
160. (For pork, 160 de-
grees is considered me-
dium; 170 to 180 de-
grees is considered well-
done.)

Pork Tenderloin with Balsamic Raisin Sauce

Doris Laubach

Doris clipped this fabulous recipe from a mail order catalog some time ago. It has become one of her wintertime favorites. It is a show-stopping, guaranteed hit with company. Plan ahead so you have ample time to soak the raisins.

½ cup raisins
1 cup dry red wine
3 tbsp. dark brown sugar
2 tbsp. balsamic vinegar, divided
1¼ cups chicken stock or canned low-salt broth
3 tbsp. olive oil
3 pork tenderloins (about 2¼ lbs. total)
½ cup onion, minced
8 shallots, minced
2 garlic cloves, minced
3 tbsp. unsalted butter
salt and pepper

1. Place raisins and wine in a heavy small saucepan. Let stand 8 hours.
2. Add brown sugar and 1 tbsp. balsamic vinegar to raisin mixture. Boil over high heat until liquid is reduced to 1 tbsp., about 7 minutes. Add chicken stock and continue to boil until mixture is reduced by half. Remove from heat. (This can be prepared up to two days ahead and stored covered in refrigerator.)
3. Preheat oven to 450 degrees. Heat olive oil in heavy, large oven-proof skillet over medium-high heat. Add tenderloin and cook until brown on bottom, about 3 minutes. Add onion and shallots and continue cooking until pork is brown on all sides and onion is tender, about 6 minutes. Add garlic.
4. Place skillet in oven and cook pork until thermometer inserted into thickest part registers 140 degrees, about 4 minutes. Transfer pork to platter and tent with foil to keep warm.
5. Put raisin mixture in the pork skillet and add 1 tbsp. vinegar. Remove from heat and whisk in butter. Season sauce with salt and pepper to taste. Keep warm.
6. Slice pork into ½-inch thick slices. Arrange in slightly overlapping rows on platter. Pour sauce over pork and serve. Sauerbrauten or roasted vegetables are a great accompaniment to this dish.

Serves 6

Glazed Cranberry Pork Roast

A spectacular entree perfect for special evenings. This adapted recipe won grand prize honors in a magazine cooking contest.

3½   lb. boneless rolled pork loin roast
½   cup chopped green onions, tops included
4   tbsp. butter, divided
¼   cup fresh squeezed orange juice
1   bay leaf
1   16-oz. can whole berry cranberry sauce
½   cup chicken stock or low-salt chicken broth
½   cup pecans, chopped
1   tbsp. cider vinegar
¼   tsp. salt
⅛   tsp. pepper
¼   cup apricot jam

1. Preheat oven to 350 degrees.
2. Place pork roast on a rack in a roasting pan and roast uncovered on a rack in the middle of the oven for 1 hour.
3. While the pork is roasting, melt 1 tbsp. butter in a skillet over medium-high heat. Sauté green onion in the butter for 1 minute. Add orange juice and bay leaf and stir constantly for 4 minutes. Add the chicken broth or stock, cranberry sauce, cider vinegar and pecans. Stir constantly until mixture thickens, about 5 minutes.
4. Reduce heat to low and stir in the salt, pepper and remaining butter. Stir until the butter is melted. Remove and discard bay leaf. Remove ¼ cup of cranberry sauce and pour into a small bowl. Cover the remaining sauce and remove skillet from heat.
5. To the cranberry sauce in the small bowl, add the apricot jam and whisk well to blend.
6. After the pork has roasted for 1 hour, brush cranberry apricot glaze over the meat. Return the roast to the oven and bake an additional 45 minutes, or until a meat thermometer inserted into the middle of the roast reads 160 degrees.
7. Remove roast from oven and let stand 15 minutes before slicing. During this time, warm the sauce reserved in the skillet over low heat, stirring occasionally. Serve the sliced pork roast with the reserved sauce.

Serves 10

The Grand Teton

At 13,770-feet, the Grand Teton is the highest peak in the Teton Range—but not the highest summit in Wyoming. That honor belongs to 13,804-foot Gannett Peak in the Wind River Range.

Pork Ribs
Caroline Janney

Caroline says this is an old Japanese recipe. These ribs could put Bubba's out of business: they're that good.

    3   lbs. baby back pork ribs
    3   cloves garlic, minced
    ¼   cup vinegar
    ⅓   cup each brown sugar and soy sauce
    2   tbsp. olive oil

1. Cut ribs into three pieces.
2. Pour olive oil into large pot and add minced garlic, stirring to distribute. Add ribs and place pot on stove over medium heat. Cook until ribs are browned, turning occasionally to evenly brown.
3. Pour vinegar over ribs and stir well before adding other ingredients. Stir again, then bring mixture to a full boil. Reduce heat and simmer for 1 hour, stirring occasionally. Serve hot over rice.

Serves 6

Grilled Mongolian Pork Chops
Susie Rauch

Susie got this wonderful recipe from Tom Roach, a noted baker from California's Napa Valley.

    6   boneless pork loin chops, ½ - ¾ inches thick
    1   cup rice wine vinegar
    ½   cup soy sauce
    2   tbsp. brown bean sauce
    1   cup chopped scallions or green onions
    ½   cup chopped cilantro
    2   tsp. fresh chives, chopped
    5   garlic cloves, minced or pressed
    1   tsp. ground coriander

1. In a large bowl, combine everything but the pork chops and stir to blend. Pour into a large, heavy-duty sealable plastic bag.
2. Add pork chops and turn to coat. Seal bag and place flat inside large, shallow baking pan (in case the bag leaks). Marinate 1-2 hours at room temperature, turning the bag occasionally, or up to 24 hours in the refrigerator.
3. Cook on a hot grill until chops are white in the center but still moist, about 12 minutes, Turn once during cooking time. Serve warm with chutney, rice and a green salad.

Serves 6

Roast Beef with Herb Crust

The herb rub imparts fantastic flavor. A spectacular way to present roast beef!

- 4 lb. boneless beef rump roast, tied
- 4 shallots, finely minced
- ¼ cup fresh parsley, finely chopped
- 2 tbsp. fresh thyme, chopped or 2 tsp. dried
- 1 tbsp. fresh sage leaves, chopped, or 1 tsp. dried
- 2 tbsp. extra-virgin olive oil
- 1 tbsp. grated lemon peel
- 1 tsp. salt
- ½ tsp. pepper

1. Preheat oven to 325 degrees.
2. In a small bowl, mix together all ingredients except the roast. Rub over roast, pressing gently to adhere herbs.
3. Put roast on a roasting rack inside a shallow roasting pan. Place pan in the center of the oven and roast uncovered for 1 hour, 45 minutes (or until thermometer inserted in the center of the roast reads 140 degrees) for medium rare. Let sit 15 minutes before carving.

Serves 10-12

The Kissengers

William S. Kissenger homesteaded near Kelly Warm Springs in 1898. To "prove up" his claim he constructed a 16 x 20-foot, three-room log house, a stable and a log shed. He also dug a four-mile ditch from Ditch Creek to his homestead to irrigate 65 acres of his property.

Kissenger Cabin, early 1900s.

Imperial Beef Tenderloin
Martha Hansen

Wyoming's former First Lady relies on this recipe for special occasions. She shared it years ago in a cookbook published by the state of Wyoming.

1	4-6 lb. beef tenderloin
¼	cup melted butter
1	clove garlic, pressed
1	tbsp. Worcestershire sauce
4	oz. blue cheese, crumbled
½	cup softened butter

1. Preheat oven to 450 degrees.
2. Trim fat from tenderloin. Place on a rack set in a shallow roasting pan and brush generously with melted butter. Roast 45-60 minutes, or until meat thermometer reaches 140 degrees.
3. Shortly before tenderloin is done, mix garlic, Worcestershire sauce, bleu cheese and butter together until well blended.
4. Remove tenderloin from oven. Spread cheese mixture on top. Serve immediately.

Note: Half of the cheese mixture is enough for the smaller sized loin.

Serves 8-12

Marinated Flank Steak

Great for summer grilling. This flavorful meal is easy to prepare, but requires a minimum of 3 hours to marinate the steak.

¼	cup fresh squeezed orange juice
2	tbsp. chili sauce
2	tbsp. light soy sauce
2	tbsp. extra-light or mild olive oil
1	tsp. sugar
1	tsp. grated orange rind
2	cloves garlic, pressed or finely minced
½	tsp. salt
⅛	tsp. hot pepper sauce
1½	lbs. flank steak
1	medium orange, sliced thin

1. Combine everything except the steak and orange slices in a small bowl. Whisk to blend.

2. Place steak in a heavy-duty, sealable plastic bag. Pour in marinade. Turn meat to coat. Top meat with orange slices. Seal plastic bag, squeezing out excess air. Place bag inside a pan and put in refrigerator. Marinate 3 hours to overnight, turning occasionally. When ready to grill, remove the orange slices and pour off the marinade. Discard both.

3. Heat a gas grill to medium-high. If using charcoal, the coals are ready when you can hold your hand, palm-side down, 4-inches above them for about 4 seconds. Grill steak 10-12 minutes, turning once, for medium rare.

4. Remove from heat. Let sit for 5 minutes before cutting thin slices across the grain of the meat. Fan slices on warmed plates. Garnish with thick oranges slices and sprigs of cilantro, if desired. Serve with Island Fruit Salsa, page 80.

Serves 4

Monarch Butterfly

The familiar orange wings with striking black veins and borders make the monarch one of the most recognizable butterflies in Jackson Hole and throughout most of North America. Monarchs winter in California and Mexico.

Steak Fajitas

Easy enough for a weeknight, good enough for company. This recipe is an adapted version of a recipe developed by the California Culinary Academy.

    1   cup thinly sliced onions
    1   cup sliced mushrooms
    1   tsp. canola oil
    ⅓   cup dry cooking sherry
    1   lb. sirloin tip steak, trimmed of fat
    2   jalapeno chiles, seeded and minced fine
    ½   tsp. cumin
    ¼   tsp. coriander
    2   tsp. cilantro leaves, minced
    4   large flour tortillas
        salsa
    ½   avocado, peeled, seeded and sliced thin
    1   cup nonfat sour cream

1. In a large skillet, heat oil and sherry over medium-high heat. Add onions and mushrooms and sauté for 10 minutes, stirring occasionally. While vegetables are cooking, cut steak into 1½-inch strips.

2. Add steak strips to skillet and sauté 2 minutes, stirring occasionally.

3. Add chiles, cumin, coriander and cilantro and cook an additional 3 minutes, stirring often. Reduce heat to low to keep mixture warm.

4. Heat tortillas in a microwave or conventional oven according to package directions.

5. Put salsa, yogurt and avocado in small bowls at the table. Place warm tortillas on plates and spoon the meat mixture down the middle. Have everyone assemble their own fajitas with the condiments on the table. Serve fajitas with traditional beans and rice and/or pico de gallo (recipe on page 82).

Serves 4

Slow Cooked Beef Burritos

Pop the meat in a crock pot before leaving for work, and these terrific slow-cooked burritos are essentially done by the time you return home.

2 lb. London broil, trimmed of fat
1 1¼-oz. pkg. taco seasoning
   vegetable cooking spray
1 cup chopped onion
1 tbsp. white vinegar
1 4.5-oz. can chopped mild green chiles
8 large flour tortillas
1½ cups shredded Monterey Jack cheese
1½ cups plum (roma) tomatoes, chopped
¾ cup light or fat-free sour cream

1. Spray crock pot or electric slow-cooker with vegetable heat and turn on to low setting.

Teton Pass Summit, 1915.

2. Rub taco seasoning over both sides of the London broil and place in slow cooker. Add onion, vinegar and green chiles. Cover and cook for 9 hours.
3. Remove meat from slow cooker and place in a shallow baking pan. Shred with two forks, then pour liquid from slow cooker into pan and stir well to blend.
4. Heat tortillas according to package instructions. Spoon a heaping portion of beef in the center of each tortilla. Top with cheese, tomato and sour cream and roll up. Serve with a side of rice and refried beans or a crisp green salad.

Serves 8

Baked Short Ribs

Joyce Lucas

Joyce's lip-smackin' recipe for ribs was featured as a Cowbelle Recipe of the Month in the *Jackson Hole Guide* years ago. It's as good today as it was then. Beef lovers can find a collection of recipes from the Jackson Hole Cowbelles, an organization formed in the 1950s to promote beef, in the groups *Feeding the Herd* cookbook. For ordering information, see the acknowledgments section.

Uncle Nick Wilson

Elijah "Uncle Nick" Wilson and his family moved to Jackson Hole in 1889, beginning a substantial migration of Mormons into the valley. Wilson, the namesake of the small town nestled at the foot of Teton Pass, claimed Native Americans raised him. His colorful life included riding for the Pony Express.

    4   lbs. beef short ribs
    ½   cup flour
    ¼   tsp. pepper
    ¼   tsp. salt
    1   medium yellow onion, thinly sliced
    ¾   cup ketchup
    ¾   cup water
    ½   cup sugar
    5   tbsp. soy sauce
    2   tbsp. white vinegar
    2   tbsp. Worcestershire sauce

1. Place flour, salt and pepper in a sturdy bag. Add batches of ribs to bag and shake well to coat ribs in the seasoned flour. Place ribs in a 13x9-inch baking dish in a single layer. Top ribs with thinly sliced onion. Set aside.
2. In a medium-sized bowl, mix together remaining ingredients. Stir well to blend.
3. Pour sauce evenly over the ribs and onions. Cover tightly with aluminum foil.
4. Place ribs in a rack in the middle of the oven, turn temperature to 300 degrees, and cook for 3 hours or until ribs are tender and cooked through. Serve with coleslaw and warm, crusty rolls.

Serves 6

The Tetons, 1890.
W.H. Jackson photo

Pioneer photographer William Henry Jackson was a member of the Snake River Division of the 1872 Hayden Survey, led by James Stephenson. Jackson shot many of the first images of the Teton Range and Jackson Hole.

Caribbean Grilled Fish

Lisa Robertson

3 large cloves garlic, coarsely chopped
1 tsp. salt
1 tsp. dried thyme
¼ tsp. ground allspice
¼ cup orange juice
2-3 tbsp. lemon juice
2 tbsp. dry white wine (optional)
¼ tsp. Tabasco sauce
¼ cup olive oil
6 6-oz. fish steaks of choice (salmon, halibut or swordfish are good)

1. Combine all ingredients (except fish!) in a jar, cover and shake well.
2. Pour marinade over fish steaks of choice and marinate in the refrigerator at least one hour.
3. Grill over medium heat, turning once, until fish is cooked through. Serve hot with lemon wedges.

Serves 6

Grilled and Baked Fish

Chef Karen Norby

Karen was given this superb technique for preparing fish by her friend and fellow chef Steve Carlyle, who produces dishes for the Rosemary Inn at the Olympic Park Institute in Washington. It works particularly well with halibut or salmon

⅓-½ lb. of fresh fish per person
butter or olive oil
garlic cloves, crushed or pressed
fresh grated ginger
fresh lemon juice

1. Preheat oven to 500 degrees.
2. Heat a large skillet or frying pan over high heat. When hot, place butter or olive oil in pan and quickly add crushed garlic and grated ginger, stirring to blend.
3. Throw in fish, skin side up/flesh side down, and cook just until the surface has browned, less than 1 minute.
4. Remove fish and place on ungreased baking sheet, skin side down/ flesh side up. Sprinkle with lemon juice and place sheet on top rack in the preheated oven. Bake 10 minutes per inch of thickness, or until the fish appears done when flaked with a fork and the temperature at the thickest part of the fillet reaches 140 degrees. Do not overcook!

5. Remove fish and serve immediately. Garnish with finely chopped, fresh parsley or springs of cilantro, if desired.

Grilled Salmon with Cucumber Relish

Donna Spurlock

A summertime treat, when grilling is easy and cucumbers are plentiful. Donna adapted this recipe from a Betty Crocker® cook booklet.

Cucumber relish
    1   cucumber, seeded and chopped
    2   tbsp. peeled and chopped red onion
    2   tbsp. white vinegar
    2   tbsp. water
    1   tsp. sugar
   ½   tsp. salt
Salmon
    1   large salmon fillet or 6 6-oz fillets
    2   tbsp. extra-virgin olive oil
 1½   tsp. fresh, snipped dill weed or ½ tsp. dried dill weed
       salt and pepper to taste

1. Mix relish ingredients together in a nonmetal bowl. Cover and refrigerate a minimum of 1 hour but no longer than 24 hours. Drain before serving.
2. Heat grill to a medium temperature.
3. Place fillet(s) on heavy-duty aluminum foil large enough to completely wrap fillets. Brush fillet(s) with olive oil and sprinkle with dill and salt and pepper. Wrap securely in foil and place on grill rack 4-6 inches from heat source. Close cover and grill for 25-30 minutes, or until salmon flakes easily with a fork. Remove fillet(s) from grill and place on platter covered with green lettuce leaves and lemon slices. Serve with cucumber relish.

Serves 6

Cooking Fish

To determine how long to cook fish—whether broiling, frying, grilling, poaching or steaming—measure a fillet at the thickest point, then allow 10 minutes per inch.

Removing Fish
Odors

To get rid of the smell of
fish on your hands rub
them against a stainless
steel spoon or sink. To
remove odor from cut-
ting boards, rub a cut
lemon over the surface.

Miso Mirin Glazed Salmon
Mary Howley, R.D.

Sensational and easy. This is one of Mary's favorite recipes.

6-8 oz. of salmon per person
      mirin (Japanese cooking wine)
      light or dark miso
      orange juice concentrate or fresh-squeezed orange juice
½ tsp. fresh grated ginger for every 2 servings, or to taste
1 clove garlic, finely minced, for every 2 servings, or to taste

1. Preheat oven to broil.
2. In a small bowl, mix together equal parts of mirin, miso and orange juice concentrate or fresh squeezed orange juice to make a
paste. Amounts will vary with number of servings being prepared.
Stir in grated fresh ginger and garlic to taste. Brush on salmon.
3. Place salmon, skin side down if you are preparing a large fillet, on
a broiler pan lightly sprayed with cooking oil. Place pan 4-6 inches
from heat and broil 5-7 minutes, or until fish flakes easily with a
fork. Watch carefully so you don't overcook. Serve immediately
with rice and fruit salsa, couscous or a salad.

Servings vary

Salmon Loaf
Val Lefebre

"People always ask me for this recipe."

½ cup mayonnaise
1 can condensed cream of celery soup
2 eggs
½ cup chopped onion
¼ cup chopped green pepper
1 tbsp. lemon juice
    salt and pepper
2 cups flaked salmon, skin and bones removed
½ cup ground macadamia nuts
1 cup bread crumbs
2 tbsp. butter

1. Preheat oven to 350 degrees. Butter a loaf pan and set aside.
2. In a large bowl, stir the mayonnaise, soup and eggs together until
well blended. Add the chopped onion and lemon juice and stir
until blended. Salt and pepper to taste.
3. Stir in the flaked salmon, macadamia nuts and bread crumbs.

4. Spoon into prepared pan and pat into a loaf. Bake for 1 hour or until the loaf is set and the top is golden.

Serves 6

Halibut Au Gratin

Carole Travis Henikoff

Carole's father, Chef Carl Anderson, developed this recipe when he operated the famous Chatam restaurant in Hollywood. It's been a favorite ever since.

Great Horned Owl

The Great Horned Owl is a common resident of Jackson Hole and Yellowstone National Park throughout the year. It lives in cliffs, canyons and broken forested terrain. Great Horns prey on small rodents, birds, grouse, squirrels, hares and even marmots—activity aided by powerful eyesight, keen hearing and finely-toothed feathers that permit almost soundless flight.

4   6-8 oz. halibut fillets, boned and skinned (any firm white fish can be used in this recipe)
    butter
    lemon juice
    salt and pepper
6   tbsp. butter, divided (no margarine!)
3   tbsp. flour
1¼ cups half-and-half
1   cup fresh bread crumbs
    fresh, finely grated Parmesan cheese

1. Preheat oven to 350 degrees.
2. Heavily butter a baking dish just large enough to hold the fillets in a single layer. Place fillets in dish and sprinkle with lemon juice, salt and pepper.
3. In a medium-sized saucepan, melt 4 tbsp. butter over moderate heat. Add flour and cook for 2 minutes, stirring constantly. Add a third of the cream. Stir until smooth, then add the rest of the cream and stir until the mixture is very thick, about 5 minutes. Season to taste with salt and pepper and set aside.
4. In a skillet, melt 2 tbsp. butter over moderate heat. Add bread crumbs and cook and stir until the crumbs are a light golden color. Remove from heat.
5. Measure the fried bread crumbs into a small bowl and add an equal amount of grated Parmesan cheese.
6. Spoon the cream sauce down the center of the fillets (do not spread the mixture). Top the sauce with the bread crumb mixture and bake for 20 minutes or until the fish is cooked through and flakes easily with a fork.

Serves 4

Chopping Nuts

To crush nuts quickly without using a food processor, place them in a self-sealing plastic bag and roll with a rolling pin.

Pecan-Crusted Trout

For a nice change from pan fried fish, try this tasty easy-to-make baked dish. The recipe is adapted from *Bon Appétit* magazine.

  ½ cup pecans
  1 tbsp. plus 1 tsp. sesame seeds
  4 8-10 inches fresh, boned trout fillets, skin on
  4 tsp. butter
  1 garlic clove, minced
  2 tbsp. vegetable oil
     salt and pepper to taste

1. Line a large baking sheet with aluminum foil. Set aside.
2. Finely chop pecans in a food processor, using on/off turns. Place in shallow bowl and mix in the sesame seeds.
3. Place butter and garlic in a small saucepan over low heat and stir until butter melts. Remove from heat.
4. Place trout fillets skin side down on prepared baking sheet and brush with garlic butter. Season with salt and pepper to taste. Sprinkle with nut mixture, then press lightly to adhere nuts to the fish. Chill, uncovered, for 30 minutes.
5. Just before trout is done chilling, preheat oven to 400 degrees. Place baking sheet on middle rack and bake until trout is opaque in the center and flakes easily, 5-6 minutes.
6. Garnish with fresh snipped parsley, if desired. Serve warm with wild rice.

Serves 4

Vietnamese Shrimp with Rice Noodles

Claudia Burkhardt

Wonderfully spicy and flavorful. Claudia, a professional caterer, shared this recipe with the Jackson Hole Cowbelles in their *Feeding the Herd* cookbook. For information on ordering that publication, or contacting Claudia, please see the acknowledgments section.

  1½ lbs. medium shrimp, cleaned and dried
   2 tsp. minced, fresh ginger
  1½ tsp. fish sauce
  1½ lbs. thin rice stick noodles, prepared according to package instructions
  2½ tbsp. vegetable oil
   4 cups bean sprouts, rinsed and drained
   1 cup chopped green onions
   ⅓ cup dry roasted peanuts, coarsely chopped
   ¼ cup fresh cilantro, chopped

Vietnamese dressing
- ¾ cup fish sauce
- ⅔ cup Japanese rice vinegar
- 1-2 small red hot chile peppers, seeded and finely minced
- 3 tbsp. minced garlic
- 5½ tbsp. sugar or to taste

1. Combine all dressing ingredients in a bowl and stir to dissolve the sugar. Chill, covered in refrigerator. Dressing will keep up to a week.
2. Prepare rice stick noodles and place in ample-sized serving bowl. In a separate bowl, toss the shrimp, ginger and 1½ tsp. of fish sauce together until shrimp are well coated. Set aside.
3. Heat a wok or heavy skillet over high heat. When the pan is hot, add 1 tbsp. of vegetable oil and cook the green onions and bean sprouts for 15 seconds, stirring constantly. Remove pan from heat and sprinkle the onions and sprouts over the noodles.
4. Return pan to heat, add 1½ tbsp. of oil and reheat pan until very hot. Add shrimp and cook just until the shrimp turns pink, about 2-3 minutes. Remove from heat and spoon shrimp over the noodles. Top with peanuts and cilantro. Spoon dressing over top and toss gently to mix.

Serves 4

Kneedy Flour Mill

The Kneedy Flour Mill in Kelly produced the first barrel of flour in Jackson Hole on July 10, 1919. The endeavor began two years earlier when Milton K. Kneedy, a miller by trade, purchased a 20-barrel capacity flour mill and a gristmill to make feed for livestock. A fire in October of 1921 destroyed the mill and tons of flour and wheat; the business was never rebuilt. On May 18, 1927, three members of the Kneedy family lost their lives in the Kelly Flood after ignoring urgent advice to evacuate.

Kneedy dam and mill, 1927.

Florentine Squash Bake

A super squash dish, adapted from *Cooking Light* magazine.

¼ cup flour
⅛ tsp. pepper
2 cups skim milk
   vegetable cooking spray
½ cup yellow onion, chopped
3 cloves garlic, minced
½ cup freshly grated Gruyère cheese
1 10-oz. pkg. frozen chopped spinach, thawed and squeezed dry
1 2-3 lb. spaghetti squash
⅔ cup diced ham

1. Prick squash 4-5 times with a fork, place on microwave safe plate and microwave on full power for 7-9 minutes. Turn over and microwave an additional 7-9 minutes. Remove from microwave and let sit for 5 minutes. Halve squash with a sharp knife and remove seeds. Using a fork, scoop 5 cups of spaghetti-like strands into a bowl. Save any remaining squash for a different use.
2. Preheat oven to 375 degrees and spray 13x9-inch baking dish with vegetable spray.
3. Put flour and pepper in a medium-sized mixing bowl and gradually pour in milk, whisking mixture to a smooth consistency. Set aside.
4. Spray a large skillet or saucepan with vegetable spray and heat over a medium-high burner. Sauté onion and garlic for 1 minute. Add set aside milk mixture and cook and stir constantly until mixture thickens, about 6 minutes. Add cheese and spinach and stir well to blend.
5. Remove pan or skillet from heat and stir in the 5 cups of squash and chopped ham. Put in prepared baking dish and bake for 20 minutes, or until hot and bubbly.

Serves 6.

Easy Chicken Quesadillas

Yummy and fast.

2½ cups cooked chicken, shredded with two forks
⅔ cup salsa
⅓ cup sliced green onion, tops included
¾ tsp. cumin
½ tsp. each, salt and oregano
4 large, soft flour tortillas

¼	cup melted butter
1	8-oz. pkg. shredded Monterey Jack cheese (2 cups)
	sour cream

1. Preheat oven to 475 degrees. Lightly grease two rimmed baking sheets. Set aside.
2. Place the chicken, salsa, green onions, cumin, salt and oregano in a large skillet over medium heat. Stir to blend. Cook 10 minutes or until heated, stirring occasionally.
3. Brush one side of tortillas with melted butter and place butter side down on a baking sheet. Spoon a fourth of the chicken mixture evenly over half of the unbuttered tortilla. Sprinkle with a fourth of the cheese and fold the unbuttered plain side over the cheese. Repeat with the remaining three tortillas, placing two folded tortillas on each baking sheet. Bake 10 minutes or until the tortillas are crisp and golden. Cut into 3 or 4 wedges from the folded seam with a pizza cutter. Top with a dollop of sour cream. Serve with guacamole, beans and rice.

Serves 4 generously.

Vegetable Quesadillas
Therese Metherell, R.D.

1	small onion, chopped
1	small zucchini, thinly sliced
1	small yellow squash, thinly sliced
1-2	garlic cloves, minced
1	can fat-free refried beans
8	large whole wheat tortillas
½	cup shredded reduced fat cheddar cheese
1	cup salsa
	low-fat sour cream (optional)

1. Coat large skillet with cooking spray and warm over medium heat. Add vegetables and cook until tender, stirring occasionally. Remove vegetable mixture from heat.
2. Spread beans evenly over all eight tortillas. Spoon vegetable mixture evenly on top of the beans on four tortillas. Sprinkle cheese over the vegetables, then top each with one of the remaining tortillas.
3. Place one quesadilla in the skillet. Cover and cook over low heat, turning once, for 5 minutes or until heated thoroughly. Place in 200 degree oven to keep warm and repeat with remaining quesadillas. Cut into wedges and serve with a dollop of low-fat sour cream and salsa.

Serves 6-8

Pronghorn

Pronghorn are named for their slightly curved horns, each with a single prong propelling forward. They are found chiefly in sagebrush flats, where they dine on sagebrush and other vegetation. Pronghorn are able to sustain speeds of 40 m.p.h., making them second only to the cheetah as the fastest mammal on Earth.

Potato Bacon Pizza

Just watch slices of this award-winning pizza disappear! The recipe below is an adaptation of a grand prize winner printed in a cooking magazine.

3   medium baking potatoes, peeled and diced
1   large Boboli® pizza crust
¼   cup milk
½   tsp. salt
1   lb. turkey bacon, diced
1   large onion, chopped
½   cup red bell pepper, seeded and chopped
1½   cups grated cheddar cheese
1½   cups grated Mozzarella cheese
     low-fat sour cream, optional

1. Place potatoes is a large saucepan, add enough water to cover, and bring water to a boil over medium heat. Cook, uncovered, until very tender, about 20 minutes.
2. While potatoes are cooking, place bacon in a large skillet and partially cook over medium heat, about 3 minutes. Add onion and red pepper and continue to cook until bacon is crisp and vegetables are tender. Drain grease and set aside.
3. When potatoes are tender, remove from heat and drain. Add milk and salt and whip with a mixer until smooth.
4. Preheat oven to 375 degrees.
5. Place Boboli® crust on an ungreased cookie sheet. Spread potatoes over crust. Evenly disperse bacon mixture over potatoes and top with cheeses.
6. Bake pizza until cheese is melted and pizza is heated through, about 20 minutes. If desired, serve with sour cream.

Serves 4-6

Red Beans and Rice   *Lokey Lytjen*

This is one of Lokey's favorite recipes. It came from her grandmother, Two Mama, who grew up in Jefferson Parish, Louisiana. She has substituted turkey bacon and heart-healthy oil without affecting the taste. Lokey recommends serving it with "a salad, French bread or corn bread, and cool jazz."

½   lb. turkey bacon, cooked crisp and crumbled
     rice for six, prepared according to package directions
1   large onion, chopped medium dice
1   tbsp. olive oil

2   15-oz. cans dark red kidney beans, undrained
½   tsp. Lea & Perrins Worcestershire sauce
    salt, pepper and Tabasco to taste

1. Prepare rice according to package directions; keep warm.
2. Cook bacon until crisp. Drain, crumble and set aside.
3. Heat a large skillet over medium-high heat until hot. Add olive oil and sauté onion, stirring often, until soft and translucent, about 3 minutes.
4. Add undrained kidney beans, crumbled bacon, Worcestershire sauce and salt and pepper to taste. Stir to blend. Reduce heat to low and simmer 30 minutes, or until hot and heated through, stirring occasionally. Serve over rice.

Lokey sometimes adds one or all of the following, based on Jeff Smith's *The Frugal Gourmet Cooks American*: minced garlic, chopped parsley, chopped celery, cayenne pepper, dried thyme, oregano, cumin or bell pepper.

Serves 4

Mexican Lentil Casserole   *Judy Eddy*

Hearty and healthy (not to mention good!).

½   cup chopped onion
½   cup chopped green pepper
½   cup chopped celery
4   cups water
1   cup uncooked lentils
1½ cups cooked brown rice
1   6-oz. can tomato paste
1   1¼-oz. packet taco seasoning mix
½   tsp. chili powder

1. In medium saucepan, combine onion, green pepper, celery and water. Bring to boil over medium heat. Stir in lentils. Cover pot, reduce heat to low and simmer 40 minutes.
2. Preheat oven to 375 degrees. Lightly oil or spray with nonstick cooking spray a 1¾-qt. baking dish.
3. Remove lentil mixture from heat and stir in remaining ingredients, mixing well. Spoon into prepared casserole.
4. Bake uncovered for 25 minutes. Let stand 5 minutes before serving.

Serves 6

Wolverine

The wolverine has a fearsome reputation of being able to down animals many times its size, robbing traps and destroying food caches. Yet, little has actually been documented about this elusive member of the weasel family. Wolverines weigh between 35-60 pounds and are covered with thick fur. If not for their bushy tail, they could be mistaken for a small bear.

Asparagus

Keep fresh asparagus clean, cold and covered. Trim the stem end about a quarter- inch and thoroughly rinse in warm water. Pat dry and place in moisture-proof wrapping. Refrigerate and use within 2-3 days.

Veggie Stir Fry with Brown Rice

Low calorie and lovin' it.

2	carrots, peeled
2	celery stalks
1	medium yellow onion
1	medium broccoli bunch
½	lb. (8-oz.) mushrooms
½	cup canola or light olive oil
½	cup water
1¼	tsp. salt
½	tsp. sugar
	brown rice

1. Follow package directions to prepare six servings of brown rice.
2. While the rice is cooking, prepare your vegetables. Cut carrots in half crosswise, then into lengthwise matchlike strips. Cut celery crosswise into thirds, then lengthwise into matchlike strips. Thinly slice onions and separate into individual rings. Leave 1½-inches of stem below the broccoli flowerets; save cut off stems for soups or other uses. Divide flowerets in half. Cut cleaned mushrooms in half or quarters, depending on mushroom size.
3. In a large skillet or Dutch oven, heat oil over high heat. When oil is hot but not smoking, add the carrots, celery, onion and broccoli. Stir quickly and often for 4 minutes. Add the mushrooms, water, salt and sugar. Stir, then cover and cook, stirring occasionally, until the vegetables are crisp-tender, about 5 minutes. Remove from heat and spoon stir-fry over brown rice. Serve with warm rolls.

Serves 4

Penne with Spinach and Asparagus

Barbara Trachtenberg

Pasta fans will love this dish. Barbara is an accomplished home chef who has donated numerous gourmet dinners to the Teton Science Schools' auction. She enjoys experimenting with ethnic foods.

1	lb. penne pasta
2	cups fresh baby spinach leaves, solidly packed
12-15	asparagus spears, ends trimmed
3	large garlic cloves, crushed
¼-½	cup extra virgin olive oil
¼	cup each chopped fresh parsley and fresh basil
	salt and pepper to taste
	fresh grated Parmesan cheese (optional)

1. Prepare pasta according to package directions. Time to be cooked, drained (not rinsed) and ready shortly after vegetables are cooked.
2. In large skillet or wok, heat 2 tbsp. olive oil to high temperature but not to the smoking point. Add crushed garlic and asparagus and cook quickly 2-3 minutes. Add two more tablespoons olive oil and the spinach and cook until spinach is totally wilted. Add parsley and basil and mix well. Salt and pepper to taste. Remove vegetables from heat.
3. When pasta is cooked and ready, reheat vegetables, add pasta and mix well. Add another 2 tbsp. to ¼ cup olive oil to taste. Sprinkle with freshly grated Parmesan cheese (optional) and serve at once.

Serves 8

Fettuccine with Walnut Sauce   *Dave Bloom*

Dave discovered this mouthwatering recipe in an out-of-print Italian cookbook. He uses pre-made pasta noodles to shorten preparation time. It is best prepared with tagliatelle, a long, narrow egg noodle, but regular fettuccine is fine.

    1   12-oz. pkg. tagliatelle or fettuccine
    1   4¼-oz. pkg. finely chopped walnuts
    2   tbsp. olive oil
        salt and pepper
    1   stick unsalted butter
    3   tbsp. tomato paste diluted in 1 cup warm water
    6   tbsp. freshly grated Parmesan cheese

1. Place walnuts, olive oil and a sprinkling of salt and pepper in a saucepan over medium heat and cook, stirring frequently, until walnuts are well toasted, about 5-7 minutes.
2. Add butter and the diluted tomato paste and bring to a boil, stirring frequently.
3. Lower heat and simmer uncovered about 20 minutes, or until sauce thickens. Keep warm.
4. Cook pasta according to package instructions. Drain and place on a warm serving platter or wide, shallow pasta bowl. Add walnut sauce and toss, then top with grated Parmesan. Serve hot with a green salad, wine and crusty bread.

Serves 6

Perfect Pasta

Perfectly cooked pasta is "al dente," or firm to the bite, yet cooked through. The firmer texture is more pleasing to the palate, and vitamins and minerals lost with longer cooking times are preserved. If the pasta is to be used as part of a dish that requires further cooking, undercook it by a third of the cooking time specified on the package.

The only time you should
rinse pasta after draining
is when you are using it
in a cold dish, or when
you are not going to
serve it immediately. In
these cases, rinse the
pasta under cold water
to stop the cooking pro-
cess and drain well.

Creamy Fettuccine with Artichoke Hearts and Mushrooms

Therese Metherell, R.D

As Therese put it, this is a "decadent-tasting recipe without cream" that is "elegant enough to impress out-of-town visitors." She's right.

- 1 cup quartered, unmarinated artichoke hearts, drained and coarsely chopped
- 2 tbsp. balsamic vinegar
- ¼ cup defatted chicken or vegetable broth
- 2 tbsp. minced garlic
- 1 cup fresh mushrooms, sliced
- ½ red bell pepper, seeded and sliced
- 4 tbsp. fresh parsley, snipped
- ½ cup fat-free sour cream mixed with ½ tsp. cornstarch salt and pepper to taste
- 4 cups hot cooked fettuccine noodles

1. Marinate artichoke hearts in vinegar for 20 minutes. Drain and set aside.
2. Bring chicken or vegetable stock to boil in a large skillet or wok over medium-high heat. Add garlic, artichokes, mushrooms and red pepper. Cook, stirring frequently, until vegetables are soft, about five minutes. Remove from heat.
3. Add parsley, sour cream mixture and salt and pepper to taste. Toss with hot pasta and serve immediately.

Serves 4

Macaroni and Cheese
Chef Karen Norby

Forget the boxed stuff. This recipe elevates mac-and-cheese to gourmet fare. Serve with a crisp green salad for a complete meal.

1	12-oz. pkg. dried elbow macaroni
2	slices whole wheat bread
1	tbsp. grated Parmesan cheese
¾	tsp. paprika
1	cup chopped onion
¼	cup flour
2	cans evaporated nonfat milk
1	cup vegetable broth
3	cups shredded reduced fat sharp cheddar cheese
	ground nutmeg
	salt and pepper

1. Cook macaroni in 2 quarts boiling water until tender to bite. Drain.
2. Tear bread into ½-inch chunks. Combine bread, Parmesan cheese and paprika in a food processor or blender and cut into coarse crumbs.
3. In a 5-6 quart pan over high heat, sauté onion until soft and translucent. Stir in flour.
4. Remove onion from heat and blend in milk, cheese and vegetable broth until smooth. Return to stove and cook over high heat until sauce boils, about five minutes.
5. Add nutmeg and salt and pepper to taste. Add macaroni to cheese sauce, mix well, then pour into a shallow 2 ½-quart casserole dish. Sprinkle with seasoned bread crumbs.
6. Bake in a 350 degree oven until crumbs are browned.

Serves 6

White-Footed Mouse

Easily recognized by its white feet and long tail, this medium-sized rodent is a ground dweller active primarily at night to avoid detection from predators. Its omnivorous diet includes seeds, insects and vegetation. Young are born hairless and blind after a gestation of 21-27 days.

Sandy's River Lasagna

Lokey Lytjen

This recipe wins Lokey's quick, easy and delicious award.

2	lb. carton low-fat cottage cheese
1-2	eggs (optional)
	parsley flakes (optional)
	Parmesan cheese (optional)
1	4 lb. 3-oz. jar spaghetti sauce
1	lb. shredded mozzarella cheese
2	10-oz. pkg. frozen spinach, thawed, drained and excess moisture squeezed out.
10-12	cooked lasagna noodles*

*   You can forego cooking noodles by assembling, covering with foil, and allowing to sit in refrigerator for 1-2 hours. The noodles soften by absorbing juice.

1. Spray a very large (14x10x2-inch) pan or two smaller pans with cooking oil/butter. Spread a small amount of spaghetti sauce in the bottom of the pan.
2. Preheat oven to 350 degrees.
3. Mix cottage cheese with eggs, Parmesan cheese and parsley flakes. Layer in the pan(s) twice, in this order: noodles, cottage cheese mixture, spinach, Mozzarella cheese, sauce.
4. Top the second layer of sauce with Mozzarella cheese.
5. Bake for 1 hour (1½ hour above 5,000 feet elevation).

Serves 8 generously

"When I visit my family in Savannah, Georgia, we spend as much time as possible running in the creeks and rivers off Tybee Island. My sister-in-law, Sandy, and I make this lasagna nearly every year—something we can put in the oven on "time bake" so that it will be done when we arrive home tired and hungry with little ones to feed.

The first year we put the glass dish of lasagna into the oven as we rushed out the door with our beach gear in hand. About mid-afternoon, as we rounded the south end of Little Tybee Island, I exclaimed, "Oh no! I forgot to turn down the oven temperature. It's set at 400 degrees. I hope the dish doesn't break."

Sandy calmly replied, "Don't worry. I forgot to turn on the oven."

—Lokey Lytjen
Executive Director of the
Jackson Hole Historical Society and Museum

Cheese Ravioli with Rosemary and Lemon

Judy Eddy

Creamy and delicious.

1   1-lb. pkg. frozen cheese ravioli
1   cup cottage cheese
½   cup evaporated skim milk
1   tsp. dried rosemary
¼   tsp. each salt and pepper
2   tsp. lemon juice
½   cup Parmesan cheese
3   tbsp. fresh snipped chives
1   tsp. lemon peel
    lemon wedges

1. Cook ravioli according to package directions. Drain well, transfer to serving bowl, drizzle lemon juice over hot ravioli and gently toss. Cover bowl to keep warm.
2. Blend cottage cheese, evaporated milk, rosemary and salt and pepper until smooth. Pour mixture on top of ravioli and gently toss until coated. Spoon onto individual serving plates.
3. In a small cup, combine Parmesan cheese, chives and lemon peel. Sprinkle on top of each serving. Serve with lemon wedges.

Serves 4-6

Norris Soldier Station

The Norris Soldier Station in Yellowstone National Park accommodated 20 men. It was the first and principal outpost established by the military in 1887 for a system of mounted patrols. The military protected the park until the formation of the National Park Service in 1916. The soldier station is presently home to the Museum of the National Park Ranger.

Norris Soldier Station, YNP.

Corn and Squash Pasta

Judy Eddy

One of Judy's favorite dinners.

- 1 1-lb. pkg. fettucine, penne or pasta or choice
- 4 medium yellow squash or zucchini, diced
- 3 tbsp. olive oil
  salt and fresh ground pepper to taste
- ¾ cup fresh cobbed corn
  (thawed frozen corn cobs are okay but not as good)
- 3 cloves garlic, minced
- ¼ cup chopped cilantro
- ¼ cup toasted pine nuts
- 2 tbsp. butter
- 4 tbsp. water
  juice of half a lemon
  freshly grated Parmesan cheese, optional

1. Heat a large skillet over medium-high heat. When hot, add olive oil and quickly stir in diced yellow squash or zucchini. Sauté until just tender, about 3 minutes. Add salt and freshly ground pepper to taste.
2. Add corn and garlic. Cook, stirring often, an additional 2 minutes.
3. Add cilantro, butter and water. Stir to melt butter, then lower heat and simmer.
4. Cook and drain pasta according to package directions and add it to the skillet. Mix well, then add lemon juice and pine nuts. Mix to blend and remove from heat. Sprinkle with Parmesan cheese, if desired.

Serves 4-6

Stacked Red Chili Enchiladas

Chef Karen Norby

A perfect hearty lunch or dinner for one.

- 3 blue or yellow corn tortillas
- 1 cup chopped onion
- 2 tbsp. ground New Mexico chiles (also called chili powder)
- 2 tsp. all-purpose flour
- ¾ cup vegetable stock
  salt and pepper
- ¾ cup shredded reduced fat cheddar cheese
  nonfat or low-fat sour cream (optional)
- 1 8-oz. can pinto or black beans, heated
- 1 cup shredded lettuce
- 2 tbsp. diced tomatoes

Parry's Primrose

This gorgeous, magenta alpine flower is rarely found below 10,000 feet. It thrives along moist stream banks and along the drip line of large boulders, where it soaks up rainwater run-off. Its mildly offensive odor doesn't match its visual appeal!

1. Preheat oven to 350 degrees.
2. Cook tortillas in a skillet over high heat in a single layer, turning once, until soft and lightly toasted. Set aside.
3. Reduce heat to medium, add a tablespoon of butter and sauté onions until soft, about 5 minutes. Remove from pan.
4.. Mix ground chilies and flour in pan and stir over low heat until chiles smell lightly toasted, about 2 minutes. Whisk in broth until smooth. Stir over high heat until sauce boils, about 2 minutes. Add salt and pepper to taste.
4. Dip 1 tortilla in chili sauce, coating both sides, then set in baking dish. Top tortilla with half of the onion and a third of the cheese. Repeat layers, using all tortillas and onion. Pour remaining chili sauce over stacked enchilada, then sprinkle with remaining cheese.
5. Place in oven and cook until cheese melts and tortilla is hot in the center. Top with sour cream and serve with beans, lettuce and tomato.

Serves 1

Basil Tomato Tart *Moose Head Ranch*

This luscious, easy-to-make entree is a favorite of ranch guests. It is one of the recipes featured in *Historical Recipes from The Pure Food Club of Jackson Hole*. For information on ordering the cookbook, please see the acknowledgments section.

1	9-inch pie shell
1½	cups grated Mozzarella cheese, divided
4	tomatoes
1	cup loosely packed fresh basil
4	cloves garlic
½	cup mayonnaise
¼	cup Parmesan cheese
⅛	tsp. white pepper

1. Preheat oven to 350 degrees
2. Bake pie shell according to favorite recipe or package directions.
3. Sprinkle warm baked pie shell with ½ cup of Mozzarella cheese.
4. Cut tomatoes into thin wedges and drain on paper towels. Arrange atop melting cheese. Finely chop basil and garlic in food processor. Sprinkle over tomatoes. Mix together 1 cup Mozzarella, mayonnaise, Parmesan cheese and white pepper. Spread evenly over top of basil and tomatoes.
5. Bake until top is golden, about 25 minutes. Serve warm.

Serves 6-8

Storing Tomatoes

Don't refrigerate tomatoes that aren't fully ripened. Store them stem-side down in a basket or bowl on your kitchen counter and they will continue to ripen, improving both flavor and texture. Refrigerate when desired ripeness is reached.

Mormon Row, GTNP

Named for the Mormon families that settled the area, at its peak Mormon Row had 15 home-steads, a one-room school, church and post office. The T.A. Moulton Ranch, below, was home-steaded in 1908. After 1912, it operated year-round for over 50 years, primarily as a cattle ranch. It is now owned by the National Park Service.

Jean's Chile Rellenos

Jean Jorgenson

Simple to prepare and oh, so good.

1   7-oz. can Ortega® whole green chiles
6   ozs. thinly sliced cheddar cheese
6   ozs. thinly sliced Monterey Jack cheese
4   eggs at room temperature, separated
1   13-oz. can evaporated milk
3   tbsp. flour
    salt and pepper
1   15-oz. can tomato sauce
    green chile salsa or Tabasco sauce, optional

1. Preheat oven to 350 degrees. Butter the bottom of a 3-quart, shallow baking pan or dish.
2. Open the chiles flat to remove seeds. Lay half of the opened chiles in the bottom of the prepared dish, in a single layer, and cover with the slices of cheddar cheese. Layer the remaining opened chiles on top of the cheddar cheese and cover with the Monterey Jack slices.
3. In a medium-size bowl, beat egg yolks together until blended. Add the milk, flour and salt and pepper to taste. Stir until well blended. In a separate bowl, beat egg whites until stiff but not dry. Fold the beaten egg whites into the yolk mixture to just blend, then pour the egg mixture over the pan of chiles.

T.A. Moulton Ranch House

4. Add a few drops of the optional sauces to the tomato sauce, if you'd like, and pour the tomato sauce evenly over the egg mixtures. Most of the heavier sauce will sink below the eggs. Bake covered for 1 hour, then remove the cover and bake an additional 15 minutes. Serve hot.

Serves 8

Bacon Roasted Turkey with Cornbread Dressing
Erika Muschaweck

Chambers Ranch House

This home was built in 1917 by Andy and Jim Chambers. Andy was a postman and rancher. His wife served as the Gro Vont postmistress and taught school on Mormon Row. The ranch was purchased by the National Park Service in 1956.

Aka "Turkey a la Playboy." Erika clipped this great recipe from a German edition of *Playboy* in the early nineties.

Cornbread Dressing
1   batch of 2-day old corn bread, ground to coarse crumbs in a blender
2   onions, chopped
1   tsp. ground thyme
1   tsp. dried sage leaves, crumbled
½   lb. ground veal
½   lb. ground beef
½   cup butter
¾   cup pecans, coarsely chopped
    salt and pepper to taste
Turkey
1   12-lb. turkey
1   lb. bacon
2   medium yellow onions, peeled and cut in half
3   carrots, sliced
    chopped veal bones
½   cup melted butter
1   lemon

1. Make dressing. Melt butter in a large skillet over medium heat. Add onions and sauté until they are soft and light brown, 5-6 minutes. Transfer onions with a slotted spoon to a large mixing bowl. Sprinkle evenly with thyme and sage. Stir to mix. Add cornbread crumbs and mix again. Set aside.
2. Add ground meat to the skillet and cook, breaking up the meat with a wooden spoon, until it is cooked through and lightly browned, about 10 minutes. Remove from heat and add to cornbread mixture. Stir to blend. Add chopped pecans. Mix again. Salt and pepper to taste and toss lightly to distribute seasoning. Set aside.

Removing Dressing

To remove all of the stuffing from the turkey, place a piece of cheese cloth inside the turkey before putting in the stuffing. When the turkey is done, pull out the cheese cloth. Viola! No more digging.

3. Preheat oven to 325 degrees.
4. Rinse turkey well and pat dry. Cut lemon in half and generously rub turkey cavity with the cut lemon. Stuff the body and neck cavities with the stuffing. Skewer or sew the body cavity shut.
5. Arrange the chopped veal bones, onions and sliced carrots in the bottom of a roasting pan. These will flavor the pan juice for the gravy. Gently place the turkey on the bed of bones and vegetables. Tuck the neck skin flap under the turkey to close the neck opening. Pour 2 cups of water into bottom of the pan.
6. Generously baste the turkey with the melted butter. Sprinkle with salt and pepper, then cover turkey with strips of uncooked bacon. Place in oven and roast 18 minutes per pound, or approximately 3½ hours for a 12-lb. turkey. Baste well with melted butter once an hour. When turkey is done, transfer to a heated platter, cover loosely with a tent made out of aluminum foil, and let rest for 10-15 minutes.
7. While the turkey is resting, make gravy. Discard the bones and vegetables. Strain pan juices through a sieve into a 4-cup or larger glass measuring cup. Discard any solids in the sieve. Add hot water to bring pan juice measurement up to 3 cups. Pour mixture into saucepan. Whisk in 2 tbsp. of cornstarch. Bring to a boil over medium heat, stirring constantly, then reduce heat and simmer for 5 minutes, or until mixture is thickened. Season with salt and pepper to taste. Pour gravy into a gravy or sauceboat and serve with turkey.

Serves 8

Dessert

Jackson, 1918

Strawberries tend to spoil quickly. If you can't use them right away, remove the leaves and berry stems. Rinse berries in a colander, then pour boiling water over them. The boiling water kills the bacteria that molds the berries. Drain and place the strawberries in a covered plastic container in the refrigerator. Use as soon as possible.

Ed Opler's Strawberries Romanoff   *Pat Opler*

Maximum "wow" for minimum effort. This is sure to become one of your entertaining favorites.

4-5	pints fresh strawberries
2	tbsp. sugar
1	pint whipping cream
1	tsp. confectioners' sugar
	juice of ½ lemon
1	oz. dark rum
2½	oz. Cointreau
1½	quarts best-quality vanilla ice cream, softened

1. Wash and dry whole or halved berries.
2. Place berries in large bowl; sprinkle with sugar. Toss lightly to coat.
3. In a separate bowl, add confectioners' sugar to whipping cream and beat until almost stiff. Fold in lemon juice, rum and Cointreau.
4. In a large bowl, fold whipped cream mixture into softened ice cream.
5. Spoon ice cream mixture over berries in individual serving bowls.

Serves 12

Peaches and Cream   *Janet Graham*

Fresh peaches define the bounty of summer. This recipe showcases the prize of warm, lazy days admirably.

2	tbsp. butter
3	tbsp. light brown sugar, packed
1	tbsp. fresh lemon juice
3	medium peaches, peeled and sliced
1	tsp. vanilla
	vanilla ice cream or heavy cream

1. Combine butter, sugar and lemon juice in a small, heavy skillet and cook over medium heat, stirring occasionally, until hot and bubbly, approximately 5-7 minutes.
2. Add peaches and cook until peaches are heated through but still firm enough to keep their shape, about 4 minutes. Remove from heat and stir in vanilla.
3. Serve warm over vanilla ice cream, or place in bowl and top with heavy cream. A sprinkling of fresh raspberries adds both flavor and visual appeal.

Serves 4-6

Strawberries with Brown Sugar & Sour Cream

This recipe could not be simpler or more luscious. Fresh, succulent strawberries dipped in sour cream and brown sugar taste like a morsel of berry-topped cheesecake.

    2   quarts fresh, ripe strawberries, tops intact
    2   cups sour cream
    1   cup light brown sugar

1. Rinse and dry strawberries and place in pretty serving bowl.
2. Whisk sour cream to a smooth consistency and transfer to small serving dish. Place brown sugar in a small serving dish.
3. Have guests dip strawberries first in sour cream then in brown sugar.

Serves 8-10

Fourth of July Berries

Red and blue berries topped with pastry stars: the perfect way to celebrate the bounty of summer and our nation's birthday! Adapted from a Pillsbury recipe.

    1   15-oz pkg. Pillsbury refrigerated piecrust
    2   tsp. plus ¼ cup sugar
    ¼   tsp. cardamom
    2   cups blueberries
    2   cups sliced strawberries
    1   tbsp. lemon juice

1. Remove one folded piecrust from package and bring to room temperature.
2. Preheat oven to 450 degrees. Line cookie sheet with foil.
3. In a small bowl, stir 2 tsp. of sugar and the cardamom together until well blended. Set aside.
4. Unfold piecrust and press dough creases together. Cut out 8 stars with a star-shaped cookie cutter. Place on prepared cookie sheet.
5. Using a small pastry brush, lightly brush stars with water, then sprinkle with the cardamom spiced sugar. Place cookie sheet in the oven and bake 6 minutes or until stars are lightly browned. Remove from oven and transfer the stars to wire racks to cool.
6. When ready to serve, combine the berries, ¼ cup sugar and lemon juice in a mixing bowl. Gently fold to mix. Divide berries into dessert bowls or plates, and top with a sugared star. Perfect!

Serves 8

Bighorn lamb

Ewes leave the herd to drop a single lamb in late May or early June, typically giving birth on a remote, protected ledge. The ewe and lamb rejoin the herd in several days. Lambs are very agile and playful shortly after birth, quickly able to jump over other lambs and even scale small cliffs. Mountain lions, bobcats and eagles occasionally prey upon the newborns.

Fisher

This reclusive, nocturnal member of the weasel family is rarely seen. Its preferred habitat is dense forest, where it dens in hollow trees, rock crevices or spaces beneath large boulders. Fishers opportunistically hunt hares, rodents and grouse, but are most well known for hunting porcupines. They attack them by clamping onto the head in an attempt to turn the porcupine over and expose its soft underside. Fishers are about two feet long and sport a 12-16 inch tail.

Hot Buttered Fruit with Ice Cream
Anne Whiting Richardson

Sherry McFarland shared this recipe with Linda Bourret, who passed it on to Anne. It was taste-tested a third time (and resoundingly approved!) by the Girls' Night Out book group. The types and quantity of fruit can be varied with the season/group size.

> 1 cup raspberries
> 1 cup blueberries
> 1 banana, sliced
> 1 11-oz. can Mandarin oranges, drained or 1 large orange, peeled, white pith removed, and broken into segments
> 1 cup sliced strawberries
> 1 cup sliced almonds
> 1 cup light brown sugar
> 1½ sticks (¾ cup) butter, melted
> 1 quart good quality vanilla ice cream

1. Preheat oven to broil.
2. Mix the brown sugar and butter together. Place fruit and nuts on a baking sheet and sprinkle with the brown sugar mixture.
3. Spoon ice cream into bowls: once the fruit is started there is no turning back!
4. Place fruit on rack 6-8 inches from top of broiler and broil for 3-4 minutes, or until hot and bubbly. Watch fruit carefully, as it burns easily. Remove from oven and spoon over ice cream. Serve immediately.

Serves 10-12

Ginger Blueberry Crumble
Judy Eddy

> 1 10-oz. pkg. frozen blueberries, thawed
> 2 tbsp. brown sugar
> ½ tsp. cinnamon
> 1 tbsp. lemon juice
> ½ cup finely crumbled gingersnaps (about 8)

1. Preheat oven to 425 degrees.
2. Place blueberries in ungreased pie pan.
3. In a small bowl, combine the brown sugar, cinnamon, lemon juice and crumbled gingersnaps. Mix well, then sprinkle over berries.
4. Bake 20 minutes, or until crumble is bubbling and berries are tender. Serve warm with vanilla ice cream, if desired.

Serves 4

Classic Apple Crisp

Some desserts are classic because they are just too good to go out of style. This is one of them. Serve warm with vanilla ice cream.

Filling
- 8 cups Granny Smith or other tart apples, peeled and thinly sliced (approx. 2½ lbs.)
- ⅓ - ½ cup sugar, to taste
- ¾ cup plus 2 tbsp. flour
- 2 tsp. cinnamon

Topping
- 1 cup regular rolled oats
- ¾ cup light brown sugar, packed
- ½ cup butter, cut into small chunks
- ¾ cup toasted pecans, chopped

1. Preheat oven to 350 degrees.
2. Lightly butter a 9-inch square pan or 2-quart baking dish. Place filling ingredients in pan and toss until mixed to coat apple slices.
3. Combine all topping ingredients except pecans in a bowl. Mix with a fork or your fingers until the topping is crumbly and butter pieces cannot be distinguished. Mix in the toasted pecans. Sprinkle topping evenly over the apple mixture.
4. Bake in the middle of the oven until the apples are tender and the topping is golden brown, about 45-50 minutes. Loosely cover topping with foil if it begins to brown before apples are tender. Let crisp cool slightly before spooning the warm dessert into bowls. Top with vanilla ice cream, if desired.

Serves 8 generously

Wilson dentist

In the early 1900s, the closest dentist to Wilson, Wyoming, was in St. Anthony, Idaho. Doris Platts wrote in her book "The Pass:" that blacksmith Pap Warren Edmiston "made a pair of forceps and would, for free, oblige anyone needing a tooth pulled and thus save a trip outside."

Early Yellowstone motorists cross the Lewis River Bridge.

Sunset Pears

Pears poached in red wine taste marvelous. Serve warm with vanilla ice cream, or chilled in beautiful dessert bowls.

Ripening Pears

To ripen green pears, place 2 or 3 in a brown bag, loosely closed, and store at room tempera-ture out of direct sunlight.

6   Bosc pears
2   cups red zinfandel wine
½   cup sugar

1. Peel pears. Core by cutting a cone-shaped wedge from the bottom of each, so the pear remains whole. Do not remove stems. Discard seeds and cores.
2. Combine zinfandel and sugar in a medium, non-aluminum sauce-pan. Stir to dissolve sugar. Bring mixture to a boil over medium-high heat. Place pears upright in the wine mixture. Reduce heat to low and simmer until tender, approximately 20 minutes.
4. Gently remove fruit with a slotted spoon to a serving dish. Return syrup to a boil over medium heat and reduce to about one cup of liquid (roughly half). This takes approximately 10 minutes.
5. Pour poaching syrup over pears. Serve warm with ice cream, gar-nishing with fresh mint if desired, or refrigerate for several hours and serve chilled.

Serves 6

Russian Cream with Raspberries   *The Blue Lion*

An unbelievably good dessert. Years ago, The Blue Lion shared this recipe with the readers of *Ford* magazine. It has since surfaced in a number of local cookbooks. The restaurant graciously gave its permis-sion to include it in this publication.

1   cup whipping cream
⅓   cup granulated sugar
1   env. unflavored gelatin
¼   cup cold water
1   cup sour cream
1   tsp. vanilla
1   10-oz. pkg. sweetened raspberries, thawed, juice reserved. Mixed berries also work well.

1. Heat whipping cream and sugar in top of a double-boiler until sugar dissolves.
2. Meanwhile, dissolve gelatin in cold water. Place in small saucepan over low heat and slowly heat mixture to a warm temperature.
3. Add gelatin to cream mixture. Stir to blend, then cool to luke-warm.

4. Add sour cream and vanilla to cream mixture. Blend well, then refrigerate until set, about 3 hours.
5. Remove set cream from refrigerator and whisk to smooth consistency. Alternately layer cream with raspberries in parfait glasses or stemmed wine glasses. Garnish with fresh berries or mint leaves.

Serves 4

Bananas Foster
Dr. William Fogarty

Dr. Fogarty acquired this recipe from Brennan's restaurant in New Orleans. The presentation is spectacular.

  1 tbsp. butter
  2 tbsp. brown sugar
  1 ripe banana, split lengthwise
      dash of cinnamon
1.2 oz. banana liqueur
  1 oz. white rum

1. In a chafing dish at the table, melt butter and add brown sugar. Blend. Add banana and sauté until the banana is just hot; sprinkle on the cinnamon.
2. Pour in the banana liqueur and rum and carefully light mixture.
3. With a punch or serving ladle, pour the flaming banana and syrup into a shallow serving dish. When the flame is out, the dessert is ready. Serve plain or over vanilla ice cream.

Serves one

Ice Cream Tip

Before young birthday party guests arrive, scoop softened ice cream into muffin tins lined with cupcake liners and refreeze. You won't have to fuss later when serving cake.

Ginger Ice Cream

The perfect ending to an Asian meal.

  1 quart high-quality vanilla ice cream
 ½ cup crystallized ginger, diced fine
  1 tsp. fresh ginger juice and pulp, finely minced

1. Place ice cream in mixing bowl and allow to soften slightly, about 15 minutes. Fold in crystallized ginger, ginger juice and pulp.
2. Spoon softened mixture back into carton or comparable freezer carton. Gently press plastic wrap onto ice cream surface, then cover with carton lid. Freeze 2-4 days to develop flavor.

Serves 6

Frozen Coffee Almond Indulgence

Chef Tamalpais Roth-McCormick
The name says it all.

- 6 almond macaroon cookies
- 6 chocolate graham crackers
- 3 tbsp. dark rum
- 4 tbsp. Kahlùa
- 1 quart Häagen Dazs coffee ice cream, softened
- ⅔ cup shaved good quality dark chocolate
- 1 cup heavy whipping cream, whipped to medium peak
- 1 small handful (approx. 2 ozs.) sliced almonds, toasted

1. Crumble the macaroons and graham crackers together in a medium sized bowl. Mix in rum and kahlùa. Pat mixture in the bottom of a freezer-proof 1½ -2 quart serving dish.
2. Layer the ice cream, then the chocolate, and finally the whipped cream in the dish. Sprinkle with almonds. Freeze at least 2 hours to set.

Serves 6-8

Pink Grapefruit Sorbet

Refreshingly different, and quite addicting.

- 1½ cups each of water and sugar
- 1⅔ cups unsweetened pink grapefruit juice
- ⅔ cup lemon juice

1. Stir water and sugar in a medium saucepan over low heat until the sugar dissolves. Increase heat and bring to boil.
2. Pour sugar mixture into large bowl. Mix in pink grapefruit and lemon juices. Refrigerate juice mixture until well chilled.
3. Transfer chilled mixture to ice cream maker and process according to manufacturer's instructions. Freeze in covered container. Garnish servings with fresh raspberries and mint leaves, if desired.

Serves 4-6

Easy Crème Brulée

Crème brulée often caps a scrumptious meal at an upscale restaurant. This easy to prepare version brings this fin de siècle custard within reach of the average home cook.

2   cups (1 pint) whipping cream
4   egg yolks
½   cup sugar
1   tbsp. vanilla
Topping
¼   cup granulated sugar
1   tsp. brown sugar

1. Preheat oven to 350 degrees.
2. In a medium-sized bowl, beat egg yolks and sugar together until mixture is thick and lemony, about 3 minutes. Set aside.
3. Heat whipping cream over low heat, stirring occasionally, until bubbles form around the edge of the pan. Remove cream from heat and gradually beat it into the egg mixture. Stir in vanilla.
4. Pour mixture into six 6-oz. custard cups. Place cups in 13x9-inch baking pan and pour enough water into the pan to come about halfway up the sides of the dishes. Place in preheated oven and bake 20-25 minutes, or until custard is set in the center. Remove custard cups from baking pan and chill for 40 minutes.
5. Preheat oven broiler. Mix sugar topping.
6. Place custard cups on a baking sheet and sprinkle each cup with 2 tsp. of the sugar topping. Place baking sheet on top rack under the broiler and broil until topping caramelizes, about 30 seconds. Watch carefully so mixture doesn't burn.
7. Chill custard for 2 hours, or until topping hardens. Serve cold.

Serves 6

Bison

Approximately 800 bison live in Grand Teton National Park. They are typically spied in the sage grasslands off Antelope Flats road. Males, called bulls, can weight up to 2400 pounds and stand 6-feet tall at the shoulder. Females are somewhat smaller. Both sexes have short, black horns that curve upward. Rut activity begins in mid-July and extends into September; one or two calves are born 9-10 months later.

Sikarni

Pepper, cloves, cardamom and walnuts turns plain yogurt into something special. Plan ahead: 4-5 hours is needed to drain the yogurt.

4   cups plain yogurt
2   cups sugar
½   tsp. each of cloves, cardamom, black pepper and salt
¾   cup chopped walnuts

1. Line a large mesh strainer with cheesecloth and place strainer over a bowl. Place yogurt in strainer and drain, refrigerated, for 4-5 hours to create a light and creamy yogurt "cheese."
2. Place drained yogurt in a mixing bowl and add sugar, cloves, cardamom, pepper and salt. Whisk to a smooth consistency.
3. Divide into 6 dessert bowls and sprinkle with chopped walnuts. Serve chilled.

Serves 6

Danish Rice Pudding

Carole Travis Henikoff

Cookbook author Carole Travis Henikoff shared this fantastic pudding with *Jackson Hole Guide* readers in 1981. She graciously granted permission to include it in this publication. Don't wait for the holidays to try it!

> 2 cups milk
> 2 cups light cream or half-and-half
> ¼ cup sugar
> ½ cup long grain white rice
> ⅛ tsp. of salt
> 1 tsp. vanilla
> 2 ozs. almond paste, crumbled
> 3½ ozs. blanched, slivered almonds (approximately 1 cup)
> 1 cup whipping cream, stiffly whipped
> 2 tbsp. sugar

1. Preheat oven to 300 degrees. Generously butter 1½ quart lidded casserole. Set aside.
2. Mix milk, cream, sugar, salt and rice together in a large bowl. Pour into buttered casserole dish and bake, covered, for 1 hour.
3. Remove dish from oven, stir well, then return to oven and bake uncovered for an additional hour.
4. Remove pudding from oven and skim off milk skin that will have formed on top of the mixture. Discard skin.
5. Pour mixture into bowl and add crumbled almond paste and vanilla. Mix thoroughly to blend.
6. Cover surface of pudding with plastic wrap so skin can't form and allow to cool for 20 minutes before placing in refrigerator to thoroughly chill, at least one hour.

Standard Timber Camp, Bridger Nat. Forest, early 1900s.

7. Beat whipping cream until stiff. Add 2 tbsp. sugar and whip again until very stiff. Fold whipped cream and almonds into the pudding.
8. Pour pudding into pretty serving bowl and refrigerate, covered, until serving time.

Serves 6-8

Carrot Pudding with Hard Sauce   *Jean Jorgensen*

"When my dad served overseas, my mother made this for him. He remarked that the pudding tasted strangely gritty. As it turns out, we kids had borrowed my mother's kitchen utensils to play in the sandbox." A sumptuous, old-fashioned holiday tradition, with or without the grit!

Bald Eagle

Because 90% of the bald eagle's diet is fish, small bird and mammals, this eagle usually nests in trees bordering rivers and lakes. Eagles return to the same nest year after year, gradually expanding their home. Nests have grown as large as 15 feet across, the largest of any bird in North America. Respected naturalist Benjamin Franklin opposed designating the bald eagle as our national bird, reportedly because it steals fish from osprey and scavenges carrion.

1 cup grated carrots
1 cup sugar
½ cup butter
½ cup currants
1 tsp. cinnamon
½ tsp. nutmeg
1 cup grated potato
1 cup flour
½ cup raisins
1 tsp. baking soda
½ tsp. cloves
½ tsp. salt

1. Combine ingredients in the top of a double boiler.
2. Bring water to a boil then reduce heat and simmer for three hours or until pudding is firm. Remove from heat and let cool slightly. Serve warm with hard sauce.

Hard Sauce

⅓ cup butter, softened
1 cup powdered sugar
½ tsp. vanilla
1 tsp. brandy (optional)

1. Cream butter in a small bowl.
2. Gradually add powdered sugar, beating until light and fluffy, then beat in vanilla and brandy.

Serves 6-8

Sage Grouse

Raisin Pecan Bread Pudding with Brandy Sauce

Bread pudding is an old-standby enjoying a resurgence in popularity, often appearing on restaurant dessert menus. This one is divine.

10	slices of day-old French bread, torn into 1-inch pieces
4	cups milk, scalded
1	cup whipping cream
5	eggs
1	cup firmly packed light brown sugar
2	tsp. vanilla
1	tsp. cinnamon
½	tsp. nutmeg
½	cup butter, melted
½	cup raisins
½	cup pecans, coarsely chopped

1. Scald milk in a medium-sized saucepan and set aside.
2. Preheat oven to 350 degrees. Butter a 2-quart baking dish and set aside.
3. In a large bowl, mix together the bread, milk and cream.
4. In a separate bowl, beat eggs well then add brown sugar. Stir to blend.
5. Pour egg mixture into bread mixture and stir to blend. Add vanilla, cinnamon and nutmeg, mixing well. Stir in melted butter, raisins and pecans. Blend well.
6. Pour batter into prepared baking dish. Place dish in large pan and pour warm water into pan until it is about 1-inch deep.
7. Place pan on middle rack of preheated oven and bake for 1 hour, or until a toothpick or knife inserted into the middle of the pudding comes out clean. Serve warm with brandy sauce.

Brandy Sauce

3	egg yolks, lightly beaten
1	cup granulated sugar
1	tsp. vanilla
1½	cups milk
1	tbsp. cornstarch
½	cup water
1½	oz. brandy or brandy flavored extract

1. In a medium saucepan over low heat, combine beaten egg yolks, sugar, vanilla and milk, stirring well to blend. Heat until mixture comes to a boil, stirring frequently.
2. Add cornstarch and water to boiling mixture. Stir well. Continue

cooking, stirring often, until mixture thickens.

3. Remove from heat and stir in brandy. Allow to cool before serving over pudding.

Serves 8

Pavlova

Val and George LeFebre

"This recipe is an Australian tradition. It is attributed to an Australian chef who was so impressed with the Russian ballerina Anna Pavlova when she visited Australia that he devised a dessert to compliment her dancing."

4	egg whites
1½	cup sugar (superfine preferred)
3	tsp. white wine vinegar or lemon juice
1	tsp. vanilla
1	tsp. cornstarch
	pinch salt

1. Preheat oven to 250 degrees.
2. Mold aluminum foil inside a 9-inch diameter cake pan and lightly oil. Set aside.
3. Beat egg whites with salt until stiff. Gradually add the sugar a little at a time, beating well after each addition. Add vanilla and beat well, then add the vinegar or lemon juice a few drops at a time, beating well again.
4. Pour into the foil-covered cake pan cake pan and place pan on a cookie sheet. Bake for 2 hours, or until meringue is dry and lightly golden.
5. Cool and top with whipped cream and sliced strawberries or other fruit. May also be served with sour cream to cut the sweetness, or ice cream.

Serves 8-10

First Car in JH

An unidentified group of tourists drove the first car into Jackson Hole in 1908. They drove over Togwotee Pass on the rough Washakie Military Road, then along Jackson Lake to the Snake River Station at the south border of Yellowstone National Park— only to discover automobile traffic was prohibited in the park. Superintendent Young allowed the party to haul their vehicle to Yellowstone's west entrance on top on a freight wagon.

One of the first cars in the valley, 1910.

GTNP Superintendent
Guy Edwards, 1936

Grand Teton National
Park Superintendent
Guy Edwards models
the National Park Ser-
vice dress uniform of
1936.

Turtle Brownies
Hunter Christensen

Judges awarded 12-year-old Hunter a blue ribbon at the 2002 Teton County Fair for this delectable concoction.

Brownie layer
- ¾ cup butter
- 3 oz. unsweetened chocolate, chopped
- 3 eggs
- 1 cup sugar
- ½ cup brown sugar, firmly packed
- 1½ tsp. vanilla
- ¼ tsp. salt
- ½ cup plus 2 tsp. flour

Filling
- 36 caramels
- ½ cup heavy or whipping cream
- 2½ cups pecan halves

Chocolate frosting
- 3 oz. semisweet chocolate, chopped
- 2½ tsp. heavy cream
- 1 tsp. light corn syrup

1. Preheat oven to 350. Grease a 13x9-inch baking pan. Set aside.
2. In a medium saucepan over low heat, melt butter and chocolate, stirring constantly. Remove from heat and cool for 10 minutes.
3. In a large bowl, combine the eggs, sugar and brown sugar. Beat until well blended. Gradually beat in the cooled chocolate and salt. Add flour and stir until mixture is just blended. Spread in prepared pan and bake until the center in just firm to the touch, approximately 20-22 minutes (don't overbake!).
4. While the brownie layer is baking, combine the caramels and cream in a medium saucepan and cook over low heat until the caramels are melted and the mixture is smooth, stirring occasionally. Add pecans and stir until the nuts are well coated. Remove from heat.
5. Spread caramel layer over brownie layer. Cool to room temperature, then place in refrigerator until caramel filling is set. This takes a total of about 45 minutes.
6. In a small saucepan, combine the chocolate, cream and corn syrup. Stir constantly over low heat until the chocolate is melted and the mixture is smooth. Remove from heat. Use a wire whisk or fork to drizzle frosting over the cooled brownies. Refrigerate briefly to set chocolate.
7. Use a heavy knife to cut brownies. These are best stored in the refrigerator and served cold.

Yield: 24-30 bars

Caramel Nut Brownies

Linda Bourett

Granite Hot Springs

The Civilian Conservation Corp converted the natural hot springs at Granite Creek into a warm water swimming pool in 1935. The average temperature of the pool is 112 degrees, making it a popular winter destination for cross-country skiers and snow-smobilers.

A rich and gooey bar that pleases even the most discriminating chocolate lover.

```
4   sqs. unsweetened baking chocolate
¾   cup butter or margarine
2   cups sugar
4   eggs, beaten
1   cup flour
1   14-oz. pkg. caramels, unwrapped
⅓   cup heavy cream
2   cups walnuts or pecans, chopped
1   6-oz. pkg. of semi-sweet chocolate chips
```

1. Preheat oven to 350 degrees. Line a 13x9-inch baking pan with foil and lightly butter. Set aside.
2. Place baking chocolate and butter in a large microwave-safe bowl and microwave for 2 minutes. Remove and stir until blended and chocolate is completely melted.
3. Stir in sugar, eggs and flour. Mix well. Spread half of the batter in the prepared baking dish. Bake 25 minutes or until batter is firm to the touch. Remove from oven.
4. In a large microwave-safe bowl, microwave caramels and cream for 3 minutes. Remove and stir until smooth. Add 1 cup of the nuts.
5. Spread caramel mixture over brownie batter and sprinkle with the chocolate chips. Pour remaining brownie batter on top and sprinkle with remaining nuts. Return to oven and bake an additional 30 minutes. Cool completely before cutting.

Yield: 24 brownies

Granite Hot Springs Pool construction, 1935.

Peanut Butter Bars

Rhonda Watson

Peanut butter cups in a bar! When Teton Science School Director of Development David Watson brought these on a school excursion, they disappeared in a wink.

½   cup each of butter, sugar and brown sugar
1   egg
⅓   cup plus ¼ cup peanut butter
4   tbsp. milk
¼   tsp. salt
½   tsp. soda
½   cup powdered sugar
1   cup chocolate chips
1   cup flour
1   cup rolled oats
½   tsp. vanilla

1. Cream butter, sugar and brown sugar. Blend in egg, ⅓ cup peanut butter, soda, salt and vanilla. Add flour and oats. Mix. Spread in greased 13x9-inch pan.
2. Bake at 350 degrees for 20-25 minutes. Remove from oven and sprinkle immediately with 1 cup chocolate chips. When chips soften (about 5 minutes), spread them evenly on top of the bars.
3. Combine powdered sugar, ¼ cup peanut butter and milk. Drizzle peanut butter mixture over all. Cut into 2-inch squares.

Yield: 24 bars

Oatmeal Fudge Bars

LoyDean Barney

An old-fashioned, abundantly satisfying treat.

Fudge filling
1   12-oz. pkg. chocolate chips
1   14-oz. can Eagle brand sweetened condensed milk
2   tbsp. butter
½   tsp. salt
1   cup chopped nuts (optional)
2   tsp. vanilla
Bar crust and topping
2   cups brown sugar
¾   cup butter
2   eggs, slightly beaten
2   tsp. vanilla
2½ cups Bisquick®
3   cups quick oats

Menors Ferry

William D. Menor arrived in Jackson Hole in 1894 and homesteaded on the west side of the Snake River in Moose. He soon built a ferry across the Snake, providing one of the few safe passage points across the river for miles. Menor sold his property and ferry operation to Maude Noble in 1918. She doubled the fares to $1 for local automobiles and $2 for out-of-state plates. When a steel truss bridge was built just south of the ferry in 1927, Noble's ferry business became obsolete. She sold her property to the Snake River Land Company in 1929. A replica of the ferry operates on the historic site today.

1. Preheat oven to 350 degrees.
2. In a large mixing bowl, combine brown sugar, margarine, eggs, vanilla, Bisquick® and oats. Mix with hands or pastry cutter until crumbly. Press three-fourths of the mixture into the bottom of a 13x9-inch baking pan. Set aside.
3. Combine chocolate chips, milk and butter in a saucepan and heat over medium heat, stirring occasionally, until chocolate chips are melted, about 4 minutes. Remove from heat and stir in salt, nuts and vanilla. Spread the fudge mixture over the crust. Drop the remaining oat mixture in spoonfuls on top of the chocolate.
4. Bake for 30-35 minutes, or until the top is a light, golden brown. Cool slightly before cutting into bars.

Yield: 24 bars

Oven Rack Position

Bake bars on the middle rack in the oven and cookies on the top rack. If baking more than one pan at a time, place pans at different angles on different racks for maximum heat circulation. Alternate their placement on the racks halfway through baking time.

Cherry Bars *Louise Woods*

Nicely spiced with almond and cinnamon, these crumbly bars are a perfect accompaniment to afternoon tea or coffee.

Filling
    1¼ cups sugar
    8 tbsp. flour
    ½ tsp. almond extract
    2 20-oz. cans sour red cherries, undrained
    4 tbsp. butter
    1 tsp. cinnamon
Crust
    1 cup butter, softened
    1 cup firmly packed brown sugar
    2 cups each of flour and oatmeal
    ½ tsp. each of salt and baking soda

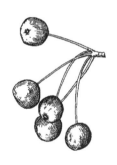

1. Preheat oven to 350 degrees.
2. In a large saucepan, combine sugar, flour, almond extract and cinnamon. Stir to blend. Add cherries and juice. Cook over medium heat, stirring constantly, until mixture thickens and boils, about 5-7 minutes. Add butter, stirring to blend, then remove from heat to cool for 15-20 minutes.
3. Combine crust ingredients and mix with hands until crumbly. Spread half of mixture in 13x9-inch baking dish and pat until firm. Spread cooled filling over crust. Crumble remaining crust over filling, patting gently to set.
4. Bake uncovered for 30-35 minutes, or until crust is golden brown. Cool before cutting into bars.

Yield: 24 bars

Lemon Cheese Bars

Donna Clinton

After *Jackson Hole Guide* food columnist J.C. Whitfield tasted these at a cookie swap in 1983, she included Donna's recipe in a December 24th column titled "Best Christmas Cookies in the Valley."

- 1 cup all-purpose flour
- ½ cup walnuts, finely chopped
- ⅓ cup brown sugar, firmly packed
- 6 tbsp. butter, softened
- 1 medium lemon
- 1 8-oz. pkg. cream cheese, softened
- ¼ cup sugar
- 1 tbsp. milk
- ½ tsp. vanilla
- 1 egg

1. Preheat oven to 350 degrees. Lightly grease 9-inch square pan. Set aside.
2. In medium bowl, measure flour, walnuts, brown sugar and butter. Knead with hands or pastry cutter until blended; mixture will be crumbly. Reserve ½ cup crumb mixture. Pat remaining crumb mixture into greased pan. Bake 12-15 minutes, or until light brown.
3. While the crumb mixture is baking, grate 1 tsp. of peel and squeeze 1 tbsp. of lemon juice into a small bowl. Add cream cheese, white sugar, milk, vanilla and egg and beat at medium speed for 2 minutes or until well blended, occasionally scraping the side of the bowl with a rubber spatula.

Togwotee Pass Highway dedication, 1918.

4. Remove crumb mixture from oven and pour cream cheese mixture over it. Top with reserved crumb mixture.
5. Put in oven and bake 25 minutes longer, or until golden brown. Refrigerate until well chilled (at least 2 hours). Cut into 24 bars. Cover pan with foil and refrigerate bars until serving. Bars may be made 4 hours before serving or up to 3 days in advance.

Yield: 24 bars

Almond Fig Squares   *Mary Howley, R.D.*

Proof that nutritious food can taste great! This dessert is rich in calcium.

  1½ cups small figs (about 24)
  ¾ cup whole wheat flour
  ¼ cup soy flour
  1 cup instant oats (or pureed whole oats)
  ½ cup chopped almonds
  ½ tsp. baking soda
  ½ tsp. salt
  ½ cup brown sugar
  ¼ cup blackstrap molasses
  1 tbsp. maple syrup
  ¼ cup canola oil
  ¼ cup calcium-fortified vanilla soy milk

1. Soak figs in ¾ cup hot water until figs are rehydrated. Drain excess water and puree. Set aside.
2. Preheat oven to 350 degrees. Lightly coat a 7x11-inch pan with canola oil and set aside.
3. Combine whole wheat flour, soy flour, oats, almonds, baking soda and salt in a large bowl. Stir until blended.
4. In a separate bowl, combine the brown sugar, molasses, maple syrup, canola oil and vanilla soy milk. Beat until creamy, then add to the flour and oat mixture.
5. Spread slightly more than half of the batter on the bottom of the prepared baking pan. The batter will be sticky. Use a wet spoon to evenly spread it in the pan.
6. Spread the pureed figs over the batter. Top with remaining batter (it will not entirely cover the fig layer).
7. Bake for 20-30 minutes, or until a toothpick inserted in the mixture comes out clean. Cool completely before cutting into 2-inch squares.

Yield: 18 bars

Hoback Canyon

The first car to travel through Hoback Canyon was driven by J. R. Jones on June 14, 1923. Esther Allen wrote in her unpublished History of Teton National Forest that "the trip through the canyon was quite a procession—the car was preceded by a plow, a ditcher and a grader with six horses hitched to each end and 12 men to help."

**Al Austin,
before 1913**

Al Austin moved to Jackson Hole around 1900. He worked for the U.S. Forest Service for many years, primarily in the protection of game animals. He became an accomplished wildlife photographer, and many of his images ended up in educational institutions on the east coast. He also kept a diary and wrote poetry during his field work, earning him the present day nickname of "wilderness poet." It is believed 74-year-old Austin died of natural causes while on a backcountry outing near Arizona Creek in November of 1940. His body was not discovered until the following June.

Frosted Coconut Macadamia Bars

Heavenly.

Crust
½	cup butter, no substitutes
1	cup flour
½	cup sugar

Filling
2	eggs
1½	cups brown sugar
1	cup macadamia nuts, coarsely chopped
½	cup flaked coconut
2	tbsp. flour
½	tsp. salt
¼	tsp. baking powder
1	tsp. vanilla

Frosting
2	tbsp. melted butter
1¼	cups powdered sugar
2	tbsp. evaporated milk

1. Preheat oven to 350 degrees.
2. Crust: Combine butter, flour and sugar in a bowl. Use knives or a pastry blender to break up and cut the butter into the flour and sugar. Dough will have pea-sized lumps. Pat dough evenly into the bottom of a 13x9-inch baking pan and bake until golden brown, about 20 minutes. Set pan on a rack to cool. Leave oven on.
3. In a large bowl, combine all filling ingredients and mix well to blend. Pour filling over cooled crust and bake 20 minutes. Remove from oven and set on rack to cool.
4. In a small bowl, mix together frosting ingredients until smooth and satiny. Use a knife or spreader to spread evenly over the cooled filling. Cut into 2-inch bars and store covered up to 1 week.

Yield: 24 bars

Almond Biscotti   *Anne Whiting Richardson*

These twice-baked treasures are great dunked in milk, coffee or tea. They are lower in fat and calories then most cookies. Anne acquired this wonderful recipe from California friend Linda Peltzman.

1	cup whole almonds
1¾	cups flour
1½	tsp. baking powder
6	tbsp. butter

1 tbsp. vanilla
½ tsp. almond extract
¼ cup brown sugar, packed
½ cup sugar
2 eggs

Baking Bars

Line pans with foil if baking bars. When bars
have cooled, lift foil out
of the pan and cut the
bars cleanly. The pans
will need only a quick
rinse and dry.

1. Spread almonds on a cookie sheet and toast in 350 degree oven until golden brown, about 5-7 minutes. (Turn after 3 minutes to brown evenly. Watch closely so the almonds don't burn. Once nuts begin to darken, they brown quickly). Remove almonds from oven and increase oven temperature to 400 degrees.
2. In a large mixing bowl, cream together the butter, vanilla and almond extract. Gradually add the brown and white sugar, hand beating well after each addition.
3. In a separate bowl, sift together the flour and baking powder. Add to the creamed mixture, mixing well. Add toasted nuts and mix well again. The batter will be slightly sticky.
4. Divide dough into two or three portions, and form flattened, oblong loaves on cookie sheet(s), leaving ample space around each loaf. Bake for 15-20 minutes, or until firm. Remove loaves from oven and reduce oven temperature to 300 degrees.
5. Let loaves cool on the cookie sheets for 10 minutes, then cut into ½-inch thick slices. Lay slices flat on cookie sheet and bake in 300 degree oven for 15-20 minutes, or until dry. Turn the oven off, open the door, and leave the slices in the oven until they are cool. Dip one end in melted chocolate if desired. Store in airtight container for up to two weeks.

Yield: 24-30 slices

Ranger Cookies   *Lucey Carissa*

This is it: the cookie that won grand champion honors at the 2002 Teton County Fair. Need we say more?

1 cup butter
1 cup sugar
1 cup brown sugar, firmly packed
2 eggs, well beaten
2 cups sifted, all-purpose flour
1 tsp. baking soda
½ tsp. each baking powder and salt
1 tsp. vanilla
2 cups each rolled oats
2 cups corn flakes
½ cup shredded or flaked coconut
½ cup each semisweet chocolate chips and chopped walnuts

Jackson Lake Ranger
Station, 1937

Teton National Forest
Superintendent F.C. Ko-
ziol was transferred to a
different forest over an
incident involving this
modest building. Or-
dered in 1943 to turn it
over to the newly cre-
ated Jackson Hole Mon-
ument, administered by
the National Park Ser-
vice, Koziol angrily re-
moved the cabinets,
doors, cupboards, plumb-
ing and an underground
well. The latter required
cutting a 4-foot hole in
the living room floor that
cut the floor joists and
left the building uninhab-
itable. The forest service
decried Koziol's action
and repaired the build-
ing.

1. Preheat oven to 350 degrees.
2. In a large bowl, cream butter and sugars together until light and fluffy. Beat in eggs.
3. In a separate bowl, sift the flour, baking powder, baking soda and salt together. Add dry ingredients to creamed mixture, stirring well to blend. Add vanilla, oats, cornflakes, coconut, chocolate chips and walnuts. Stir until well blended.
4. Drop 2½ tbsp. mounds onto ungreased cookie sheets, then flatten into 4-inch diameter rounds. Bake in middle of oven for 10-12 minutes. Cookies will be slightly soft when removed. Cool for 1 minute on baking sheet before transferring to wire racks to cool completely.

Yield: 3 dozen

Oatmeal Crinkles

Pierce Tome

The best oatmeal cookie in town. The judges awarded 10-year-old Pierce a purple ribbon at the 2002 Teton County Fair for these great cookies, earning him the right to compete in the Wyoming State Fair.

1¼	cup sugar, divided
1	tsp. ground cinnamon
1	cup shortening
1	cup firmly packed brown sugar
2	eggs
1	tsp. vanilla
¼	tsp. almond extract
2	cups all-purpose flour
1	tsp. each of baking powder, baking soda and salt
2½	cups regular oats, uncooked
1½	cups raisins

1. Preheat oven to 350 degrees. Grease cookie sheets.
2. Combine ¼ cup sugar and cinnamon in a small bowl. Stir until well blended and set aside.
3. In a large mixing bowl, cream shortening and remaining 1 cup of sugar together. Add brown sugar, eggs and vanilla and almond ex-tracts and beat until well blended.
4. In a separate bowl, sift together the flour, baking powder, baking soda and salt. Add the nuts and raisins.Stir to blend. Add dry mix-ture to creamed mixture and mix well. Add oats and stir well.
6. Shape dough into 1-inch balls and roll in reserved cinnamon sugar. Place 2-inches apart on prepared cookie sheets. Bake for 8-10 min-utes or until bottoms are browned. Cool 1 minute, then transfer cookies to racks to cool completely. Store in a covered container.

Yield: 5 dozen

Cranberry Cookies

Chef Karen Norby

Stewart Ranger
Station

Forest Service ranger Al
Austin built Stewart
Ranger Station at Bea-
ver Creek c. 1908. When
Grand Teton National
Park was created two
decades later, the build-
ing was transferred to
the new park and used
both as the park head-
quarters and as a resi-
dence. It was expanded
in 1938 and is today
used as office space. It
is the oldest forest ser-
vice building in the park.

Yum.

½ cup butter
1 cup sugar
¾ cup brown sugar
1 tsp. vanilla
1 egg
⅓ cup milk
3 cups flour
1 tsp. baking powder
¼ tsp. baking soda
½ tsp. salt
1 tbsp. grated orange rind
2½ cups fresh cranberries, coarsely chopped

1. Preheat oven to 350. Lightly grease cookie sheets and set aside.
2. In a large mixing bowl, cream the butter, sugar, brown sugar and vanilla together. Add the eggs and milk. Beat until light and fluffy.
3. In a separate bowl, sift together the flour, baking powder and baking soda. Mix in orange rind and cranberries. Add dry ingredients in batches to the wet mixture, mixing well after each addition.
4. Drop by rounded teaspoons on prepared cookie sheets. Bake until golden brown, about 8-10 minutes.

Yield: 3 dozen cookies

Stuart Ranger Station, 1920.

Iced Orange Drop Cookies
Louise Murie MacLeod

A.C. McCain

A.C. McCain was supervisor of Bridger-Teton National Forest from 1918-1936. During his tenure, he oversaw the controversial establishment of Grand Teton National Park, rode out the Great Depression and implemented many Civilian Conservation Corp projects on the forest.

"I got this recipe years ago from a Danish friend who was the wife of a naturalist in Yellowstone National Park. They're good!"

         ¾   cup butter
    1½   cups brown sugar, firmly packed
     2   eggs
     1   tsp. vanilla
    1½   tsp. grated orange peel
     ½   cup milk
     ½   tsp. baking soda
     ½   tsp. vinegar
     3   cups flour
    1½   tsp. baking powder
     ¼   tsp. salt
     ½   cup walnuts or pecans

Orange Icing
    1½   tsp. grated orange rind
     2   cups powdered sugar
     ¼   cup orange juice

1. Mix icing ingredients together until smooth. Set aside.
2. Preheat oven to 350 degrees. Grease cookie sheets and set aside.
3. Mix milk, baking soda and vinegar together. Set aside.
4. In a medium bowl, sift flour, baking powder and salt together.
5. In a large bowl, cream butter and sugar together. Add eggs, one at a time, beating well after each addition with a wooden spoon. Mix in vanilla and eggs. Add milk and stir to blend.
6. Add dry ingredients to mixture, stirring well to blend. Stir in nuts.
7. Drop by rounded teaspoons on cookie sheets. Bake for 20 minutes, or until light brown. Ice cookies while they are still warm.

Yield: 3 dozen

Soft Molasses Cookies
Georgia Woods

Old-fashioned goodness that makes your mouth happy.

    1¼   cups butter
    1¼   cups sugar, divided
     ¼   cup molasses
     1   egg
    2½   cups all-purpose flour
     2   tsp. baking soda
     ½   tsp. cream of tartar
     ½   tsp. ground cloves

1 tsp. cinnamon
1 tsp. ginger

1. Preheat oven to 350 degrees. Grease cookie sheets.
2. In a large mixing bowl, cream butter and 1 cup of the sugar until light and fluffy. Add molasses and egg and mix well.
3. In a separate bowl, sift together the flour, baking soda, cream of tartar, cinnamon, ginger and cloves. Add in batches to the creamed mixture, blending well after each addition.
4. Shape dough into 1¼-inch balls, then roll in remaining sugar. Place on prepared cookie sheet and gently flatten ball with a fork.
5. Bake 8-10 minutes. Let cookies cool for 1 minute, then transfer them to wire racks to continue cooling. Store in tightly covered container.

Yield: Approximately 4 dozen

Fresh Cookies

To keep cookies fresh, place a slice of apple in the container where they are stored.

Chocolate Ginger Cookies   *Martha MacEachern*

A time-tested favorite.

2¼ cups flour
⅓ cup cocoa
¼ tsp. salt
1 cup unsalted butter
1 cup sugar
3 tbsp. heavy cream or half-and-half
½ cup crystallized ginger, chopped fine
1 beaten egg

1. In a medium bowl, sift together flour, cocoa and salt. Set aside.
2. In a large mixing bowl, cream the butter and sugar together until well blended. Add beaten egg a little at a time, beating well after each addition to blend. Beat in cream.
3. Add dry mixture to creamed mixture by thirds, blending well after each addition. Stir in chopped ginger.
4. Divide dough into thirds and roll each portion into a log about 1½-inches in diameter. Wrap each log in wax paper and chill for 1 hour in the refrigerator, or 20 minutes in the freezer.
5. When you are ready to bake, preheat oven to 350 degrees and grease cookie sheets.
6. Remove logs from refrigerator/freezer and cut into thin slices, about ⅛-inch thick. Place slices 2-inches apart on prepared cookie sheets. Bake for 12-15 minutes.

Yield: Approximately 6 dozen

Ginger Snaps

Jan Hayse

A classic.

¾ cup shortening
1 cup brown sugar
1 tbsp. vinegar
¼ cup molasses
1 egg
2¼ cups flour
2 tsp. baking soda
½ tsp. salt
2 tsp. ginger
2 tsp. cinnamon
½ tsp. ground cloves
½ tsp. nutmeg
½ tsp. pepper

Ginger

To always have fresh ginger on hand for a recipe, freeze it either peeled or unpeeled. Thawing releases the juices and makes it easier to crush.

1. Preheat oven to 375 degrees. Grease cookie sheets and set aside.
2. In a large saucepan, mix the shortening, brown sugar, vinegar and molasses together. Bring to a boil over medium heat, then remove from heat and cool.
3. Add egg to cooled mixture. Stir to blend.
4. In a separate bowl, sift together the remaining dry ingredients.
5. Stir sifted dry ingredients into the liquid mixture.
6. Form dough into 1-inch balls and roll in granulated sugar. Place 2-inches apart on prepared cookie sheets. Bake for 8-10 minutes. Remove from oven and let sit for 1 minute before removing from cookie sheet to wire racks to cool completely.

Yield: 4 dozen

Quick & Easy Gingerbread Cookies

Mary Gridley

Great gingerbread cookies from a mix. Who knew?! Mary's recipe was included in J. C. Whitfield's "Best Christmas Cookies in the Valley"article in the December 22, 1983, edition of the *Jackson Hole Guide*.

1 pkg. Betty Crocker® gingerbread mix
⅓ cup warm water

1. Mix gingerbread and water together. Form into a ball, wrap with plastic wrap and refrigerate for 2 hours.
2. Preheat oven to 350 degrees. Lightly grease cookie sheets.

3. Take out a third of the dough. Rewrap remainder and keep refrigerated. Roll dough on a floured surface to ¼-inch thickness and cut into Christmas shapes. Place cookies on baking sheets and bake for 8-10 minutes. Repeat until all dough is used. Cool completely before decorating with piped frosting.

Yield: About 2½ dozen

Matt's Favorite Chocolate Chip Cookie

Martha MacEachern

The addition of a grated Hershey™ bar and blended oats makes this version of the classic chocolate chip cookie a standout.

1	cup butter
1	cup sugar
1	cup brown sugar
2	eggs
1	tsp. vanilla
2	cups flour
2½	cups oats, coarsely blended
½	tsp. salt
1	tsp. baking powder
1	tsp. baking soda
1	12-oz. pkg. semi-sweet chocolate chips
4	oz. grated Hershey™ bar
1½	cups chopped nuts

1. Preheat oven to 375 degrees. Grease cookie sheets and set aside.
2. In a large bowl, cream butter and sugars together.
3. Add eggs and vanilla to creamed mixture and stir until well blended.
4. Add flour, oats, salt, baking soda and baking powder. Blend well.
5. Stir in chocolate chips, the grated Hershey™ bar and nuts. Batter will be stiff.
6. Roll dough into 1-inch balls and place on greased cookie sheets.
7. Bake for 8 minutes or until cookies are golden brown. Remove from oven. Let sit for 1 minute before placing on racks to cool completely.

Yield: 5 dozen cookies

Cowboy Bar

The famous watering hole at 25 N. Cache was founded in 1936 by Joe Ruby, who named his establishment "Ruby's Cafe and Beer Garden." A year later it was sold to Benjamin F. Goe who changed the name to the present "Cowboy Bar."

Cowboy Bar, c.1940

Grandma Hays Chocolate Chip Cookies

Dick Hays

Dick shared his grandmother's chocolate chip cookie recipe with *Jackson Hole Guide* readers in 1981, when he served as Chief of Police for the Town of Jackson.

Cookie Sheets

Cool cookie sheets between batches to keep unbaked cookies from melting and thinning at the edges.

- 2 cups shortening
- 1½ cups sugar
- 1½ cups brown sugar, firmly packed
- 4 eggs
- 2 tbsp. hot water
- 2 tsp. vanilla
- 4 cups flour
- 2 tsp. baking soda
- 1 tsp. salt
- 4 cups quick oats
- 1 cup chopped nuts
- 1 12-oz. pkg. semi-sweet chocolate chips

1. Cream together shortening and sugars until light and fluffy. Add eggs, hot water and vanilla. Mix well.
2. In a separate bowl, sift together flour, soda and salt, then add to the creamed mixture.
3. Blend in oats, nuts and chocolate chips.
4. Bake 10-15 minutes in 375 degree oven. Begin baking on a lower rack, then move to a higher rack for at least half of the baking time for even browning. Let sit on cookie sheet for 1 minute, then place on wire racks to cool completely. Store in a covered container.

Yield: 4 dozen cookies

Chocolate Hazelnut Crescents

Candy Bayer

Jackson Hole Guide food columnist J.C. Whitfield named Candy's recipe one of the "Best Christmas Cookies in the Valley" in 1983.

- 1 cup flour
- 3 tbsp. unsweetened cocoa powder
- ½ cup softened butter
- ¼ cup light brown sugar
- ½ cup finely ground hazelnuts
  powdered sugar

1. Sift flour and cocoa together on wax paper. Set aside.
2. Preheat oven to 325 degrees.

3. Beat sugar and butter in a medium-sized bowl until creamy. Add ground nuts and flour mixture. Stir to blend.
4. Roll small amount of dough into 6-inch long pieces, ¼-inch in diameter. Cut in half and form into crescents. Place on ungreased cookie sheets, 1-inch apart, until dough is gone.
5. Bake for 10 minutes. Cool completely before dusting with powdered sugar.

Yield: 2 dozen crescents

Old-Fashioned Soft Sugar Cookies   *Becky Woods*

Dark-eyed Junco

Juncos prefer open forest and clearings in denser woods. Their grass-lined nests are on the ground, typically under a sheltering fir. These small birds are easily identified by their pale pink bill, dark hood and outer white tail feathers.

"This soft sugar cookie recipe has been passed down in our family for generations. The only time my father stepped into the kitchen was to whip up a batch of these cookies as the holidays approached. And I do mean whipped. My mother swears there was flour on the ceiling when he finished. The clean-up was worth every wonderful bite. For us, these cookies defined Christmas."

- 1 cup shortening
- 2 cups sugar
- 3 eggs, beaten
- 1 tbsp. white vinegar plus enough whole milk to measure 1 cup
- 1 tsp. vanilla
- 1 tsp. baking soda
- 2 tsp. baking powder
- 6 cups all-purpose flour (approximate)

1. Preheat oven to 350 degrees (375 above 6,000 ft.) Grease baking sheets and set aside.
2. In a large mixing bowl, cream together shortening, sugar and eggs until light and fluffy.
3. Add milk, vanilla, baking soda and baking powder. Stir until well blended.
4. Sift in flour, two cups at a time, beating by hand to incorporate after each addition. Dough will be sticky.
5. Lightly flour waxed paper or a pastry board and roll a portion of dough to ¼-inch thickness. Cut out with desired cookie cutters and place on greased cookie sheets. Sprinkle with granulated sugar.
6. Bake on rack in the middle of the oven for 8-10 minutes, or until the bottoms are golden brown and the center of the cookie springs back lightly when touched. Remove from oven, cool for 1 minute on cookie sheet, then transfer to wire rack to cool.

Yield: Approx. 6½ dozen

Stephen N. Leek

Stephen N. Leek moved to Jackson in 1888. He established a home-stead and ranch across from the canyon that now bears his name. His efforts to save the starving elk of Jackson Hole earned him the nickname "Father of the Elk." Leek photographed dead and starving elk during a massive die-off the winter of 1908-09. He used the photos in articles and lectures to publicize the plight of animals cut-off from traditional migration routes by settlement. The photos helped convince the state of Wyoming and the federal government to establish feedgrounds and the National Elk Refuge in 1912.

Frosted Roll Out Cookies   *Deb Hibberd*

Deb's delicious recipe earned a "Best Christmas cookies in the valley" designation from *Jackson Hole Guide* food columnist J.C. Whitfield.

Cookies
1	cup butter, softened
⅔	cup sugar
2	tsp. pure vanilla extract
2	eggs
3	cups flour
½	tsp. salt

Buttercream Frosting
2	tbsp. butter, no substitutes
1	tsp. pure vanilla extract
2-3	tbsp. half-and-half (to desired consistency)
1	box powdered sugar
	food color of choice

Elk in Jackson. S.N.Leek photo

1. Mix cookie ingredients together in a large bowl until well blended. Form into a ball, cover with plastic wrap and chill for 2 hours.
2. Preheat oven to 350 degrees. Lightly grease baking sheets.
3. Roll out portions of dough to ¼-inch thickness and cut into Christmas shapes with cookie cutters. Keep remaining dough covered and refrigerated until ready to use.
4. Place shapes on cookie sheets and bake for about 10 minutes, or until cookies are golden brown on the bottom and dough is cooked through. Remove from baking sheets and cool completely on wire racks before frosting.
5. To make frosting, combine all ingredients in a small bowl except food coloring and beat until smooth. Add food coloring, a drop at a time, until desired color is obtained. After frosting, decorate as desired with coconut, multi-colored candies, red hots, etc.

Yield: Approx. 3 dozen

Stephen Leek with fish, Jackson Lake.

To help make ends meet, Leek constructed a hunting lodge at the north end of Leigh Lake and later ran a camp on the east side of Jackson Lake near the present Leek's Marina.

Old-Fashioned Raisin Cookies   *Mardy Murie*

One of Mardy's favorite cookies. When she held her famous Christmas cookie swap, this was often her contribution.

2 cups raisins
1 tsp. baking soda
1 cup water
2 cups sugar
1 cup shortening
3 eggs
1 tsp. vanilla
4 cups flour
½ tsp. salt
¼ tsp. nutmeg
1 tsp. cinnamon
1 tsp. baking powder

1. Preheat oven to 375 degrees. Lightly grease cookie sheets.
2. In a medium-sized saucepan, combine raisins with baking soda and water. Bring to a boil over medium heat and boil until raisins are plump and most of the liquid is absorbed.
3. Pour raisin mixture into large bowl. Add remaining ingredients and stir until well blended. Drop by full teaspoons onto prepared cookie sheets. Bake until cookie is firm and bottoms are golden brown, 12-15 minutes. Cool on racks. Store in a covered container.

Yield: Approximately 3 dozen

Mountain Bluebird

The mountain bluebird is the state bird of both Idaho and Nevada. It is common in Jackson Hole and Yellowstone as well, largely due to the availability of dead trees for nesting. Fire, insect epidemics and trees killed by shifting thermal water are "beneficial disasters" to this pretty azure cavity nester.

Grove Farm Icebox Cookies

A light, crisp cookie. Serve with the farm's mint iced tea for a mid-afternoon treat (See recipe on page 45.)

½ cup butter
2 cups raw sugar*
2 beaten eggs
2¾ cups flour
1 tsp. baking soda
1 tsp. vanilla

1. Mix ingredients together and roll into cylinders about the diameter of a quarter. Wrap in waxed paper and chill in the refrigerator for about an hour. (Dough may also be frozen for future use.)
2. When ready to bake, preheat oven to 350 degrees. Grease a cookie sheet. Cut rolls into ¼-inch thick cookie rounds and place thin rounds on cookie sheets about 1-inch apart. Bake 20-25 minutes. Cookies will appear very lightly browned when done. Remove from cookie sheet immediately and place on wire racks to cool.

*Raw sugar is available in most larger grocery store and/or health food stores. Do not use regular brown or dark brown sugar. It's the coarse raw sugar that gives these cookies their unique flavor.

Yield: 5 dozen

Bird Nest Cookies
Sami Robinson

Another "Best Christmas Cookies in the Valley" winner!

1 stick butter (½ cup)
¼ cup brown sugar
1 egg, separated
1 cup flour
1 cup chopped pecans
jam or jelly

1. Preheat oven to 350 degrees. Lightly grease baking sheets.
2. In a small bowl, lightly beat egg white. Set aside.
3. In a separate bowl, cream butter and sugar together. Add egg yolk and beat until light and fluffy. Stir in flour until well blended.
4. Form dough into small balls and dip in egg white. Roll in chopped pecans.
5. Place on prepared baking sheet and press an indent in the center. Bake for 8 minutes, remove, and repress center of cookies. Return

to oven and bake an additional 10 minutes, or until bottoms are golden brown.

6. Cool cookies on rack. When completely cool, fill centers with jam or jelly of your choice.

Yield: 4 dozen

Pecan Puffs

Nancy Carson

Nancy calls these the "best Christmas cookies ever." She inherited the recipe from her mother.

- ½ cup butter, softened
- 2 tbsp. sugar
- 1 tsp. vanilla
- 1 cup coarsely ground pecans
- 1 cup flour
  powdered sugar

1. Preheat oven to 300 degrees. Grease baking sheet(s) and set aside,
2. In a medium-sized bowl, cream together the butter, sugar and vanilla until smooth.
3. Add the ground pecans and flour. Stir until well blended.
4. Roll into 1-inch balls and place on prepared baking sheets. Bake for 10-15 minutes, or until lightly browned. Remove from oven.
5. Roll hot cookies in powdered sugar and set on rack to cool. After cookies are cold, roll in powdered sugar again. Store in a cool place in a covered container.

Yield: Approximately 3 dozen

Pecan Chocolate Chip Meringues

Gertrude Brennan

Gertrude got this wonderful recipe from Mildred Buchenroth, who called the light meringues "overnight cookies." Whip up a batch before retiring, and you'll have cookies in the morning!

- 2 egg whites
- ⅛ tsp. salt
- ¼ tsp. cream of tartar
- ⅔ cup sugar
- 1 tsp. vanilla
- ¼ tsp. almond extract

Baking time

Cooking and baking times specified in most recipes are only guidelines, as temperatures can vary from oven to oven. Check your dish a few minutes before the recommended baking time. Don't keep the oven door open long. It is estimated your oven loses 25 degrees each time the door is opened.

    1   cup chopped pecans
    ¾   cup semisweet chocolate chips

1. Preheat oven to 350 degrees. Grease baking sheets.
2. In a stainless steel or copper bowl, beat egg whites until frothy. Add salt and cream of tartar and continue beating until whites are stiff but not dry (peaks should remain standing). Gradually add sugar and beat until mixture is shiny and stiff.
3. Mix in vanilla and almond extract, then gently fold in pecans and chocolate chips.
4. Drop by rounded teaspoons onto prepared sheets. Place in preheated oven and turn off heat. Leave in oven overnight. *Do not open the oven door.* Store in a covered container. Cookies keep about 1 week.

Yield: 2 dozen

Janie Camenzind's Famous Fudgy, Flourless Chocolate Torte   *Janie Camenzind*

Janie dubs this recipe "the essence of pure chocolate." Quite an endorsement from a confessed chocoholic and one of the best dessertmakers in the valley!

    7   ozs. good quality semi-sweet chocolate
    ½   cup strong black coffee
    1   cup butter
    1   cup granulated sugar
    4   eggs, slightly beaten

1. Preheat oven to 375 degrees (for Jackson altitude of 6,200 feet. Preheat to 325 degrees for lower elevations).
2. Generously flour and butter a leak-proof springform pan. (Note: If your pan is not leak-proof, wrap aluminum foil on the bottom so the mixture doesn't leak out. It is typical for the torte to leak slightly for the first five minutes or so.) Set pan aside.
3. Place chocolate and coffee in a large saucepan over medium heat. Stir occasionally until the chocolate melts and the mixture is well blended. Alternately add portions of the butter and sugar, blending well after each addition.
4. Cook blended mixture until very hot but *do not boil.*
5. Remove pan from heat and gradually add slightly beaten eggs, stirring constantly, until mixture is well blended. Batter will resemble thin brownie batter. Pour mixture through fine-mesh sieve into springform pan. Don't skip this step: it makes for a finely textured torte.

6. Place in the middle of the oven and bake until a brownie-like crust forms on top and the mixture begins to pull away from the side of the pan. Cool on rack. Cover and refrigerate until serving.

Torte may be served at room temperature or cold. To serve at room temperature, remove from refrigerator 30 minutes before serving. Serve plain or with vanilla whipped cream. Cake will be very moist.

Vanilla Whipped Cream

    2   cups cream
    2   tbsp. granulated sugar
    1   tsp. vanilla

Beat ingredients together in a narrow bowl until soft peaks form in the cream. Chill, covered, until served.

Serves 8-10

Walnut Torte   *Marcia Kunstel*

"I don't know from precisely where this came, but it is a recipe that my mother Marguerite Kunstel handed down to me. It's a drop dead dessert that my family enjoyed at special occasions."

    12 eggs, separated
    2   cups sugar
    2   tsp. vanilla
    2   tbsp. whiskey or brandy
    4   cups ground walnuts (or hazelnuts)
    2   tbsp. bread crumbs
        pinch of salt (about ¼ tsp.)
    2   cups whipping cream

1. Preheat oven to 350 degrees.
2. Prepare three round or square 8 or 9-inch pans. Butter the pans and line the bottoms with waxed paper, then butter the surface of the paper. Set aside.
3. Beat egg yolks until thick and lemon colored. Gradually add sugar and beat well. Add vanilla and whiskey. Beat thoroughly.
4. Mix ground nuts, bread crumbs and salt. Add to egg yolk mixture. (It will be very thick.) Set aside.
5. Beat egg whites until stiff. Gradually fold into batter until well mixed. Divide batter evenly among the three prepared pans.
6. Bake at 350 degrees for about one hour. Check for doneness at about 45-50 minutes. Torte is done when sides have drawn back from pan and a toothpick inserted in the center comes out clean.

Old Faithful Geyser
W.H. Jackson photo

Old Faithful was named by members of the Washburn Expedition of 1870 who were impressed by its size and frequency. It erupts every 35-120 minutes, with a present average of about once every 90 minutes. Eruptions last 1½ to 5 minutes and attain heights of 90-184 feet. The geyser expels 3,700-8,400 gallons of water each time it erupts.

When done, remove pans from oven and carefully invert the pans on racks to cool. Remove wax paper from bottom of the cakes.

7. Put cooled layers together with stiffly beaten, sweetened whipped cream, then frost the sides and, if desired, the top with whipped cream. Decorate cream on top with walnut pieces or cherry halves.

Serves 12

Hazelnut Torte with Chocolate Satin Icing

Daughter Nicola Esdorn
Submitted by Erika Muschaweck
Fabulous.

Torte
- 8¼ ozs. hazelnuts, finely chopped
- 1 cup plus 1 tbsp. sugar
- 6 extra large eggs, separated

Chocolate Satin Icing
- ½ stick butter
- 4 ozs. unsweetened chocolate
- 3 tbsp. whipping cream
- ⅔ cup powdered sugar
- 1 tsp. vanilla

1. Preheat oven to 325 degrees. Grease 8½-inch springform pan.
2. In a medium-sized bowl, beat egg yolks and sugar together until very creamy, thick and lemon colored. Set aside.
3. In a separate bowl, beat egg whites to a stiff cream. Carefully fold nuts and egg whites into the egg yolk / sugar mixture, stirring until just blended. Bake in prepared pan for 1 hour. Cool on rack.
5. Prepare the icing. Heat butter and chocolate on top of a double boiler, stirring constantly, until both are melted and blended together. Remove from heat and stir in the whipping cream. Add sugar and vanilla and stir until smooth. Spread icing on the torte when it is still warm.

Serves 8-10

Tiramisù

Tiramisù means "pick-me-up" in Italian, and this layered espresso and chocolate dessert does just that. This version, adapted from *Bon Apetit* magazine, uses cream cheese and prepared pound cake instead of traditional mascarpone cheese and ladyfingers. Allow enough preparation time to chill ingredients.

        8   ozs. good quality, semisweet chocolate
        1   cup sugar
        4   egg yolks
     1½   tsp. vanilla
        8   ozs. room temperature cream cheese, cut into pieces
    1 ¾   cups whipping cream, chilled
        1   tbsp. instant espresso powder diluted in 1¼ cups hot water,
             cooled or 1¼ cups cooled espresso
        1   12-oz. prepared pound cake, cut into 3 ½ x1x ½-inch
             strips
        1   tsp. unsweetened cocoa powder

1. Finely chop chocolate in processor and set aside.
2. Mix sugar and egg yolks in a food processor or large blender for 30
    seconds. Add vanilla and beat until pale yellow, approximately 90
    seconds. Add cheese in batches, blending until smooth after each
    addition. Transfer mixture to medium bowl. Cover and chill 1 hour.
3. Beat whipping cream until stiff. Fold into cream cheese mixture.
    Cover and refrigerate 1 hour. Note: This mixture can be prepared
    up to 2 days in advance.
4. Pour espresso into a bowl. Use a pastry brush to lightly coat all
    sides of the cake strips.
5. Arrange strips on bottom of 10-cup shallow dish, gently pressing
    strips together with fingers. Sprinkle with half of chopped choco-
    late and top with chilled cheese mixture. Sprinkle remaining choco-
    late over the top. Cover and refrigerate at least 2 hours, or up to 1
    day in advance. Just before serving, lightly dust top with unsweet-
    ened cocoa.

Serves 8

The Crow's Nest

Perched only 18 feet be-
neath the peak of the
Inn's 92-foot high lobby
ceiling, the Crow's Nest
is a separate small land-
ing where musicians
played for guests after
dinner during the early
days of the Inn. A 7.5
earthquake outside of
the park on August 17,
1959, weakened sup-
ports of the platform. It
is no longer open to the
public.

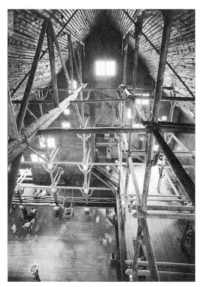

View from the Crow's Nest,
Old Faithful Inn.

Date Torte
Lois Ruosch

Date fans will love this rich, moist concoction. It's special enough to cap off a holiday feast.

1	cup chopped dates
1½	tsp. baking soda
1	cup boiling water
1	cup sugar
1	tbsp. butter
1	egg
1	cup flour
	pinch of salt
½	cup chopped nuts

1. Place dates and soda in a small bowl. Pour boiling water over the dates and stir well. Let stand until cool, about 15 minutes.
2. Preheat oven to 400 degrees.
3. In a separate bowl, cream together the sugar and butter until light and fluffy. Add the egg and blend. Pour in the date mixture; mix well. Stir in the flour and salt. Blend well. Add chopped nuts and mix well again.
4. Pour in a lightly oiled 8-inch square pan. Bake for 30 minutes, or until a toothpick inserted in the center of the pan comes out clean. Serve warm or cold. This is especially good topped with whipped cream.

Serves 12

Green Devil Cake
Marilyn Quinn

The secret to this wonderfully moist chocolate cake is green tomatoes—something many Jackson Hole gardeners have plenty of at the end of a short summer! It is reprinted with permission from Marilyn's book, *Peak Bloom: Honest Advice for Mountain and Northern Gardeners.*

2	cups flour
1	cup brown sugar
1	tsp. each baking powder, cinnamon and soda
4	oz. unsweetened chocolate, melted
1	cup sour milk
	(mix 1 tbsp. of white vinegar with enough milk to make 1 cup. Let stand five minutes.)
1	cup puréed green tomatoes
1	cup softened butter
2	eggs
1	tbsp. grated orange peel

1. Preheat oven to 350 degrees. Grease and flour a 13x9-inch pan.
2. Combine flour, brown sugar, baking powder, cinnamon and soda. Mix well.
3. Add chocolate, sour milk, tomatoes, butter, eggs and orange peel to dry mixture. Beat with electric mixer for two minutes to blend well.
4. Pour into prepared pan. Bake for 35-40 minutes, or until cake pulls away from sides of pan and a toothpick inserted into the center comes out clean.
5. Frost with your favorite chocolate icing after cake has cooled.

Serves 8

South Fork Falls

South Fork Falls plunges over 80 feet to the bottom of South Buffalo Fork Gorge, both scenic highlights of Teton Wilderness on Bridger-Teton National Forest.

Warm Chocolate Dessert with Soft Interior

Nicola Esdorn

Submitted by Erika Muschaweck

Sublime. Serve with vanilla ice cream and fresh raspberries.

 5 ozs. bittersweet chocolate, chopped (use very good chocolate like Lindt)
 ½ stick unsalted butter
 1 tablespoon cognac
 2 eggs + 2 egg yolks
 ¼ cup sugar
 1 tsp. vanilla extract
   pinch of salt
 1 tbsp. + 1 tsp. flour

1. Preheat oven to 400 degrees and butter wells of muffin pan or small cake pans.
2. Combine chocolate and butter and melt in the microwave until mixture is smooth and blended. Stir in cognac and let cool until lukewarm.
3. In another bowl, combine eggs, egg yolks, sugar, vanilla and salt. Beat on high speed until thick, about five minutes. Sift the flour over bowl and fold gently until just blended.
4. Add the chocolate mixture and fold carefully to get a smooth, blended batter.
5. Fill muffin cups or cake forms and bake until tops are firm, 9-11 minutes.
6. Cool slightly and transfer to dessert plates. Serve warm with ice cream and raspberries.

Chocolate Tips

Sometimes a grayish color, called "bloom," develops on chocolate. This indicates that the cocoa butter has risen to the surface. Flavor and quality will not be lessened and the grayish color will disappear when the chocolate is melted.

•

Melt white chocolate over very hot water — never boiling or even simmering. White chocolate will scorch at a lower temperature than bittersweet chocolate.

•

To make the best and prettiest chocolate shavings, use white or milk chocolate; they are softer in texture and curl better.

Heavenly Chocolate Cake with Chocolate Buttercream Frosting
Danielle Town

Excellent. This moist, rich cake is one of Danielle's all-time favorite recipes.

    1   8-oz. pkg. Hershey's® semi-sweet baking chocolate, broken
        into pieces, or 1 cup good quality semisweet chocolate chips
    3   cups all-purpose flour
  1½   cups sugar
    2   tsp. baking soda
    1   tsp. salt
    2   cups water
   ⅔   cup canola oil
    2   tbsp. white vinegar or lemon juice
    2   tsp. pure vanilla extract

1. Preheat oven to 350 degrees. Grease and flour two 9-inch round cake pans. Set aside.
2. Melt chocolate on top on a double boiler, watching carefully so it doesn't scorch. Cool slightly.
3. In a large bowl, combine the flour, sugar, baking soda and salt. Mix together well. Add the melted chocolate, water, oil, vinegar or lemon juice and vanilla. Beat with mixer on medium speed until thoroughly blended, about 3 minutes.
4. Pour batter into prepared pans and bake approximately 35 minutes, or until a toothpick inserted in the center of the batter comes out clean. Cool 10-15 minutes. Remove from pans and let cool completely on wire racks before frosting.

Chocolate Buttercream frosting

    3   cups powdered sugar
   ½   cup cocoa
   ½   cup (1 stick) butter, softened (no substitutions)
  5-6   tbsp. milk, divided
    1   tsp. vanilla

1. In a medium bowl, beat together 1 cup of the powdered sugar, cocoa, butter, 2 tbsp. of milk and vanilla until smooth and well blended.
2. Add remaining sugar alternately with the milk, beating after each addition until smooth. Frosts a 13x9-inch sheet cake, or 1 two-layer cake.

Serves 8-10

Chocolate Kahlua Cake

Jane Bloom

Evening Grosbeak

Sinfully good. No one will guess this easy-to-make cake starts with a cake mix.

- ¼ cup kahlua
- ½ cup chilled canola oil
- 1 egg
- ¼ cup Eggbeaters® or other egg substitute
- 1 pint nonfat sour cream
- 1 pkg. devil's food chocolate cake mix
- 1 12-oz. pkg. semi-sweet chocolate chips
  powdered sugar

1. Preheat oven to 350 degrees. Grease and flour a 10-inch bundt, tube, or angel food cake pan.
2. Combine kahlua, oil, egg, egg substitute, sour cream and cake mix in a large mixing bowl. Beat for 3 minutes or until smooth and well blended. Stir in chocolate chips.
3. Pour into prepared pan. Bake 50-60 minutes, or until a toothpick inserted into the center of the cake comes out clean. Remove pan from oven and cool on a wire rack. When the cake is still barely warm, remove the pan and invert the cake on a serving plate. Dust with powdered sugar.

Serves 12

The grosbeak's powerful bill allows it to efficiently crack tough seeds. It is called an evening grosbeak because it was once believed the bird only sang at dusk.

Pineapple Cake with Broiled Coconut Pecan Frosting

Joyce Rudd

The Rudds operated Teton Trail Rides in Grand Teton National Park for over 40 years. Joyce collected recipes from people working for them during their years in business. This is one of her favorites.

- 1½ cups sugar
- 1 egg
- ½ tsp. salt
- 2 tsp. baking soda
- 1 tsp. pure vanilla extract
- 2 cups flour
- 2 cups crushed pineapple with juice

1. Preheat oven to 350 degrees. Lightly grease 13x9-inch baking pan. Set aside.

Grizzly Bear

A male grizzly can tip the scales at over 1,000 pounds. Almost 80 percent of its diet is composed of plants, roots and berries, though it will opportunistically eat young mammals, insects and fish. Carrion—which grizzlies can smell up to 10 miles away—is sought by the bears when they emerge from hibernation in the spring.

2. Combine all cake ingredients in a large mixing bowl, stirring until well blended.
3. Pour into prepared pan and bake 40 minutes, or until cake springs back when lightly touched and a toothpick inserted into the center comes out clean.
4 Spread frosting while cake is still warm. Put frosted cake under a broiler and broil until frosting turns golden brown. Serve warm or cold.

Coconut Pecan Frosting

⅔ cup Sego® canned milk
⅔ cup sugar
1 egg, beaten
½ cup butter
1 tsp. pure vanilla extract
1 cup chopped pecans
1 cup flaked coconut

1. In a small bowl, beat egg and milk together until well blended. Stir in sugar until dissolved.
2. Melt butter in a medium-sized saucepan over medium heat. Add milk mixture and bring to a boil. Boil 6 minutes, stirring frequently.
3. Remove from heat and add vanilla, pecans and coconut. Stir to blend.

Serves 12-16

Orange Spongcake with Rum Icing   *Muffy Moore*

Muffy Moore is a former Teton County Commissioner who now lives in Cheyenne, Wyoming. This is one of her favorite desserts.

Cake
3 cups sugar
4 eggs, separated
grated rind and juice of one orange
pinch of salt
1¼ cups sifted cake flour
Rum Icing
2 egg yolks
3 cups powdered sugar
1½ sticks butter, softened
2 tbsp. rum (Myers Dark Rum is ideal. 1 tbsp. of vanilla may be substituted.)

1. Preheat oven to 375 degrees. Butter and flour 8-9" springform pan.
2. In a large mixing bowl, beat sugar into egg yolks until sugar is dissolved, then beat another 3 minutes. Add orange juice, orange peel and salt and beat until foamy. Beat in flour until well blended.
3. In a separate small bowl, beat egg white and pinch of salt together until soft peaks form. Add sugar and beat until stiff. Fold egg white mixture into the orange mixture.
4. Pour batter into springform pan and bake 30-35 minutes until delicately browned. Let cool before removing springform pan. Transfer to serving platter and frost with rum icing. To make icing, beat all ingredients together until smooth.

Serves 12

Pumpkin Bundt Cake

Dana Rogers

Mouth-wateringly good. This moist, flavorful cake netted 11-year-old Dana a highly-sought-after purple ribbon at the 2002 Teton County Fair, earning her the right to enter her cake in the Wyoming State Fair.

2	cups all-purpose flour
2	tsp. baking powder
2	tsp. cinnamon
½	tsp. salt
1	tsp. baking soda
2	cups sugar
4	eggs
2	cups canned pumpkin
1	cup vegetable oil

1. Preheat oven to 350 degrees. Lightly grease and flour a bundt pan or 10-inch tube pan and set aside.
2. In a large bowl, mix together the sugar and eggs until well blended. Add the pumpkin and oil. Stir well to blend.
3. In a separate bowl, sift together the flour, baking powder, baking soda, cinnamon and salt. Add to the pumpkin mixture and stir until thoroughly blended.
4. Pour batter into prepared pan and place on a rack in the middle of the oven. Bake for 30 minutes, or until the cake springs back when lightly touched. Cool completely before slicing. Frost with cream cheese frosting, if desired.

Serves 12

Cake Topper

For a pretty and quick cake topping, place a paper doily on top and dust with powdered sugar. Carefully remove the doily so you don't smudge the design.

Lantelme Cake

Ann Laubach

Cake Tip

To prevent nuts and fruits from sinking to the bottom of a cake during baking, warm them in the oven and toss with flour. Shake off excess flour before mixing them into the batter.

"This recipe has been handed down from my great-grandparents, who operated a restaurant in New York City around the turn of the century. We have always called it Lantelme Cake, Lantelme being our family's last name. It is a traditional pound cake, though I think it has a much nicer texture than the kind you get in the store. It can be served plain or fancied up with ice cream, any kind of sauce or fruit."

1	cup butter, no substitutes
2	cups sugar
4	eggs, separated
3	cups flour
2½	tsp. baking powder
1	cup milk
¼	tsp. salt
1	tsp. pure vanilla extract, or ½ tsp. almond extract and ½ tsp. vanilla

1. Preheat oven to 350 degrees. Grease and lightly flour a bundt pan.
2. In a small bowl, beat egg whites until stiff peaks form. Set aside.
3. In a large mixing bowl, cream together the butter and sugar. Add egg yolks one at a time, beating well after each addition.
4. In a separate bowl, sift the flour, baking powder and salt together.
5. Stir vanilla/almond extract(s) into the milk.
6. Add dry ingredients alternately with the milk mixture to the moist batter, mixing well after each addition. Fold in egg whites. Bake for approximately one hour, or until the cake is golden brown and a toothpick inserted near the center comes out clean. Remove from oven and cool slightly before removing from pan. Place on wire rack to cool completely.

Serves 8-10

Pound Cake

Chef Tamalpais Roth-McCormick

"There are two pound cake recipes that I love and I truly believe are worthy of a queen. I settled on the one that I can't imagine living without." For an equally delectable lemon variation of the above, add lemon zest and lemon juice in place of the vanilla.

1¾	stick soft, unsalted butter
1½	cups superfine sugar
1½	cups cake flour
1½	tsp. baking powder
¼	cup milk, at room temperature

4 large eggs, at room temperature
2 tsp. pure vanilla extract

1. Preheat oven to 350 degrees. Butter a loaf pan with butter wrappers and set aside.
2. Cream the butter and sugar until fluffy. Add milk and blend, then add eggs one at a time, beating only until incorporated and very light.
3. Add flour and baking powder and mix for roughly one minute, then mix in the vanilla.
4. Bake for approximately 1 hour or until the sides pull away from the edges of the pan and a wooden toothpick inserted in the center comes out clean. Serve warm or cold.

Serves 8

James Rosner's World Famous Chocolate Chip Pound Cake *Chef Karen Norby*

Aka "MMM! That Smells Good." Karen says dunking pound cake in milk is a must!

4 eggs
4 oz. soft cream cheese
1 stick of butter
1½ cups all-purpose flour
1 cup sugar
1 tbsp. pure vanilla extract
1 tbsp. fresh lemon or orange zest
1 tsp. baking powder
1 cup chocolate chips

1. Preheat oven to 350 degrees. Butter and flour a loaf pan.
2. In a large bowl, cream butter and cream cheese together until there are no lumps and mixture has a smooth consistency. Add eggs and sugar and mix well, then add vanilla and citrus zest. Mix again.
3. Add flour and baking powder. Mix well, then add chocolate chips.
4. Pour batter into loaf pan and bake until golden brown on top and firm to the touch, about 1 hour. Serve warm or cold.

Serves 8

Quaking Aspen

This attractive, sun-loving tree is one of the few deciduous trees in the valley. It successfully reproduces by sending suckers, or clones, up from its extensive, shallow root system. The greenish-white bark is photosynthetic, allowing the tree to produce food year-round. In exposed sites, the tree produces a white powder that covers its bark to protect the tree from ultraviolet radiation. Native Americans were known to use the powder for sunscreen.

Prevent soggy crust
when making a custard-
style pie, such as coco-
nut or pumpkin, by care-
fully breaking one of the
eggs for the pie filling
into the unbaked pastry
shell. Swirl the raw egg
around so the egg white
covers the entire sur-
face, then pour the egg
into the filling mixture.

Creamy Coconut Pie

Bertie Millward

An all-time favorite cream pie.

4	eggs, well beaten
1¼	cups sugar
1	tbsp. flour
1	stick of butter, melted
1	tsp. white vinegar
1	tsp. vanilla
⅛	tsp. salt
1	cup flaked coconut
1	9-inch pie shell, unbaked

1. Preheat oven to 350 degrees.
2. Combine all ingredients in a large bowl and stir well to blend. Pour into pie shell.
3. Bake 50 minutes or until filling is set and pastry is brown. Serve slightly warm or chilled. Top with a dollop of whipped cream and toasted coconut, if desired.

Serves 8

Perfect Peach Pie

Chef Tamalpais Roth-McCormick

"This recipe is one of my favorite pies ever. It comes to me only a few times each year—when peaches are at the height of their greatness. A puddle of warm pie juices mingling with melting ice cream is one of the most gratifying summer pleasures."

Butter-crust dough
2	cups all-purpose flour
¼	cup sugar
½	tsp. salt
1	cup chilled unsalted butter in ½-inch cubes
4-8	tbsp. ice water

Peach Filling
7	cups peeled and sliced peaches
⅔	cup sugar
⅓	cup flour
¼	tsp. freshly grated nutmeg
¼	tsp. salt
3	tbsp. fresh lemon juice
2	tbsp. butter
1	tbsp. sugar for garnish

1. Combine flour, sugar and salt in a bowl. Add butter and work into

242

flour mixture with a pastry knife until mixture looks like bread crumbs with a few pea-size pieces of butter. Sprinkle water evenly over the mixture, tossing with a fork until the dough comes together. (Begin with 4 tbsp. and add more as needed.) Divide dough in half and let rest in the refrigerator for 10 minutes.

2. Working on a floured surface, roll half the dough from the center out and transfer to pie pan. Roll out top crust to a thickness of ⅛-inch and at least 1-inch larger than the pie pan.

3. Preheat oven to 400 degrees.

4. Place peaches in a large bowl. In a separate bowl, combine the sugar, flour, nutmeg and salt and stir to blend. Add dry ingredients to peaches and stir to evenly coat. Add lemon juice and stir to mix.

5. Mound peach filling into pie shell and dot with 2 tbsp. butter. Place top crust over filling and firmly press crust together. Cut off excess crust and crimp as desired. Cut vents in crust.

6. Bake for 10 minutes, then reduce heat to 350 degrees and bake for an additional 50 minutes or until the filling is bubbling up through the vents and the crust is golden brown. About 15 minutes before the pie is done, sprinkle the crust with 1 tbsp. of sugar. Let pie rest for at least 45 minutes after baking to let the juices thicken. Serve warm or cold.

Serves 8

Key Lime Pie

Divinely simple. Simply divine. This light, cool dessert is a great way to end a spicy meal.

    2   14-oz. cans sweetened condensed milk
    2   eggs at room temperature
    1   cup lime juice
  1½   cups graham cracker crumbs
    ¼   cup sugar
    ½   cup butter, melted
    1   lime and whipped cream for garnish

1. Preheat oven to 350 degrees.
2. Combine graham cracker crumbs, melted butter and sugar in a 9-inch pie pan, stirring well to mix. Press evenly over bottom and up sides of pan. Bake for 20 minutes. Remove from oven and cool.
3. Coddle eggs. Fill a small saucepan with enough water to cover the eggs and bring to a boil. Place eggs, one at a time, on a tablespoon and lower into the boiling water. Turn off the burner, cover the saucepan and let sit for 1 minute. Remove eggs from water and break immediately into large bowl. The eggs will be very runny. Whip.

Measuring Pie Crust

Use waxed paper to measure pie dough. The standard pie pan is 9 inches in diameter so you'll need a 12-inch circle of dough. Since wax paper comes in a 12-inch width, simply tear off a piece 12 inches long, then roll your circle of dough so it touches the center of all four sides of the square.

Buffalo Bill Dam, 1911.

The Buffalo Bill dam near Cody, Wyoming, was built between 1905-1910. Upon its completion, the 325-foot high structure was the tallest dam in the world. Its crest extends 200 feet across. The dam was added to the National Register of Historic Places in 1973.

4. Add condensed milk to eggs and whisk to blend. Stir in lime juice.
5. Pour into baked and cooled graham cracker crust and refrigerate 3 hours to set. Garnish, if desired, just before serving. Ring perimeter of pie with dollops of whipped cream. Cut lime into thin circles, cut halfway into the slices, and twist ends in opposite directions. Place lime twist in dollops of whipped cream.

Serves 8

Cranberry Nut Pie
Dick Hays

A rich, easy-to-make crustless pie. Serve warm with vanilla ice cream.

    1¼ cups fresh cranberries
    ¼   cup brown sugar
    ¼   cup chopped walnuts
    1   egg
    ½   cup sugar
    ½   cup whole wheat flour
    ½   cup melted butter

1. Preheat oven to 325 degrees.
2. Butter a 9-inch pie pan and layer cranberries on bottom. Sprinkle with brown sugar and walnuts.
3. In a medium-sized bowl, beat egg until thick. Gradually add sugar, beating until thoroughly blended. Stir in flour and melted butter; mix well. Pour mixture over cranberries.
4. Bake 45 minutes, or until pie is firm.

Serves 8

Heavenly Lemon Pie

A light and lemony creation cradled in a cloud of meringue. Perfect!

Meringue crust
    4   egg whites
    ½   tsp. cream of tartar
    1   cup sugar
Filling
    4   egg yolks
    ½   cup sugar
    4   tbsp. fresh lemon juice
        grated rind of 1 lemon
    1   cup whipping cream, whipped

1. Preheat oven to 300 degrees.
2. In a copper or stainless steel bowl, beat egg whites until frothy. Add cream of tartar and continue beating whites. As the whites begin to stiffen, add 2 tbsp. of sugar at a time until the entire cup has been added, beating well after each addition.
3. Place meringue in an ungreased, deep pie dish and use a spatula to mold an even "crust" on the bottom and up the sides. Bake 40 minutes, then cool on a rack.
4. While the shell is cooling, make the filling. Heat water over medium low heat in the bottom of a double boiler until hot but not boiling. As the water is heating, beat the egg yolks until thick and lemony. Add the sugar, lemon juice and rind. Stir to blend. Pour yolk mixture into the top of the double boiler and cook, stirring constantly, until the filling mixture thickens and develops a spongy texture. Remove from heat and cool.
5. Fold whipping cream into the cooled filling mixture. Spread filling evenly into baked meringue crust. Refrigerate at least 20 minutes before serving. Garnish with thin twisted slices of lemon and mint leaves, if desired.

Serves 8

Pumpkin Cheesecake with Caramelized Walnuts

JHCA

Truly extraordinary. This special dessert is from the Jackson Hole Conservation Alliance's *Jackson Hole A La Carte* cookbook, a great collection of 100+ recipes. Plan ahead: you must refrigerate this dessert overnight before serving. For information on the alliance and ordering *Jackson Hole A La Carte*, please see the acknowledgments section.

Crust
    1   cup graham cracker crumbs
    ¼   cup crushed ginger snaps
    ¼   cup sugar
    ¼   cup melted butter
Filling
   1½ lbs. cream cheese
    1   cup light brown sugar
    ½   cup sugar
    5   eggs
    1   1 lb. can pumpkin
    1   tsp. cinnamon
    ¼   tsp. each of nutmeg and cloves
    ¼   cup whipping cream

Minidoka Project

The Minodka Project is a water irrigation/power system in southeastern Idaho/northwest Wyoming initiated by the Bureau of Reclamation in 1904 and completed in 1939. Jackson Lake is one of five storage reservoirs. American Falls Reservoir is the project's largest storage reservoir and holds up to 1.7 million acre-feet of water. The project includes two dams, two power plants, and over 900 miles of canals that serve 1.1 million acres of farmland on both sides of the Snake River in the 300 mile area from Ashton to Bliss, Idaho.

All women Minidoka Project Survey crew, 1918.

245

Cutting Cheesecake

For perfectly clean-cut slices of cheesecake, briefly run a thin-bladed slicing knife through an open flame, then cut. Wipe the blade and reheat between cuts.

Caramelized walnuts
- ¼ cup butter
- ½ cup light brown sugar
- 1 tsp. lemon juice
- 1 cup perfect walnut halves

1. Preheat oven to 350 degrees.
2. Combine crust ingredients and press onto the bottom and 1-inch up the sides of a 9-inch springform pan. Bake 10 minutes, or until lightly browned. Set on a rack to cool. Lower oven temperature to 325 degrees.
3. For filling, beat together the cream cheese and sugar until smooth and creamy. Gently mix in eggs, one at a time, until blended. Mix in the pumpkin, spices and cream. Pour evenly into crust. Bake in the center of the oven for 1½ hours. Turn off the oven and let cheesecake sit in the oven, with the door closed, 30 minutes longer. Place on a rack to cool.
4. While the cheesecake is cooling, caramelize the walnuts. Bring butter, sugar and lemon juice slowly to a boil in a heavy saucepan, stirring often to dissolve sugar. Stir in walnuts and let mixture boil slowly for 5 minutes. Remove from heat.
5. Decorate top of cooled cheesecake with the caramelized walnuts. Refrigerate overnight before serving.

Serves 12-16

Confections

Signal Mountain Lookout

"Photographing in High Places," 1872

William Henry Jackson's horsepacker took this picture of Jackson near the top of Table Mountain in 1872. Jackson, a photographer who traveled with the Hayden Surveys, took the first pictures of the Grand Teton from this vantage point.

Cream Cheese Mints
Latitia Roskatool

These are tasty, pretty and easy to make. If made with decorative holiday candy molds, they make a great gift or nice addition to a special gathering.

1   3-oz. pkg. cream cheese, softened to room temperature.
3   cups confectioners' sugar
½   tsp. peppermint flavoring
      sugar
      food color as desired

1. Mix all ingredients except food color together in a large bowl. Knead well to blend. Divide dough into smaller portions, place in bowls and add different food colors to each portion, if desired.
2. Roll into ½-inch balls, then roll in granulated sugar. Press with a fork to flatten. Or, press small amounts of mixture into decorative rubber or plastic candy molds dusted with powdered sugar. Allow mints to dry overnight.

Tip: Work with small amounts of dough at a time so it doesn't dry out before it is formed. Keep remainder of dough in a plastic bag or lidded container until you are ready to work with it.

Yield: Varies with mold size. Approximately 3 dozen mints.

Peppermint Bark
Cindy Fischer

A Christmastime favorite.

10   1-oz. white chocolate baking squares
½   cup crushed peppermint candies or candy canes

1. Cover a large baking sheet with aluminium foil. Set aside.
2. Place baking squares in a heavy saucepan over low heat. Stir constantly until squares are just melted, about 7 minutes.
3. Remove from heat and pour on foil-covered baking sheet, using a thin spatula to evenly spread the melted chocolate about ¼-inch thick. Sprinkle chocolate with crushed candy. Lightly press into chocolate with a spatula.
4. Refrigerate for 10 minutes or until chocolate has set. Break into pieces and store refrigerated in a covered container. Keeps up to 5 days.

Yield: About 2½ dozen pieces

Mounds™ *Simone Christensen*

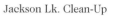
Jackson Lk. Clean-Up

After the completion of Jackson Lake dam in 1919, rising waters killed over 7,000 acres of lodgepole pine trees, creating unsightly log-jams along the shore. CCC crews were employed to remove the logs the summers of 1933-1937, finally completing one of the biggest undertakings in the program's history.

Coconut lovers will go wild over the homemade version of this famous candy. The recipe earned 16-year-old Simone reserve champion honors at the 2002 Teton County Fair.

- 1 cup sweetened condensed milk
- 1 envelope unflavored gelatin
- 1 14-oz pkg. flaked coconut
- 1 6-oz. pkg. milk chocolate chips

1. In a medium sized bowl, combine sweetened condensed milk, gelatin and coconut. Stir to blend, cover, and chill for 2 hours in the refrigerator.
2. Shortly before you are ready to assemble the candy, melt the chocolate on top of a double boiler. When melted and smooth, remove from heat source.
3. Remove coconut mixture from refrigerator. Roll into small balls, stick with toothpick and dip into melted chocolate. Place on cookie sheet lined with wax paper. When all candies have been made, place cookie sheet in refrigerator to harden chocolate. Store covered in a cool place. To make Almond Joys™, shape coconut mixture around a whole almond before dipping in chocolate.

Yield: 2 dozen

Jackson Lake, 1872. Photo by
W.H. Jackson

Elk antlers, 1912

Chocolate Truffles

Putzi Harrington

Divine decadence.

¼ cup heavy cream
2 tbsp. Grand Marnier or other liqueur
1 6-oz. pkg. chocolate chips
4 tbsp. butter, softened
unsweetened, powdered cocoa

1. In a small, heavy saucepan over low heat, bring cream to a boil. Continue boiling until cream is reduced to 2 tbsp.
2. Remove from heat and stir in liqueur and chocolate chips. Return to low heat and stir until chocolate melts. Whisk in softened butter until mixture is smooth.
3. Pour into shallow bowl and refrigerate until firm, about 40 minutes.
4. Scoop chocolate up with a teaspoon or melon baller to shape into 1-inch balls. Roll in unsweetened cocoa and place in paper candy cups. Cover and store in refrigerator.

Yield: 2 dozen truffles

White Chocolate Truffles

Ditto above.

1½ lbs. white confectionary coating
(sometimes called almond bark or candy coating)
9 tbsp. butter, no substitutes
2 tbsp. whipping cream
¼ cup powdered sugar
additional powdered sugar

1. Melt confectionary coating, butter and cream in the top of a double boiler over low heat, stirring frequently until smooth.
2. Add sugar and stir until incorporated.
3. Pour into 8-inch square baking pan. Cover and chill for 20 minutes or until lightly hardened.
4. Use a teaspoon or small melon ball to scoop out and form into 1-inch balls. Roll in powdered sugar. Refrigerate in an airtight container until ready to be served.

Yield: 4 dozen

Maple Walnut Creams

Easy to make chocolates with a creamy maple center.

- 1 cup butter, softened (no substitutions)
- 3½ cups powdered sugar
- 2 tbsp. pure maple syrup
- 2 cups chopped walnuts
- 2 cups semisweet chocolate chips
- 1 cup butterscotch chips

1. In a medium bowl, cream butter, powdered sugar and maple syrup together until smooth and well blended. Stir in chopped walnuts. Form into 1-inch balls and place on cookie sheets lined with wax paper. Freeze until firm but not frozen, about 30 minutes.
2. Melt chips on top of a double boiler.
3. Roll each candy in chocolate and put back on baking sheets. Refrigerate cookie sheets until chocolate has hardened. Store, covered, in the refrigerator.

Yield: 5 dozen

Christmas Caramels
Donna Spurlock

A nice gift...if you can get smuggle them away from home!

- 2 cups sugar
- 1 cup firmly packed light brown sugar
- 1 cup butter, softened
- 1 cup milk
- 1 cup whipping cream
- 1 cup light corn syrup
- 1 tsp. pure vanilla extract

1. Butter a 13x9-inch baking pan and set aside.
2. In a 4-quart, heavy saucepan, combine all ingredients except vanilla. Stir to blend. Cook over low heat, stirring occasionally, until sugar is dissolved and the butter is melted. Continue cooking mixture, without stirring, until a candy thermometer reaches 248 degrees or a small amount of the caramel mixture dropped into ice water forms a firm ball.
3. Remove mixture from heat and beat in vanilla. Pour into prepared pan and cool completely. Cut into ¾ x 2-inch pieces and wrap in colored cellophane, plastic wrap or wax paper (securely twisting ends closed).

Yield: 6 dozen

Candy Success

Using the correct equipment when making candy spells the difference between yum and yucky results. Use the size saucepan specified in the recipe. If your pan is too small, the candy mixture may boil over; too large, and it might not cover the candy thermometer's bulb, giving an inaccurate reading. A thermometer is indispensable for candy-making, removing the guesswork from candy temperatures. Candy recipes are based on a precise balance between ingredients and temperature. Measure accurately and don't substitute ingredients. Don't rush a candy mixture by cooking it at higher temperatures than the recipe directs, or slow it down by reducing the heat.

Pecan Toffee Triangles

An easy-to-make treat that appeals to both adults and kids.

American White
Pelican

This large, white migratory bird is seen at Oxbow Bend and Jackson Lake spring through fall. Pelicans use their enlarged pouches as a fish scoop. Small groups work cooperatively to herd fish into shallower water for easier fishing.

24 2-inch graham cracker squares
½ lb. butter (no substitutes)
1 cup light brown sugar
1½ cup chopped pecans
1 6 oz. pkg. semi-sweet chocolate chips

1. Preheat oven to 350 degrees.
2. Place graham crackers on a large, rimmed ungreased cookie sheet.
3. In a heavy saucepan, melt butter and brown sugar over medium heat, stirring occasionally. Once melted, stir constantly until mixture comes to a boil. Boil for 5 minutes, continuing to stir constantly.
4. Remove from heat and spread evenly over graham crackers. Sprinkle with chocolate chips and pecans and place in preheated oven. Bake for 10 minutes.
5. Remove from oven and let cool on wire rack for 10 minutes. Cut between each graham cracker square, then diagonally across the cracker to make 48 triangles. Remove from sheet and cool completely on wire racks. Store in covered container.

Yield: 48 triangles

Award-Winning Toffee *Simone Christensen*

This excellent confection garnered a purple ribbon at the 2002 Teton County Fair.

1 cup pecans, chopped
½ cup butter
¾ cup brown sugar, firmly packed
½ cup semisweet chocolate chips

1. Generously butter an 8 or 9-inch square pan. Spread pecans on the bottom of the pan. Set aside.
2. Put butter and brown sugar in a saucepan. Place over medium heat and stir constantly until mixture comes to a boil. Boil for 7 minutes, continuing to stir constantly.
3. Remove from heat and immediately spread over nuts.
4. Sprinkle chocolate chips over the hot mixture. Wait 1 minute, then evenly spread melted chips with a spoon. Cool completely before cutting into 1½-inch squares.

Yield: 36 pieces

Chocolate Pecan Clusters

Easy and delicious.

1½ lbs. good-quality chocolate, broken into pieces
1 7-oz. jar marshmallow creme
5 cups sugar
1 13-oz. can evaporated milk
½ cup butter (no substitutes)
6 cups pecan halves

1. Place chocolate and marshmallow creme in a large bowl. Set aside.
2. Combine sugar, evaporated milk and butter together in a heavy saucepan. Bring to a boil over medium heat, stirring constantly. Continue to cook and stir for 8 minutes.
3. Remove from heat and pour hot mixture into marshmallow creme and white chocolate mixture, stirring until well blended. Add pecans and stir until incorporated.
4. Drop by teaspoons onto wax paper and cool until set. Store in covered container.

Yield: 10-12 dozen

Miracle Fudge

Judy Schmitt

A traditional, rich chocolate fudge.

1 cup semi-sweet chocolate chips
1 8-oz. Hershey's™ milk chocolate bar, broken in pieces
1 small jar marshmallow creme
1 6-oz. can evaporated milk
2 cups sugar
1 tsp. pure vanilla extract
½ cup chopped nuts (optional)

1. Put chocolate chips and milk chocolate bar pieces in a large heat-proof bowl. Set aside. Butter a 13x9-inch or larger pan.
2. Combine sugar, evaporated milk and marshmallow creme in a heavy saucepan. Bring to a boil over medium heat. Boil for 8 minutes, stirring often.
3. Remove from burner and pour hot mixture into bowl containing chocolate. Stir vigorously with a wooden spoon to blend. Add vanilla and nuts; stir to blend.
4. Spread evenly in prepared pan. Chill in refrigerator to harden before cutting into 1-inch squares.

Yield: Varies with pan size

Soft Fudge

If your batch of fudge doesn't harden, refrigerate it then crumble it into pieces. Store in a sealed bag in the freezer. Use the frozen pieces in cookie dough or brownies as you would chocolate chunks or chips.

**Huckleberry
Fire Lookout**

In 1938, CCC crews built this two-story, 15 x 17-foot lookout on Huckleberry Ridge, one of six fire lookouts on the northern portion of Bridger-Teton National Forest. It was last used as an active lookout the summer of 1957. The rustic structure was added to the National Register of Historic Places in the 1980s.

Walnut Date Chews   *Marcia Woods*

A scrumptious confection, perfect for gift-giving or hoarding yourself.

1	cup chopped, pitted dates
1	cup chopped walnuts
½	cup brown sugar, lightly packed
2	tbsp. flour
½	tsp. baking soda
1	tsp. cream of tartar
1	egg, beaten
	granulated sugar

1. Preheat oven to 350 degrees. Grease a 9-inch square pan. Set aside.
2. In a large bowl, combine everything except granulated sugar. Stir to blend.
3. Press mixture evenly into prepared pan. Bake for 20 minutes.
4. Let cool just enough to handle, about 10 minutes. Scoop out with a teaspoon and form into 1-inch balls. Roll in granulated sugar. Store in a covered container in a cool place.

Yield: Approximately 2½ dozen

Hard Suckers   *Jed Christensen*

Fun on a stick! Jed's recipe for this time-honored pleasure won a purple ribbon at the 2002 Teton County Fair, earning him the right to enter his suckers in the Wyoming State Fair.

2	cups sugar
½	cup corn syrup
	food coloring of choice
½	cup water
1	tsp. flavored oil of choice

1. Grease sucker molds and cookie sheet, or lightly spray sheet with cooking spray. Arrange molds on cookie sheet.
2. In a medium saucepan, combine sugar, water and corn syrup. Cook over medium heat, stirring constantly until sugar is dissolved. Continue cooking until a candy thermometer reaches 300 degrees.
3. Remove mixture from heat and add flavored oil and food coloring. Pour into arranged molds and insert sucker sticks. Set until firm before removing molds.

Yield: Approximately 20 suckers. Recipe can be doubled.

Appendix

Snake River Ferry, 1916

Ingredient Equivalents

Quick! How many slices of bread makes 1 cup of soft bread crumbs? If you don't know off the top of your head (and why *would* you!), the yield chart below will help you out

When the recipe specifies: **You Need:**

Apple, 1 cup sliced .... 1 medium-sized apple
Banana, 1 cup mashed .... 3 medium-sized bananas
Beans and peas, 2¼ cup cooked .... 1 cup dried
Bread crumbs
    1 cup soft .... 2 slices fresh bread
    1 cup cubed .... 2 slices fresh bread
Butter or margarine
    ¼ cup or 4 tbsp. .... ½ stick
    2 cups or 4 sticks .... 1 pound
Cabbage, 4 cups shredded .... 1 small cabbage
Carrot
    1 cup grated .... 1 large carrot
    2½ cups sliced .... 1 lb. raw carrots
    2 cups cooked .... 7-9 raw carrots
Cheese
    Blue, 1 cup .... 4 oz. crumbled
    Cottage cheese, 1 cup .... 8 ozs.
    Cream cheese, 1 cup .... 8 ozs.
    Parmesan, 1¼ cups grated .... 4 ozs.
    Swiss or cheddar, 2 cups shredded .... 8 ozs.
Cherries, 2 cups pitted .... 1 quart
Chocolate
    1 square .... 1 ounce
    3-4 tbsp., grated .... 1 square
Chocolate chips, 1 cup .... 6-oz. package
Cocoa, 4 cups... 1 pound
Coconut, 2⅔ cups .... 8 oz. package
Corn Flakes, 1 cup crushed .... 3 cups uncrushed
Crumbs, 1 cup finely crumbled
    chocolate wafer .... 19 wafers
    graham.. 14 squares
    vanilla wafer .... 22 cookies
    soda crackers.. 28 crackers
    Zweiback crackers... 4 crackers
Cornmeal, 3 cups .... 1 pound
Crackers, saltine, 1 cup crumbs .... 14 squares
Cucumbers, 1 pound .... 2 6-inch cucumbers
Dates, pitted, 2 cups .... 1 lb. package
Egg whites, 1 cup .... 6-7 large eggs
Flour, all-purpose sifted, 4 cups .... 1 pound

Grapefruit
    juice, ⅔ cup .... 1 medium grapefruit
    grated rind, 3-4 tbsp. .... 1 medium grapefruit
Green or red bell pepper, 1 cup chopped .... 1 large pepper
Green Beans, 4 cups cooked fresh cut .... 1 pound beans
Horseradish, 1 tbsp. fresh .... 2 tbsp. bottled
Lemon
    1 tsp. grated rind .... 1 medium-sized lemon
    2 tbsp. lemon juice .... 1 medium-sized lemon
    1 cup lemon juice .... 6 medium lemons
Lime ....
    juice, 2 tbsp. .... 1 medium lime
    grated rind, 2 tsp. .... 1 medium lime
Milk
    condensed, 1¼ cups .... 14-oz. can
    evaporated, ⅔ cup .... 6-oz. can
    evaporated, 1⅔ cup .... 14½-oz. can
Noodles, 1½ cups cooked .... 1 cup raw
Nuts
    almonds, 3½ cups .... 1 pound. chopped
    walnuts broken, 3 cups .... 1 pound chopped
    walnuts or pecans, 4 cups chopped .... 1 pound shelled
Onion, 1 cup chopped .... 1 large onion
Orange
    grated rind, 4 tsp. .... 1 medium orange
    juice, 1 cup fresh squeezed .... 3 medium oranges
Pasta
    elbow macaroni, 4 cups cooked .... 8 ozs.
    medium-wide noodles, 3¾ cups cooked .... 8 ozs.
    fine noodles, 5½ cups cooked .... 8 ozs.
    spaghetti, 4 cups cooked .... 8 ozs.
Peaches, 2 cups sliced .... 4 medium-sized peaches
Peanuts, 1 cup .... 5 ozs.
Potatoes, 1 cups sliced, raw .... 1 medium-sized potato
Prunes, 4 cups cooked .... 1 pound package
Raisins, 3½ cups .... 1 pound package
Raspberries, 2¼ cups .... 1 pint
Rice
    white, 3 cups cooked .... 1 cup uncooked
    instant, 1½ cups cooked .... 1 cup uncooked
    brown, 3-4 cups cooked .... 1 cup uncooked
Strawberries, 2 cups sliced .... 1 pint
Sugar
    granulated, 2 cups .... 1 pound
    brown, firmly packed, 2¼ cups .... 1 pound
    confectioners or powder, 4½ cups .... 1 pound
Tomato, 1 cup chopped .... 1 large tomato
Whipped cream, 2 cups .... 1 cup heavy cream

Measurement Equivalents

Measure   **Equals**

Teaspoons, dry ingredients
    under 1/8 tsp. .... dash or pinch
    1½ tsp. .... ½ tbsp.
    3 tsp. .... 1 tbsp.
Tablespoons, dry ingredients
    1 tbsp. .... 3 tsp.
    4 tbsp. .... ¼ cup
    5⅓ tbsp. .... ⅓ cup
    8 tbsp. .... ½ cup
    10⅔ tbsp. .... ⅔ cup
    16 tbsp. .... 1 cup
Cups, dry ingredients
    ¼ cup .... 4 tbsp.
    ⅓ cup .... 5½ tbsp.
    ½ cup .... 8 tbsp.
    ⅔ cup .... 10⅔ tbsp.
    1 cup .... 16 tbsp.
Cups, liquid ingredients
    1 cup .... ½ pint
    2 cups .... pint
    4 cups .... 1 quart
Ounces, solid ingredients
    16 ounces, solid .... 1 pound
Liquid measurements
    1 fluid ounce .... 2 tbsp.
    1 jigger .... 3 tbsp.
    2 fluid ounces .... ¼ cup
    4 fluid ounces .... ½ cup
    8 fluid ounces .... 1 cup
    2 cups .... 1 pint
    4 cups .... 1 quart
    4 quarts .... 1 gallon
Liquid and solid measurements
    8 quarts .... 1 peck
    4 pecks .... 1 bushel

Metric to U.S. Conversions

Milliliters	U.S. Equivalent
5 ml.	1 tsp.
15 ml.	1 tbsp.
30 ml.	2 tbsp.
60 ml.	¼ cup
80 ml.	⅓ cup
90 ml.	6 tbsp. or ⅜ cup
120 ml.	½ cup
160 ml	⅔ cup
180 ml	¾ cup
240 ml	1 cup or 8 ounces, dry
240 ml	1/2 pint or 8 fluid ounces
480 ml	1 pint or 2 cups
.473 liter (480 ml)	1 pint or 16 fluid ounces
960 ml or .95 liter	2 pints or 1 quart
1 liter	1.05 quarts or .26 gallons
3.8 liters	4 quarts or 1 gallon

Grams	U.S. Equivalent
28 grams	1 ounce
454 grams	1 pound

Celsius to Fahrenheit Conversions

Celsius	Fahrenheit
93 degrees	200 degrees
106 degrees	225 degrees
121 degrees	250 degrees
135 degrees	275 degrees
149 degrees	300 degrees
163 degrees	325 degrees
176 degrees	350 degrees
191 degrees	375 degrees
205 degrees	400 degrees
218 degrees	425 degrees
231 degrees	450 degrees
246 degrees	475 degrees
260 degrees	500 degrees
288 degrees	550 degrees

Substitutions

You are in the middle of whipping up that special holiday dish, and discover the sour cream is so outdated it's become a science experiment. It's happened to all of us. What to you do when you discover you are missing an important ingredient? Check to see if the solution is in this list of in-a-pinch substitutions.

Ingredient	Substitution
Allspice, 1 tsp.	½ tsp. cinnamon + ½ tsp. cloves
Baking powder, 1 tsp.	¼ tsp. baking soda + ½ tsp. cream of tartar + ¼ tsp. cornstarch
Brown sugar, 1 cup firmly packed	1 cup sugar + 2 tbsp. molasses
Buttermilk or sour milk, 1 cup	1 tbsp. vinegar or lemon juice + enough milk to make 1 cup. Stir and let rest for 5 minutes.
Cake flour, 1 cup	1 cup less 2 tbsp. all-purpose flour
Chocolate, 1 square unsweetened	3 tbsp. unsweetened cocoa powder + 1 tbsp. butter or margarine
Corn syrup, 1 cup	1 cup sugar + ¼ cup additional liquid used in recipe
Cornstarch, 1 tbsp.	2 tbsp. flour or 2 tbsp. quick-cooking tapioca
Flour, self-rising, 1 cup	1 cup all-purpose flour + ½ tsp. salt + 1 tsp. baking powder
Fruit liqueur, 1 tbsp.	1 tbsp. fruit juice
Garlic, 1 clove	¼ tsp. garlic powder
Gingerroot, grated, 1 tsp.	¼ tsp. ground ginger
Herbs, fresh, 1 tbsp.	1 tsp. dried herbs
Honey, 1 cup	1¼ cups sugar plus ¼ cup water
Ketchup, 1 cup (for cooking)	1 cup tomato sauce + ½ cup sugar and 2 tbsp. vinegar
Lemon juice, 1 tsp.	¼ tsp. vinegar (not balsamic)
Molasses, 1 cup	1 cup honey
Milk, whole, 1 cup	½ cup evaporated milk + 1 cup water
Mushrooms, 1 cup fresh	1 6-oz. can mushrooms, drained
Mustard, 1 tbsp. prepared	1 tsp. dry mustard + 1 tbsp. water
Onion, 1/4 cup chopped	1 tbsp. instant minced, rehydrated
Powdered sugar, 1 cup	1 cup granulated sugar + 1 tsp. cornstarch
Pumpkin Pie Spice, 1 tsp.	½ tsp. cinnamon + ¼ tsp. ginger + ⅛ tsp. allspice + ⅛ tsp. nutmeg
Sour cream, 1 cup (for baking)	1 cup plain yogurt
Tomato juice, 1 cup	½ cup tomato sauce + ½ cup water
Tomato paste, 1 tbsp.	1 tbsp. tomato ketchup
Tomato sauce, 2 cups	¾ cup tomato paste + 1 cup water
Tomato soup, 1 103/4-oz. can condensed	1 8-oz. can tomato sauce + ¼ cup water
Vanilla bean, 1 inch	1 tsp. vanilla extract
Yogurt, 1 cup	1 cup buttermilk

Baking Dish and Pan Sizes

Pay attention to what size pan a recipe specifies. A larger, shallower pan means your creation may bake or cook sooner. A deeper, smaller pan may mean it needs more time. Adjust accordingly. If you don't have a speciality pan, pick a pan with similar dimensions and volumes. Manufacturers measure pans across the top.

Specialty Pans by Dimension

Tube pans
    7½ x 3-in. bundt .... 6 cups
    9 x 3½-in. bundt .... 9 cups
    9 x 3½-in. angel cake .... 12 cups
    10 x 3¾-in. bundt .... 12 cups
    10 x 4-in. angel cake .... 18 cups
Molds ....
    7 x 5½ x 4-in. mold .... 6 cups
    8 x 2¼-in. ring mold .... 4½ cups
    9¼ x 2¾-in. ring mold .... 8 cups
Springform pans
    8½ x 3-in. .... 12 cups
    9¾ x 3-in. .... 14 cups
    10⅛ x 3-in. .... 15 cups
Tart pan, removable bottom
    9 x 1-in .... 4 cups
Jelly-roll pan
    15¼ x 10 .... 10 cups
Loaf pan
    8½ x 3⅝-in .... 6 cups
    9¼ x 5¼-in .... 7½ cups

Pans by volume

4-5 cup pan
    9-inch pie plate
    8-inch round cake pan
    7⅜ x 3⅝-in. loaf pan
6-cup pan
    9-inch round cake pan
    10-inch pie plate
    8½ x 3⅝-in. loaf pan
8-cup pan
    8-inch square pan
    11 x 7-inch baking pan
10-cup pan
    9-inch square pan
    11¾ x 7½-in. baking pan
12-cup and over pans
    13½ x 8½-in glass pan .... 12 cups
    13 x 9-in metal pan .... 15 cups
    14 x 10½-in roasting pan .... 19 cups

Spice Life

Spices last indefinitely, but begin losing strength as they age. They are best used within the time frame listed below.

Extracts .... 4 years, except vanilla, which has unlimited shelf life
Seasoning blends .... 1-2 years
Dried herbs .... 1-3 years
Whole spices .... 4 years
Ground spices .... 3 years
Poppy and Sesame seeds .... 2 years
Other seeds .... 4 years

A Well-Stocked Kitchen

Certain spices and ingredients are used over and over in recipes. It is helpful to keep these items in stock. Buy sizes you will use up in a reasonable time frame, so you don't end up throwing things out. Remember: these are just suggestions. If you would never use currants, don't buy them.

Spices and Herbs
Allspice
Basil
Bay leaves
Cardamom
Celery seeds
Chili powder
Cinnamon, ground
Cinnamon sticks
Cloves
Curry
Dill
Dry Mustard
Ginger, ground &
  crystallized
Mace
Marjoram
Nutmeg, ground
  and whole
Oregano
Paprika
Pepper, black, red
  flakes, white and
  cayenne
Peppercorns
Poppy Seeds
Rosemary
Sage
Salt, table and
  kosher
Sesame Seeds
Tarragon
Thyme
Turmeric

Baking Items
Almond extract
Almonds
Baking powder
Baking soda
Bisquick
Cake flour

Chocolate chips
Chocolate, squares
Cocoa, unsweetened
Coconut
Cooking spray
Corn syrup
Cornmeal
Cream of tartar
Currants
Dates
Decorating sugars,
  sprinkles
Flour, all-purpose
Gelatin, unflavored
Hazelnut extract
Maple extract
Milk: evaporated &
  condensed
Molasses
Oatmeal
Peanuts
Pecans
Pinenuts
Raisins
Shortening
Sugar, granulated,
  brown, powdered,
  superfine
Vanilla Extract
Vanilla beans
Walnuts
Yeast

**Condiments
and Sauces**
Fudge sauce
Hoisin sauce
Honey
Horseradish
Ketchup
Mustard
Soy Sauce

Tabasco sauce
Teriyaki sauce
Worcestershire sauce

General Pantry
Artichokes: hearts
  and bottoms
Beans, canned
  baked
  kidney
  garbanzo
Beans, dried
  Great Northern
  navy
Bouillon cubes
  beef and chicken
Bread crumbs
Broth, canned
  chicken, beef
  and vegetable
Capers
Cereal
Chiles, canned
Clams, chopped or
  whole
Crackers and chips
Coffee and tea
  Fruit, canned
Lentils
Liqueurs, amaretto,
  Grand Marnier,
  port
Maple Syrup
Oils: vegetable,
  olive, peanut
Olives, black and
  green
Onions
Oysters, canned
Pastas of choice
Peanut butter
Pesto, jarred

Potatoes
Powdered drink
  mixes
Pumpkin, canned
Preserves and jams
Rice: white, brown
  and wild
Roasted red pepper,
  jarred
Spaghetti sauce
Sun-dried tomatoes
Tapioca
Tomatoes, canned
  sauce, paste and
  whole
Tuna
Vinegar: white, red
  wine, balsamic,
  rice, cider
Water chestnuts
Wines
  sherry
  Marsala
  dry white
  dry red

Refrigerator Stock
Butter, regular and
  unsalted
Capers
Cheese: cheddar,
  Swiss, Parmesan
Cream cheese
Eggs
Half and half
Mayonnaise
Milk, skim & whole
Pickles
Sour Cream
Tortillas
Whipping cream
Yogurt

Index

Gros Ventre School, 1905-1916

A

Acorn Squash with Apples 112
Almond
  Almond Biscotti 216
  Almond Fig Squares 215
  Frozen Coffee Almond Indulgence 204
  Mandarin Orange Salad with Sugared
    Almonds 87
  Raspberry Almond Streusel Muffins 27
  Red Pepper-Almond Pesto 83
Amaretto 56
Amish Friendship Bread 33
Appetizers
  Artichoke-Green Chile Dip 71
  Best-Ever Guacamole 74
  Black Bean and Corn Salsa 81
  Blue Cheese Dip 72
  Brandied Raisin Brie 68
  Bruschetta 66
  Cheesy Onion Dip 72
  Chili Chips 78
  Chinese Spring (Egg) Rolls 63
  Chutney Curry Cheese Ball 69
  Crabmeat hors d'oeuvres 62
  Creamy Roasted Red Pepper Salsa 80
  Cucumber Rounds with Sour Cream
    and Chutney 67
  Dare-Deviled Eggs 67
  Deans Favorite Snack 68
  Eight Layer Fiesta Dip 74
  Fresh Tomato Salsa 81
  Garlic Bagel Chips 77
  Gingered Chicken Satay 62
  Hot Pecan Dip 72
  Island Fruit Salsa 80
  Mango White Bean Salsa 79
  Mexican Pinwheels 61
  Mushrooms Hana 60
  Peach Salsa 79
  Peppered Pecans 70
  Pico de Gallo 82
  Pita Crisps with Tuna Tapenade 75
  Roasted Eggplant Spread 70
  Roasted Garlic 66
  Roasted Red Pepper and
    Cream Cheese Dip 73
  Sausage Cheese Balls 61
  Sicilian-Style Caponata 65
  Stuffed Mushrooms 60
  Toasted Walnut Bites 69
  Veggie Pizza Bites 76
Apple
  Acorn Squash with Apples 112
  Baked Apples and Butternut Squash
    127
  Baked Cinnamon Apple French Toast 5
  Classic Apple Crisp 201
  Glazed Apple Nut Bread 31
  Smoked Salmon and Apple Quesadilla
    Wedges with Horseradish Creme 76
  Sparkling Apple Cider 44
Apricot
  Apricot-Cashew Couscous 115
  Ricotta Parmesan Stuffed Chicken with
    Apricot Sauce 161
Artichoke
  Artichoke-Green Chile Dip 71
  Creamy Fettuccine with Artichoke
    Hearts and Mushrooms 188
  Frozen Lemon-Blue Cheese Salad with
    Marinated Artichokes 98
Asparagus
  Penne with Spinach and Asparagus 186
  Potato Soup with Asparagus 134
Avocado
  Avocado and Tomato Salad 91
  Best-Ever Guacamole 74
  Chicken and Avocado Soup 144
  Patty's Cold Avocado Soup 133
  White Gazpacho with Crab, Avocado
    and Tomato 132
Award-Winning Toffee 252

B

Bacon
  Bacon Roasted Turkey with Cornbread
    Dressing 194
  Potato Bacon Pizza 184
  Spinach and Bacon Stuffed Tomatoes
    120
Bagel
  Garlic Bagel Chips 77
Baked Apples and Butternut Squash 127
Baked Chicken Reuben 167
Baked Cinnamon Apple French Toast 5

Baked Eggplant, Roasted Red Peppers, Tomatoes and Cucumber in Pita 156
Baked Short Ribs 175
Baked Tomatoes with Herbs 119
Baking Pan Sizes 261
Balsamic Orange Salad Dressing 105
Banana
    Baked Banana 8
    Bananas Foster 203
    Best Banana Blueberry Bread 30
Barley
    Booktrader Barley 118
    Steamed Brown Rice and Barley 118
Basic Vinaigrette 104
Basil
    Basil Tomato Tart 193
    Marilyn's Pesto 83
    Tomato Basil Soup 139
Beans
    Bean and Seashell Pasta Salad 99
    Bean Me Up Soup 141
    Black Bean and Corn Salsa 81
    Black Bean Soup 140
    Kale and Bean Soup 142
    Mango White Bean Salsa 79
    Old Settler Beans 125
    Red Beans and Rice 184
    Southwestern Bean Salad 100
    Teton Trail Ride Beans 126
Beef
    Baked Short Ribs 175
    Cabbage and Beef Soup 146
    Imperial Beef Tenderloin 172
    Marinated Flank Steak 172
    Roast Beef Sandwiches with Roasted Red Onions 155
    Roast Beef with Herb Crust 171
    Slow Cooked Beef Burritos 174
    Spicy Beef Stew 147
    Steak Fajitas 173
Beer Biscuits 39
Best Banana Blueberry Bread 30
Best-Ever Guacamole 74
Beverages
    Amaretto 56
    Chai (Tea Latte) 48
    Cranberry Liqueur 57
    Cranberry Tea Punch 52
    Ginger Lemonade 44

    Hot Buttered Rum 54
    Hot Vanilla 52
    Iced Toffee 49
    Kahlua 57
    Lucilla and Diego's Orange Margaritas 56
    Mexican Chocolate 51
    Mint Iced Tea 45
    Mocha Frappuccino 51
    Old Fashioned Christmas Egg Nog 55
    Peach Smoothie 44
    Peaches and Cream Liqueur 58
    Perfect Hot Toddy 54
    Raspberry Mint Crush 48
    Southern Iced Tea 45
    Sparkling Apple Cider 44
    Sparkling Spiced Ice Tea 46
    Sports Energy Drink 47
    Teton Tea 53
    Ultimate Mocha 50
    Vanilla Iced Coffee 49
    Watermelon Cooler 46
    White Hot Chocolate 52
Biscotti
    Almond Biscotti 216
Biscuits
    Beer Biscuits 39
    Cloud Biscuits 40
    Sourdough Buttermilk Biscuits 38
Black Bean and Corn Salsa 81
Black Bean Soup 140
Blue Cheese Dip 72
Blueberry
    Best Banana Blueberry Bread 30
    Blueberry Bran Muffins 23
    Ginger Blueberry Crumble 200
Bookbinder's Light Fish Chowder 150
Booktrader Barley 118
Bran
    Blueberry Bran Muffins 23
    Molasses Bran Bread 38
Brandied Raisin Brie 68
Brandied Sweet Potatoes 112
Brandy Sauce 208
Bread
    Amish Friendship Bread 33
    Best Banana Blueberry Bread 30
    Bishops Bread 32
    Cranberry Orange Raisin Bread 35

Bread, cont.
  Easy Herb Bread 40
  Focaccia 41
  French Bread 37
  Garlic Bread 41
  Glazed Apple Nut Bread 31
  Glazed Lemon Pecan Bread 34
  Mango Macadamia Nut Bread 29
  Molasses Bran Bread 38
  Peanut Butter Bread 30
  Perfect Corn Bread 42
  Zucchini Bread with Gingered Cream
    Cheese 32
Brie
  Brandied Raisin Brie 68
Broccoli
  Citrus Broccoli Slaw 92
  Crunchy Broccoli Salad 99
Brownies
  Caramel Nut Brownies 211
  Turtle Brownies 210
Bruschetta 66
Buckwheat Waffles 12
Burritos
  Slow Cooked Beef Burritos 174
Butter
  Hot Buttered Fruit with Ice Cream 200
  Hot Buttered Rum 54
  Strawberry Butter 9
Buttercream Frosting 226
Buttercream Syrup 13
Buttermilk
  Oatmeal-Buttermilk Pancakes 9
  Sourdough Buttermilk Biscuits 38
  The Old Painted Porch Pancakes 11
Butternut Squash Purée 113

C

Cabbage
  Cabbage and Beef Soup 146
  Company Cabbage 119
Cake
  Chocolate Kahlua Cake 237
  Green Devil Cake 234
  Heavenly Chocolate Cake with
    Chocolate Buttercream Frosting 236

James Rosner's World Famous
  Chocolate Chip Pound Cake 242
  Lantelme Cake 240
  Orange Spongecake with Rum Icing 238
  Pineapple Cake with Broiled Coconut
    Pecan Frosting 237
  Pound Cake 241
  Pumpkin Bundt Cake 239
Candy, see also confections
  Hard Suckers 254
  Christmas Caramels 251
  Miracle Fudge 253
  Mounds 249
Caponata, Sicilian-Style 65
Caramel
  Christmas Caramels 251
  Caramel Nut Brownies 211
Caramelized
  Onions 123
  Pecans 86
  Walnuts 246
Caribbean Grilled Fish 176
Carrots
  Carrot Pudding with Hard Sauce 207
  Carrot Tarragon Soup 134
  Ginger Carrot Bisque 135
  Roasted Carrots and Parsnips 123
Cashew
  Apricot-Cashew Couscous 115
Cauliflower Soup 140
Chai (Tea Latte) 48
Cheese
  Blue Cheese Dip 72
  Cheese Ravioli with Rosemary and
    Lemon 191
  Cheesy Onion Dip 72
  Chutney Curry Cheese Ball 69
  Frozen Lemon-Blue Cheese Salad with
    Marinated Artichokes 98
  Macaroni and Cheese 189
  Sausage Cheese Balls 61
Cheesecake, Pumpkin 245
Cherry
  Cherry Bars 213
  Cherry Yogurt Muffins 21
Chicken
  Baked Chicken Reuben 167
  Chicken and Avocado Soup 144
  Chicken and Walnuts 167

Chicken Corn Chowder 145
Chicken Marsala 164
Chicken Teriyaki 165
Chicken with Hazelnuts and
    Mushrooms 162
Chicken with Lime Butter 166
Curried Chicken Salad 96
Easy Chicken Quesadillas 182
Flat Creek Ranch Grilled Curried
    Chicken Sandwiches 154
Gingered Chicken Satay 62
Key Lime Chicken 160
Linda's Southwestern Chicken
    Vegetable Soup 143
Parmesan Dijon Chicken 164
Ricotta Parmesan Stuffed Chicken with
    Apricot Sauce 161
Santa Fe Grilled Chicken Salad with
    Honey Lime Vinaigrette 94
Southwestern Grilled Chicken 160
Walnut Chicken Salad 93
White Chicken Chili 153
Chile
    Artichoke-Green Chile Dip 71
    Green Chile Stew 148
    Jean's Chile Rellenos 194
Chili
    Chili Chips 78
    Stacked Red Chili Enchiladas 192
    White Chicken Chili 153
Chilled Cucumber Soup 133
Chinese Spring (Egg) Rolls 63
Chinese Vegetable Salad with Honey
    Sesame Dressing 96
Chocolate
    Chocolate Ginger Cookies 221
    Chocolate Kahlua Cake 237
    Chocolate Pecan Clusters 253
    Chocolate Satin Icing 232
    Chocolate Truffles 250
    Green Devil Cake 234
    Heavenly Chocolate Cake with
        Chocolate Buttercream 236
    Janie Camenzind's Famous Fudgy,
        Flourless Chocolate Torte 230
    Mexican Chocolate 51
    Warm Chocolate Dessert with Soft
        Interior 235

Chocolate chip
    Chocolate Chip Coffee Cake 18
    Chocolate Chip Orange Muffins 20
    Espresso Chip Muffins with Mocha
        Cream 25
    Grandma Hays Chocolate Chip
        Cookies 224
    James Rosner's World Famous
        Chocolate Chip Pound Cake 242
    Matt's Favorite Chocolate Chip Cookie
        223
    Pecan Chocolate Chip Meringues 229
Chokecherry Syrup 13
Chowder
    Chicken Corn Chowder 145
    Fish, Bookbinder's Light 150
Christmas Caramels 251
Chutney
    Chutney Curry Cheese Ball 69
    Cucumber Rounds with Sour Cream
        and Chutney 67
Cinema Salad 89
Cinnamon
    Baked Cinnamon Apple French Toast 5
    Cinnamon Sugar Muffins 22
Citrus Broccoli Slaw 92
Classic Apple Crisp 201
Cloud Biscuits 40
Cocktails/Alcoholic drinks
    Hot Buttered Rum 54
    Lucilla & Diego's Orange Margaritas 56
    Perfect Hot Toddy 54
    Old Fashioned Christmas Egg Nog 55
Coconut
    Creamy Coconut Pie 242
    Frosted Coconut Macadamia Bars 216
    Mounds 249
    Nutty Coconut Brunch Cake 17
Coconut Pecan Frosting 238
Coffee
    Espresso Chip Muffins with Mocha
        Cream 25
    Frozen Coffee Almond Indulgence 204
    Iced Toffee 49
    Mocha Elegantissimo 50
    Mocha Frappuccino 51
    Vanilla Iced Coffee 49
Coffee Cake
    Chocolate Chip Coffee Cake 18

Cream Cheese Coffee Cake 18
Maple Nut Danish 19
Nutty Coconut Brunch Cake 17
Sour Cream Coffee Cake 16
Yogurt Poppy Seed Coffee Cake 16
Cold Dilled Peas 101
Company Cabbage 119
Condiments, see also sauces/salsas
Curry Mayonnaise 157
Zesty Hamburger Relish 84
Confections, see also candy
Award-Winning Toffee 252
Chocolate Pecan Clusters 253
Chocolate Truffles 250
Christmas Caramels 251
Cream Cheese Mints 248
Maple Walnut Creams 251
Miracle Fudge 253
Mounds 249
Pecan Toffee Triangles 252
Peppermint Bark 248
Walnut Date Chews 254
White Chocolate Truffles 250
Cookies
Almond Biscotti 216
Almond Fig Squares 215
Bird Nest Cookies 228
Cherry Bars 213
Chocolate Ginger Cookies 221
Chocolate Hazelnut Crescents 224
Cranberry Cookies 219
Frosted Coconut Macadamia Bars 216
Frosted Roll Out Cookies 226
Ginger Snaps 222
Grandma Hays Chocolate Chip Cookies
  224
Grove Farm Icebox Cookies 228
Iced Orange Drop Cookies 220
Lemon Cheese Bars 214
Matt's Favorite Chocolate Chip Cookie
  223
Oatmeal Crinkles 218
Oatmeal Fudge Bars 212
Old-Fashioned Raisin Cookies 227
Old-Fashioned Soft Sugar Cookies 225
Peanut Butter Bars 212
Pecan Chocolate Chip Meringues 229
Pecan Puffs 229
Quick & Easy Gingerbread Cookies 222

Ranger Cookies 217
Soft Molasses Cookies 220
Corn
Black Bean and Corn Salsa 81
Chicken Corn Chowder 145
Corn and Squash Pasta 191
Corn Pudding 124
Grits Soufflé 14
Perfect Corn Bread 42
Coucous, Apricot-Cashew 115
Crab
Crabmeat Hors d'oeuvres 62
White Gazpacho with Crab, Avocado
  and Tomato 132
Cranberry
Cranberry Cookies 219
Cranberry Liqueur 57
Cranberry Maple Vinaigrette 106
Cranberry Nut Pie 244
Cranberry Orange Raisin Bread 35
Cranberry Ricotta Pancakes 10
Cranberry Tea Punch 52
Glazed Cranberry Pork Roast 169
Grilled Turkey, Cheddar and Cranberry
  Sandwiches 158
Teton Tea 53
Toasted Walnut Cranberry Stuffing 129
Cream
Mocha Cream 25
Lemon Cream 6
Russian Cream with Raspberries 202
Vanilla Whipped Cream 231
Cream cheese
Cream Cheese Coffee Cake 18
Cream Cheese Mints 248
Gingered Cream Cheese
Roasted Red Pepper and Cream Cheese
  Dip 73
Creamed Tomato Soup with Cognac 138
Creamy Coconut Pie 242
Creamy Fettuccine with Artichoke Hearts
  and Mushrooms 188
Creamy Roasted Red Pepper Salsa 80
Crème Brulée, Easy 204
Crème Fraîche 163
Croutons, Herb 106
Crunchy Broccoli Salad 99
Cucumber
Baked Eggplant, Roasted Red Peppers,

Tomatoes and Cucumbers in Pita 156
Chilled Cucumber Soup 133
Cucumber and Yogurt Salad 98
Cucumber Rounds with Sour Cream
   and Chutney 67
Grilled Salmon with Cucumber Relish
   177
Curry
   Chutney Curry Cheese Ball 69
   Curried Chicken Salad 96
   Curried Fruit 127
   Flat Creek Ranch Grilled Curried
      Chicken Sandwiches 154
   Mango Curry Tuna Salad 92
   Curry Mayonnaise 157
   Pumpkin Curry Soup 136
Custard
   Easy Crème Brulée 204

Pink Grapefruit Sorbet 204
Sikarni 205
Strawberries with Brown Sugar and
   Sour Cream 199
Sunset Pears 202
Tiramisù 232
Turtle Brownies 210
Walnut Torte 231
Warm Chocolate Dessert with Soft
   Interior 235
Dips
   Artichoke-Green Chile Dip 71
   Best-Ever Guacamole 74
   Blue Cheese Dip 72
   Cheesy Onion Dip 72
   Eight Layer Fiesta Dip 74
   Hot Pecan Dip 72
   Roasted Red Pepper and Cream Cheese 73
Distinctly Different Slaw 91

D

Danish
   Maple Nut Danish 19
Danish Rice Pudding 206
Dare-Deviled Eggs 67
Dates
   Date Puree 24
   Date Torte 234
   Oatmeal Date Nut Muffins 24
   Walnut Date Chews 254
Deans Favorite Snack 68
Dessert, see also cakes, cookies, pies
   Bananas Foster 203
   Caramel Nut Brownies 211
   Classic Apple Crisp 201
   Date Torte 234
   Easy Crème Brulée 204
   Ed Opler's Strawberries Romanoff 198
   Fourth of July Berries 199
   Frozen Coffee Almond Indulgence 204
   Ginger Blueberry Crumble 200
   Ginger Ice Cream 203
   Hazelnut Torte with Chocolate Satin
      Icing 232
   Janie Camenzind's Famous Fudgy,
      Flourless Chocolate Torte 230
   Pavlova 209
   Peaches and Cream 198

E

Easy Chicken Quesadillas 182
Easy Crème Brulée 204
Easy Herb Bread 40
Ed Opler's Strawberries Romanoff 198
Eggplant
   Baked Eggplant, Roasted Red Peppers,
      Tomatoes and Cucumber in Pita 156
   Roasted Eggplant and Red Bell Pepper
      Soup 137
   Roasted Eggplant Spread 70
   Sicilian-Style Caponata 65
Eggroll, Chinese 63
Eggs
   Breakfast Casserole 15
   Dare-Deviled Eggs 67
   Sassy Eggs 2
   Spinach Ham Quiche 14
   Wildflower Baked Eggs with Herbs 2
Eight Layer Fiesta Dip 74
Elizabeth McCabe's Spinach Salad 88
Enchiladas, Stacked Red Chili 192
Equivalents, Ingredients 256
Equivalents, Measurements 258
Espresso Chip Muffins with Mocha Cream
   25

F

Fajitas
  Steak Fajitas 173
Feta cheese
  Mixed Greens with Pickled Beets,
    Pineapple and Feta 97
  Red Onion, Pear and Feta Salad with
    Caramelized Pecans 86
Fettuccine with Walnut Sauce 187
Fish
  Bookbinder's Light Fish Chowder 150
  Caribbean Grilled Fish 176
  Grilled and Baked Fish 176
  Grilled Salmon with Cucumber Relish
    177
  Halibut Au Gratin 179
  Miso Mirin Glazed Salmon 178
  Pecan-Crusted Trout 180
  Salmon Loaf 178
  Spicy Fish and Pumpkin Stew 151
Flat Creek Ranch Grilled Curried Chicken
  Sandwiches 154
Florentine Squash Bake 182
Focaccia 41
Fourth of July Berries 199
French Bread 37
French Toast
  Amber's Peach French Toast 3
  Baked Cinnamon Apple French Toast 5
  Orange French Toast 3
  Honey Pecan French Toast 4
Fresh Apple Muesli 5
Fresh Huckleberries with Lemon Cream 6
Fresh Tomato Salsa 81
Frosted Coconut Macadamia Bars 216
Frosted Roll Out Cookies 226
Frosting
  Buttercream Frosting 226
  Chocolate Buttercream Frosting 236
  Chocolate Satin Icing 232
  Coconut Pecan Frosting 238
  Rum Icing 238
Frozen Coffee Almond Indulgence 204
Frozen Lemon-Blue Cheese Salad with
  Marinated Artichokes 98
Fruit
  Baked Apples and Butternut Squash 127
  Baked Banana 8

Bananas Foster 203
Cherry Bars
Chokecherry Syrup 13
Classic Apple Crisp 201
Curried Fruit 127
Date Puree 24
Ed Opler's Strawberries Romanoff 198
Fourth of July Berries 199
Fresh Huckleberries with Lemon Cream
  6
Fruit and Nut Granola 6
Ginger Blueberry Crumble 200
Hot Buttered Fruit with Ice Cream 200
Island Fruit Salsa 80
Oranges with Marmalade 8
Peaches and Cream 198
Raspberries, with Russian Cream 202
Strawberries with Brown Sugar & Sour
  Cream 199
Sunset Pears 202
Fudge
  Miracle Fudge 253
  Oatmeal Fudge Bars 212

G

Garlic
  Garlic Bagel Chips 77
  Garlic Bread 41
  Mashed Potatoes with Garlic 108
  Roasted Garlic 66
Gazpacho, White with Crab, Avocado and
  tomato 132
Ginger
  Chocolate Ginger Cookies 221
  Ginger Blueberry Crumble 200
  Ginger Carrot Bisque 135
  Ginger Ice Cream 203
  Ginger Lemonade 44
  Ginger Snaps 222
  Gingerbread Pancakes 10
  Gingered Chicken Satay 62
  Gingered Cream Cheese 32
  Quick & Easy Gingerbread Cookies 222
  Zucchini Bread with Gingered Cream
    Cheese 32
Glazed Apple Nut Bread 31
Glazed Cranberry Pork Roast 169
Golden Parmesan Potatoes 110

Gorgonzola Walnut Dressing 103
Grandma Hays Chocolate Chip Cookies
     224
Granola
    Fruit and Nut Granola 6
Grapefruit
    Pink Grapefruit Sorbet 204
    Summer Salad 90
Green bean
    Fresh Green Bean and Mushroom
        Casserole 124
Green Chile Stew 148
Green Devil Cake 234
Grilled and Baked Fish 176
Grilled Mongolian Pork Chops 170
Grilled Salmon with Cucumber Relish
     177
Grilled Turkey, Cheddar and Cranberry
     Sandwiches 158
Grits Soufflé 14
Grove Farm Icebox Cookies 228
Guacamole, Best-Ever 74
Guissy's Salad 89

H

Halibut Au Gratin 179
Ham
    Breakfast Casserole 15
    Florentine Squash Bake 182
    Spinach Ham Quiche 14
Hamburger
    Zesty Hamburger Relish 84
Hard Sauce 207
Hard Suckers 254
Hash Browns
    Breakfast Casserole 15
Hazelnut
    Chocolate Hazelnut Crescents 224
    Hazelnut Torte with Chocolate Satin
        Icing 232
    Chicken with Hazelnuts and Mush-
        rooms 162
Heavenly Chocolate Cake with Chocolate
     Buttercream 236
Heavenly Lemon Pie 244
Herbs
    Baked Tomatoes with Herbs 119
    Easy Herb Bread 40

Herb Croutons 106
Roast Beef with Herb Crust 171
Zingy Herbed Squash 114
Honey
    Honey Dressing 103
    Honey French Dressing 102
    Honey Pecan French Toast 4
    Honey Lime Vinaigrette 94
    Honey Sesame Dressing 96
Horseradish Creme 76
Hot Buttered Fruit with Ice Cream 200
Hot Buttered Rum 54
Hot Pecan Dip 72
Hot Vanilla 52
Huckleberry
    Fresh Huckleberries with
        Lemon Cream 6
    Huckleberry Muffins 22

I

Iced Orange Drop Cookies 220
Iced Tea
    Mint Iced Tea 45
    Southern Iced Tea 45
    Sparkling Spiced Iced Tea 46
Iced Toffee 49
Imperial Beef Tenderloin 172
Ingredient Equivalents 256
Insalata Capricciosa 90
Island Fruit Salsa 80

J

James Rosner's World Famous Chocolate
     Chip Pound Cake 242
Janie Camenzind's Famous Fudgy,
Flourless Chocolate Torte 230
Jean's Chile Rellenos 194

K

Kahlua 57
Kale and Bean Soup 142
Key Lime Chicken 160
Key Lime Pie 243

L

Lantelme Cake 240
Lasagna, Sandy's River 190
Leeks, Scalloped with Potatoes 108
Lemon
  Lemon Cream 6
  Frozen Lemon-Blue Cheese Salad with
    Marinated Artichokes 98
  Glazed Lemon Pecan Bread 34
  Heavenly Lemon Pie 244
  Lemon Cheese Bars 214
Lemonade
  Ginger Lemonade 44
Lentil
  Mexican Lentil Casserole 185
  Simple Lentil Soup 142
Lime
  Chicken with Lime Butter 166
  Honey Lime Vinaigrette 94
  Key Lime Chicken 160
  Key Lime Pie 243
  Lime Salad Dressing 104
Linda's Southwestern Chicken Vegetable
    Soup 143
Liqueur
  Amaretto 56
  Cranberry Liqueur 57
  Kahlua 57
  Peaches and Cream Liqueur 58
Lucilla and Diego's Orange Margaritas 56

M

Macadamia
  Frosted Coconut Macadamia Bars 216
  Mango Macadamia Nut Bread 29
Macaroni and Cheese 189
Mandarin Orange Salad with Sugared
    Almonds 87
Mango
  Island Fruit Salsa 80
  Mango Curry Tuna Salad 92
  Mango Macadamia Nut Bread 29
  Mango Turkey Wraps with Curry
    Mayonnaise 157
  Mango White Bean Salsa 79

Maple
  Cranberry Maple Vinaigrette 106
  Maple Nut Danish 19
  Maple Vinaigrette 105
  Maple Walnut Creams 251
Margarita, Orange 56
Marilyn's Pesto 83
Marinated Flank Steak 172
Marmalade
  Oranges with Marmalade 8
Mashed Potatoes with Garlic 108
Matt's Favorite Chocolate Chip Cookie
    223
Measurement Equivalents 256
Metric conversions 259
Mexican
  Eight Layer Fiesta Dip 74
  Easy Chicken Quesadillas 182
  Jean's Chile Rellenos 194
  Mexican Chocolate 51
  Mexican Lentil Casserole 185
  Mexican Pinwheels 61
  Pico de Gallo 82
  Slow Cooked Beef Burritos 174
  Stacked Red Chili Enchiladas 192
  Steak Fajitas 173
  Vegetable Quesadillas 183
Mint
  Cream Cheese Mints 248
  Mint Iced Tea 45
  Minted Caesar Salad 86
  Peppermint Bark 248
  Raspberry Mint Crush 48
Miracle Fudge 253
Miso Mirin Glazed Salmon 178
Mixed Greens with Pickled Beets,
    Pineapple and Feta 97
Mocha
  Mocha Cream 25
  Mocha Frappuccino 51
  Ultimate Mocha 50
Molasses
  Molasses Bran Bread 38
  Soft Molasses Cookies 220
Mounds 249
Mozzarella
  Insalata Capricciosa 90
Muesli
  Fresh Apple Muesli 5

Muffins
  Blueberry Bran Muffins 23
  Cherry Yogurt Muffins 21
  Chocolate Chip Orange Muffins 20
  Cinnamon Sugar Muffins 22
  Espresso Chip Muffins 25
  Huckleberry Muffins 22
  Oatmeal Date Nut Muffins 24
  Pumpkin Spice Muffins 26
  Raspberry Almond Streusel Muffins 27
  Rhubarb Muffins 28
Mulligatawny Soup 146
Mushrooms
  Chicken with Hazelnuts and Mush-
    rooms 162
  Creamy Fettuccine with Artichoke
    Hearts and Mushrooms 188
  Fresh Green Bean and Mushroom
    Casserole 124
  Mushrooms Hana 60
  Stuffed Mushrooms 60

N

Nut, see also individual nuts
  Caramel Nut Brownies 211
  Chocolate Hazelnut Crescents 224
  Cranberry Nut Pie 244
  Fruit and Nut Granola 6
  Glazed Apple Nut Bread 31
  Mango Macadamia Nut Bread 29
  Maple Nut Danish 19
  Oatmeal Date Nut Muffins 24
  Peppered Pecans 70
  Toasted Walnut Bites 69
Nutty Coconut Brunch Cake 17

O

Oat
  Oatmeal-Buttermilk Pancakes 9
  Oatmeal Crinkles 218
  Oatmeal Date Nut Muffins 24
  Oatmeal Fudge Bars 212
  Scottish Oat Scones 28
  Super Oatmeal 7
Old Fashioned Christmas Egg Nog 55
Old Settler Beans 125

Old-Fashioned Raisin Cookies 227
Old-Fashioned Soft Sugar Cookies 225
Onions
  Caramelized Onions 123
  Cheesy Onion Dip 72
  Red Onion, Pear and Feta Salad with
    Caramelized Pears 86
  Roast Beef Sandwiches with Roasted
    Red Onions on Sourdough 155
  Roasted Red Onions 122
  Roasted Vidalia Soup 138
  Sherried Onions 122
Orange
  Balsamic Orange Salad Dressing 105
  Chocolate Chip Orange Muffins 20
  Citrus Broccoli Slaw 92
  Cranberry Orange Raisin Bread 35
  Iced Orange Drop Cookies 220
  Lucilla and Diego's Orange Margaritas
    56
  Mandarin Orange Salad with Sugared
    Almonds 87
  Orange French Toast 3
  Orange Spongcake with Rum Icing 238
  Oranges with Marmalade 8
  Whipped Citrus Winter Squash 114
Oysters
  Oyster Dressing 128
  Scalloped Oysters 128

P

Pan sizes 261
Pancakes
  Cranberry Ricotta Pancakes 10
  Gingerbread Pancakes 10
  Oatmeal-Buttermilk Pancakes 9
  The Old Painted Porch Pancakes 11
Pantry, suggested 262
Papaya
  Island Fruit Salsa 80
Parmesan
  Golden Parmesan Potatoes 110
  Parmesan Dijon Chicken 164
  Peppery Parmesan Dressing 104
  Ricotta Parmesan Stuffed Chicken with
    Apricot Sauce 161

Parsnips
  Roasted Carrots and Parsnips 123
Pasta
  Bean and Seashell Pasta Salad 99
  Cheese Ravioli with Rosemary and
    Lemon 191
  Corn and Squash Pasta 191
  Creamy Fettuccine with Artichoke
    Hearts and Mushrooms 188
  Fettuccine with Walnut Sauce 187
  Macaroni and Cheese 189
  Penne with Spinach and Asparagus 186
  Sandy's River Lasagna 190
  Summer Pasta Salad 100
Patty's Cold Avocado Soup 133
Pavlova 209
Peach
  Amber's Peach French Toast 3
  Peach Salsa 79
  Peach Smoothie 44
  Peaches and Cream 198
  Peaches and Cream Liqueur 58
  Perfect Peach Pie 242
Peanut Butter
  Peanut Butter Bars 212
  Peanut Butter Bread 30
Pears
  Red Onion, Pear and Feta Salad with
    Caramelized Pears 86
  Sunset Pears 202
  Sweet Potatoes and Pears with Streusel
    Topping 111
Peas
  Cold Dilled Peas 101
Pecan
  Caramelized Pecans 86
  Chocolate Pecan Clusters 253
  Glazed Lemon Pecan Bread 34
  Honey Pecan French Toast 4
  Hot Pecan Dip 72
  Pecan Chocolate Chip Meringues 229
  Pecan Puffs 229
  Pecan Toffee Triangles 252
  Pecan-Crusted Trout 180
  Peppered Pecans 70
  Raisin Pecan Bread Pudding with
    Brandy Sauce 208
  Red Onion, Pear and Feta Salad with
    Caramelized Pecans 86

Toasted Pecan Pilaf 116
Penne with Spinach and Asparagus 186
Peppermint Bark 248
Peppery Parmesan Dressing 104
Perfect Corn Bread 42
Perfect Hot Toddy 54
Perfect Peach Pie 242
Pesto
  Marilyn's Pesto 83
  Red Pepper-Almond Pesto 83
Pickled beets
  Mixed Greens with Pickled Beets,
    Pineapple and Feta 97
Pico de Gallo 82
Pie
  Cranberry Nut Pie 244
  Creamy Coconut Pie 242
  Heavenly Lemon Pie 244
  Key Lime Pie 243
  Perfect Peach Pie 242
Pineapple
  Island Fruit Salsa 80
  Mixed Greens with Pickled Beets,
    Pineapple and Feta 97
  Pineapple Cake with Broiled Coconut
    Pecan Frosting 237
Pink Grapefruit Sorbet 204
Pita Crisps with Tuna Tapenade 75
Pizza
  Potato Bacon Pizza 184
  Veggie Pizza Bites 76
Poppy Seed
  Yogurt Poppy Seed Coffee Cake 16
  Raspberry Poppy Seed Salad Dressing
    102
Pork
  Glazed Cranberry Pork Roast 169
  Grilled Mongolian Pork Chops 170
  Pork Ribs 170
  Pork Tenderloin with Balsamic Raisin
    Sauce 168
Potato
  Chili Chips 78
  Golden Parmesan Potatoes 110
  Mashed Potatoes with Garlic 108
  Potato Bacon Pizza 184
  Potato Soup with Asparagus 134
  Roasted New Potatoes 109
  Scalloped Leeks and Potatoes 108

Spicy Oven Fries 110
Pound Cake 240
Pudding
    Carrot Pudding with Hard Sauce 207
    Corn Pudding 124
    Danish Rice Pudding 206
    Raisin Pecan Bread Pudding with
        Brandy Sauce 208
Pumpkin
    Pumpkin Bundt Cake 239
    Pumpkin Cheesecake with
        Caramelized Walnuts 245
    Pumpkin Curry Soup 136
    Pumpkin Spice Muffins 26
    Spicy Fish and Pumpkin Stew 151

Q

Quesadillas
    Easy Chicken Quesadillas 182
    Smoked Salmon and Apple Quesadilla
        Wedges with Horseradish Creme 76
    Vegetable Quesadillas 183
Quiche
    Basil Tomato Tart 193
    Spinach Ham Quiche 14
Quick & Easy Gingerbread Cookies 222
Quick Breads
    Best Banana Blueberry Bread 30
    Bishops Bread 32
    Cranberry Orange Raisin Bread 35
    Glazed Apple Nut Bread 31
    Glazed Lemon Pecan Bread 34
    Mango Macadamia Nut Bread 29
    Peanut Butter Bread 30
    Perfect Corn Bread 42
    Zucchini Bread with Gingered Cream
        Cheese 32

R

Raisin
    Brandied Raisin Brie 68
    Cranberry Orange Raisin Bread 35
    Old-Fashioned Raisin Cookies 227
    Pork Tenderloin with Balsamic Raisin

Sauce 168
Raisin Pecan Bread Pudding with
    Brandy Sauce 208
Ramen noodles
    Distinctly Different Slaw 91
Ranger Cookies 217
Raspberry
    Raspberry Almond Streusel Muffins 27
    Raspberry Mint Crush 48
    Raspberry Poppy Seed Salad Dressing
        102
    Russian Cream with Raspberries 202
Ravioli
    Cheese Ravioli with Rosemary and
        Lemon 191
Red Beans and Rice 184
Red Onion, Pear and Feta Salad with
    Caramelized Pears 86
Red Pepper
    Baked Eggplant, Roasted Red Peppers,
        Tomatoes and Cucumbers in Pita 156
    Creamy Roasted Red Pepper Salsa 80
    Red Pepper-Almond Pesto 83
    Roasted Eggplant and Red Bell Pepper
        Soup 137
    Roasted Red Pepper and Cream Cheese
        Dip 73
Red Rice, Savannah 185
Relish
    Zesty Hamburger Relish 84
Rhubarb Muffins 28
Ribs
    Baked Short Ribs 175
    Pork Ribs 170
Rice
    Danish Rice Pudding 206
    Red Beans and Rice 184
    Savannah Red Rice 115
    Steamed Brown Rice and Barley 118
    Toasted Pecan Pilaf 116
    Veggie Stir Fry with Brown Rice 186
    Wild Rice Supreme 117
Ricotta
    Cranberry Ricotta Pancakes 10
    Ricotta Parmesan Stuffed Chicken with
        Apricot Sauce 161
Roast
    Roast Beef Sandwiches with Roasted
        Red Onions on Sourdough 155

Roast Beef with Herb Crust 171
Roasted Carrots and Parsnips 123
Roasted Eggplant and Red Bell Pepper
    Soup 137
Roasted Eggplant Spread 70
Roasted Garlic 66
Roasted New Potatoes 109
Roasted Red Onions 122
Roasted Vidalia Soup 138
Roasted Red Peppers
    Baked Eggplant, Roasted Red Peppers,
        Tomatoes and Cucumber in Pita 156
    Creamy Roasted Red Pepper Salsa 80
    Roasted Red Pepper and Cream Cheese
        Dip 73
Rockin' Moroccan Stew 149
Rum
    Hot Buttered Rum 54
    Rum Icing 238
Russian Cream with Raspberries 202

S

Salad
    Avocado and Tomato Salad 91
    Bean and Seashell Pasta Salad 99
    Chinese Vegetable Salad with Honey
        Sesame Dressing 96
    Cinema Salad 89
    Citrus Broccoli Slaw 92
    Cold Dilled Peas 101
    Crunchy Broccoli Salad 99
    Cucumber and Yogurt Salad 98
    Curried Chicken Salad 96
    Distinctly Different Slaw 91
    Elizabeth McCabe's Spinach Salad 88
    Frozen Lemon-Blue Cheese Salad with
        Marinated Artichokes 98
    Guissy's Salad 89
    Insalata Capricciosa 90
    Mandarin Orange Salad with Sugared
        Almonds 87
    Mango Curry Tuna Salad 92
    Minted Caesar Salad 86
    Mixed Greens with Pickled Beets,
        Pineapple and Feta 97
    Red Onion, Pear and Feta Salad with
        Caramelized Pecans 86
    Santa Fe Grilled Chicken Salad with

Honey Lime Vinaigrette 94
    Southwestern Bean Salad 100
    Summer Pasta Salad 100
    Summer Salad 90
    Walnut Chicken Salad 93
Salad dressing
    Balsamic Orange Salad Dressing 105
    Basic Vinaigrette 104
    Cranberry Maple Vinaigrette 106
    Gorgonzola Walnut Dressing 103
    Honey Dressing 103
    Honey French Dressing 102
    Honey Lime Vinaigrette 94
    Honey Sesame Dressing 96
    Lime Salad Dressing 104
    Maple Vinaigrette 105
    Peppery Parmesan Dressing 104
    Raspberry Poppyseed Dressing 102
Salmon
    Grilled Salmon with Cucumber Relish 177
    Miso Mirin Glazed Salmon 178
    Salmon Loaf 178
    Smoked Salmon and Apple Quesadilla
        Wedges with Horseradish Creme 76
Salsa
    Black Bean and Corn Salsa 81
    Creamy Roasted Red Pepper Salsa 80
    Fresh Tomato Salsa 81
    Island Fruit Salsa 80
    Mango White Bean Salsa 79
    Peach Salsa 79
    Pico de Gallo 82
Sandwich
    Baked Eggplant, Roasted Red Peppers,
        Tomatoes and Cucumbers in Pita 156
    Flat Creek Ranch Grilled Curried
        Chicken Sandwiches s 154
    Grilled Turkey, Cheddar and Cranberry
        Sandwiches 158
    Mango Turkey Wraps with Curry
        Mayonnaise 157
    Roast Beef Sandwiches with Roasted
        Red Onions on Sourdough 155
Sandy's River Lasagna 190
Santa Fe Grilled Chicken Salad with
    Honey Lime Vinaigrette 94
Sassy Eggs 2
Sauces
    Apricot Sauce 161

Brandy Sauce 208
Hard Sauce 207
Sausage
  Sausage Cheese Balls 61
  Turkey Sausage Stew 152
Savannah Red Rice 115
Scalloped Leeks and Potatoes 108
Scalloped Oysters 128
Scones
  Scottish Oat Scones 28
Seafood
  Seafood Stew with Tomatoes and Basil
    150
  Vietnamese Shrimp with Rice Noodles
    180
Sesame
  Honey Sesame Dressing 96
Sherried Onions 122
Shrimp
  Vietnamese Shrimp with Rice Noodles
    180
Sicilian-Style Caponata 65
Sikarni 205
Simple Lentil Soup 142
Slow Cooked Beef Burritos 174
Smoked Salmon and Apple Quesadilla
    Wedges with Horseradish Creme 76
Smoothie
  Peach Smoothie 44
Soft Molasses Cookies 220
Soufflé
  Grits Soufflé 14
Soup
  Bean Me Up Soup 141
  Black Bean Soup 140
  Bookbinder's Light Fish Chowder 150
  Cabbage and Beef Soup 146
  Carrot Tarragon Soup 134
  Cauliflower Soup 140
  Chicken and Avocado Soup 144
  Chicken Corn Chowder 145
  Chilled Cucumber Soup 133
  Creamed Tomato Soup with Cognac
    138
  Ginger Carrot Bisque 135
  Kale and Bean Soup 142
  Lentil Soup, Simple 142
  Linda's Southwestern Chicken Veg-
    etable Soup 143

Mulligatawny Soup 146
Patty's Cold Avocado Soup 133
Potato Soup with Asparagus 134
Pumpkin Curry Soup 136
Roasted Eggplant and Red Bell Pepper
    Soup 137
Roasted Vidalia Soup 138
Squash Soup 136
Tomato Basil Soup 139
White Gazpacho with Crab, Avocado
    and Tomato 132
Sour Cream
  Cucumber Rounds with Sour Cream
    and Chutney 67
  Strawberries with Brown Sugar & Sour
    Cream 199
Sour Cream Coffee Cake 16
Sour milk 260
Sourdough
  Molasses Bran bread 38
  Sourdough Baking 36
  Sourdough Buttermilk Biscuits 38
Southern Iced Tea 45
Southwestern Bean Salad 100
Southwestern Grilled Chicken 160
Sparkling Apple Cider 44
Sparkling Spiced Iced Tea 46
Spice, shelf life 259
Spicy Beef Stew 147
Spicy Fish and Pumpkin Stew 151
Spicy Oven Fries 110
Spinach
  Elizabeth McCabe's Spinach Salad 88
  Florentine Squash Bake 182
  Penne with Spinach and Asparagus 186
  Spinach and Bacon Stuffed Tomatoes
    120
  Spinach Gratin 120
  Spinach Ham Quiche 14
Sports Energy Drink 47
Spring rolls
  Chinese Spring (Egg) Rolls 63
Squash
  Acorn Squash with Apples 112
  Baked Apples and Butternut Squash
    127
  Butternut Squash Purée with Pomegran-
    ates and Scallions 113
  Corn and Squash Pasta 191

Florentine Squash Bake 182
Squash Soup 136
Whipped Citrus Winter Squash 114
Zingy Herbed Squash 114
Stacked Red Chili Enchiladas 192
Steak
　Marinated Flank Steak 172
　Steak Fajitas 173
Steamed Brown Rice and Barley 118
Stew
　Green Chile Stew 148
　Rockin' Moroccan Stew 149
　Seafood Stew with Tomatoes and Basil
　　150
　Spicy Beef Stew 147
　Spicy Fish and Pumpkin Stew 151
　Turkey Sausage Stew 152
　White Chicken Chili 153
Stir fry
　Veggie Stir Fry with Brown Rice 186
Strawberry
　Ed Opler's Strawberries Romanoff 198
　Strawberries with Brown Sugar and
　　Sour Cream 199
　Strawberry Butter 9
Streusel
　Raspberry Almond Streusel Muffins 27
　Sweet Potatoes and Pears with Streusel
　　Topping 111
Stuffed Mushrooms 60
Stuffing
　Bacon Roasted Turkey with Cornbread
　　Dressing 194
　Oyster Dressing 128
　Toasted Walnut Cranberry Stuffing 129
Substitutions 260
Summer Pasta Salad 100
Summer Salad 90
Sunset Pears 202
Super Oatmeal 7
Sweet Potatoes
　Brandied Sweet Potatoes 112
　Sweet Potato Fries 111
　Sweet Potatoes and Pears with Streusel
　　Topping 111
Syrup
　Buttercream Syrup 13
　Chokecherry Syrup 13

T

Tea, see also Iced Tea
　Chai (Tea Latte) 48
　Cranberry Tea Punch 52
　Mint Iced Tea 45
　Southern Iced Tea 45
　Teton Tea 53
Teriyaki
　Chicken Teriyaki 165
Teton Tea 53
Teton Trail Ride Beans 126
The Old Painted Porch Pancakes 11
Tips
　Apples 5
　Asparagus 186
　Avocado 132
　Baking Time 239
　Baking time 229
　Barley Yields 118
　Basil 139
　Bell Peppers 73
　Biscuits, square 41
　Browning Stew Ingredients 149
　Cake Tips 240
　Candy Success 251
　Canned Broth 145
　Cauliflower 140
　Cheesecake , Cutting 246
　Chicken 164
　Chocolate Tips 236
　Choosing Broccoli 99
　Chopping Nuts 180
　Coffee 50
　Cookie Sheets 224
　Cookies, Fresh 221
　Cooking Fish 177
　Cooking Pork 168
　Corn, Fresh 124
　Corn, Storing 81
　Cucumbers 67
　Dressings, Oil in 103
　Eggplant, Selecting 137
　Eggs 2
　Fish, Removing Odors 178
　Frozen Spinach 120
　Fruit, Freezing 44
　Fudge, Soft 253
　Garlic, Removing skin 77

Ginger 222
Honey, Measuring 103
Ice Cream Tip 203
Lettuce 89
Mangoes 29
Muffins , Removing 25
Muffins, Tender 22
Nuts, Storing 86
Onions, No Tear 123
Onion Odor 155
Oranges 8
Oven Rack Position 213, 217
Pancakes 11
Pasta, Perfect 187
Pasta, Rinsing 188
Pears 202
Pie Crust, ;Avoiding Soggy 242
Pie Crust, Measuring 243
Potatoes, Storing 11
Soup, Preventing Curdling 134
Soup, Refrigerating 143
Soup or Stew, Leftover 150
Squash, Selecting 114, 182
Sweet Potatoes ,Peeling 112
Tomatoes, Quick Ripening 90
Tomatoes, Storing 193
Stuffing, Removing 129, 196
Vinaigrette, Smooth 104
Yeast 37
Tiramisù 232
Toasted Pecan Pilaf 116
Toasted Walnut Bites 69
Toasted Walnut Cranberry Stuffing 129
Toffee
Award-Winning Toffee 252
Pecan Toffee Triangles 252
Tomato
Avocado and Tomato Salad 91
Baked Eggplant, Roasted Red Peppers,
Tomatoes and Cucumber in Pita 156
Baked Tomatoes with Herbs 119
Basil Tomato Tart 193
Creamed Tomato Soup with Cognac
138
Fresh Tomato Salsa 81
Insalata Capricciosa 90
Pico de Gallo 82
Spinach and Bacon Stuffed Tomatoes
120

Tomato Basil Soup 139
White Gazpacho with Crab, Avocado
and Tomato 132
Torte
Date Torte 234
Hazelnut Torte with Chocolate Satin
Icing 232
Janie Camenzind's Famous Fudgy,
Flourless Chocolate Torte 230
Walnut Torte 231
Trout
Pecan-Crusted Trout 180
Truffles
Chocolate 250
White Chocolate 250
Tuna
Mango Curry Tuna Salad 92
Pita Crisps with Tuna Tapenade 75
Turkey
Bacon Roasted Turkey with Cornbread
Dressing 194
Grilled Turkey, Cheddar and Cranberry
Sandwiches 158
Mango Turkey Wraps with Curry
Mayonnaise 157
Turkey Sausage Stew 152
Turtle Brownies 210

U

Ulimate Mocha 50

V

Vanilla
Hot Vanilla 52
Vanilla Iced Coffee 49
Vanilla Whipped Cream 231
Vegetable Quesadillas 183
Vegetables, see also individual vegetables
Acorn Squash with Apples 112
Baked Tomatoes with Herbs 119
Brandied Sweet Potatoes 112
Company Cabbage 119
Corn and Squash Pasta 191

Fresh Green Bean and Mushroom
    Casserole 124
Golden Parmesan Potatoes 110
Mashed Potatoes with Garlic 108
Roasted Carrots and Parsnips 123
Roasted New Potatoes 109
Roasted Red Onions 122
Scalloped Leeks and Potatoes 108
Sherried Onions 122
Spicy Oven Fries 110
Spinach and Bacon Stuffed Tomatoes
    120
Spinach Gratin 120
Sweet Potato Fries 111
Sweet Potatoes and Pears with Streusel
    Topping 111
Veggie Pizza Bites 76
Veggie Stir Fry with Brown Rice 186
Whipped Citrus Winter Squash 114
Zingy Herbed Squash 114
Vietnamese Shrimp with Rice Noodles
    180
Vinaigrette
    Basic Vinaigrette 104
    Cranberry Maple Vinaigrette 106
    Guissy's Vinaigrette 89
    Honey Lime Vinaigrette 94
    Maple Vinaigrette 105

Pumpkin Cheesecake with Caramelized
    Walnuts 245
Toasted Walnut Bites 69
Toasted Walnut Cranberry Stuffing 129
Walnut Chicken Salad 93
Walnut Date Chews 254
Walnut Torte 231
Warm Chocolate Dessert with Soft Interior
    235
Watermelon Cooler 46
Whipped Citrus Winter Squash 114
White Chicken Chili 153
White Chocolate
    White Chocolate Truffles 250
    White Hot Chocolate 52
White Gazpacho with Crab, Avocado and
    Tomato 132
Wild Rice Supreme 117
Wildflower Baked Eggs with Herbs 2

W

Waffles
    Buckwheat Waffles 12
Walnut
    Chicken and Walnuts 167
    Fettuccine with Walnut Sauce 187
    Gorgonzola Walnut Dressing 103

Y

Yogurt
    Cherry Yogurt Muffins 21
    Cucumber and Yogurt Salad 98
    Sikarni 205
    Yogurt Poppy Seed Coffee Cake 16

Z

Zesty Hamburger Relish 84
Zingy Herbed Squash 114
Zucchini
    Zucchini Bread with Gingered Cream
    Cheese 32

Acknowledgments

Sportsmen with Trout and Elk Antlers, 1905

Recipe Contributors

Many thanks to the 120 plus contributors listed below.
Without them, "Jackson Hole Cooks" would not exist.

Bed and Breakfasts

The Wildflower Inn

The Wildflower is a beautiful log inn located only minutes away from Jackson Hole Ski Resort, Grand Teton National Park and the town of Jackson. The attractive B&B is set on three acres graced by aspens, ponds and mountain views. It has been nationally recognized by Sunset, Glamour, Bon Appétit, National Geographic Traveler and Time magazines for its setting, food, décor and hospitality of innkeepers Sherrie and Ken Jern, who built the Wildflower in 1989. Each of the inn's five rooms has its own bath, deck and television. Guests enjoy the Inn's hot tub, solarium and cozy fireplace.

Contact Information:
The Wildflower Inn
3725 Teton Village Road
Box 11000, Jackson, Wyoming 83002
Phone: 307-733-4710
email: jhwildflowerinn@cs.com
www.jacksonholewildflower.com

Huff House Inn Bed and Breakfast

The historic Huff House was built in 1917 for Jackson's first full-time doctor, Charles Huff. It was opened as a bed and breakfast by Jackie and Weldon Richardson in 1995. The inn has three large rooms in the main house and four guest cottages, all with private bath. Breakfasts are served family style in the formal dining room and the casual breakfast room.

Contact information:
P.O. Box 1189, Jackson, WY 83001
Phone: (307) 733-4164
email: huffhousebnb@blissnet.com
www.jacksonwyomingbnb.com

Sassy Moose Inn

The Sassy Moose Inn is an ideal choice for a romantic getaway or a family vacation. Children are welcomed and easily accommodated in Polly and Craig Kelley's lovely log home, centrally located between the town of Jackson and Grand Teton National Park. Each of the six rooms has a private bath. Guests enjoy the inn's gourmet breakfasts, large hot tub, fireplaces and laundry facilities. From November 1 through April 30, parties can "rent the inn," perfect for family vacations and reunions.

Contact information:
The Sassy Moose Inn
3859 Miles Road
Jackson Hole, Wyoming 83014
Phone: 307-733-1277; (800) 356-1277
email: craigrwy@aol.com
www.sassymoose.com

Teton Tree House

Teton Tree House is a charming, multi-level home reminiscent of a tree house. It is nestled in the trees at the base of Teton Pass, centrally located eight miles from the town of Jackson and nine miles from the south entrance of Grand Teton National Park. A gentle 95-step climb brings guests to the front door of this wooded retreat. Six guest rooms all have their own private path, deck and window seat. An outdoor hot tub is available. Innkeeper Denny Becker treats guests with fresh fruit, tasty breakfasts and western hospitality.

Contact information:
P.O. Box 550, Wilson, WY 83014
Phone: (307) 733-3233
email: tetontreehouse@aol.com
www.cruising-america.com/
tetontreehouse

Former Innkeepers

Martha and Matt MacEachern ran the popular Painted Porch Bed and Breakfast in Jackson before deciding to sell the inn to move on to other endeavors and have more time to raise their young family. Martha graciously shared recipes that were a hit with her guests. Similarly, Susan and Mark Nowlin retired their Nowlin Creek Inn Bed and Breakfast a number of years ago so Mark could concentrate on their business, The Master's Studio, and Susan could devote more time to art. (In a former life, she was an exhibit designer for the Smithsonian.) Susan shared one of Nowlin Creek's favorite breakfast items: Orange French Toast.

Guest Ranches

Brooks Lake Lodge

Rated one of America's Ten Best Adventure Lodges by *Outside Magazine* in 2002, historic Brooks Lake Lodge and Guest Ranch offers an exclusive getaway for people who love the outdoors *and* luxurious accommodations. Located near Jackson Hole, Wyoming and Yellowstone National Park, Brooks Lake offers horseback riding, pack trips, fly-fishing and hiking in the summer, and snowmobiling, cross-country skiing, snowshoeing and dogsled tours in the winter. The main lodge houses six rooms with private baths. Newly remodeled cabins feature private bathrooms, wood burning stoves and electric heat. Guests enjoy spectacular views of the Pinnacles, Brooks Mountain and Brooks Lake. Gourmet meals are served in the dining room.

Contact information:
458 Brooks Lake Road
Dubois, WY 82513
Phone: (307) 455-2121
email: brookslake@wyoming.com
www.brookslake.com

Flat Creek Ranch

Elegantly appointed after an extensive restoration completed in 2001, Flat Creek Ranch is listed in the National Register of Historic Places. Five cabins nestled in a gorgeous wilderness setting offer an unforgettable spot for families, small retreats, fly fishing parties and special gatherings. Getting there is your first adventure—a 15-mile route across the National Elk Refuge and into the mountains over a rigorous jeep track. At the end of the road you reach a true wilderness haven that in the 1920s served as a hideaway for flamboyant countess and newspaper publisher, Cissy Patterson. Guests hike, fish, horseback ride, enjoy the western library of owners Joe Albright and Marcia Kunstel, or just blissfully relax.

Contact information:
P.O. Box 9760, Jackson WY 83002
Phone: (307) 733-0603
Toll-free: 1-866-522-3344
www. flatcreekranch.com

Moose Head Ranch

Moose Head Ranch is one of only a few privately owned guest ranches completely surrounded by Grand Teton National Park. With a panoramic view of the Tetons as a backdrop, guests stay in modern log cabins tucked among pine and cottonwood trees. Moose Head is known for its fine food, served family-style in the warm and welcoming spacious lodge. Supervised small group rides, stocked trout ponds for catch and release fly fishing, hiking in Grand Teton National Park and the surrounding national forests, whitewater float trips down the Snake River, touring through Grand Teton and Yellowstone National Park, or visiting the shops and art galleries of Jackson are easily arranged diversions. Minimum five nights stay. The ranch is open June 14-August 20.

Contact information:
Summer phone: (307) 733-3141
Winter phone: (850) 877-1431
www.wyomingdra.com/moosehead

Restaurants

The Blue Lion

In a town where restaurants come and go, The Blue Lion has been a local tradition for over 20 years. The popular restaurant is located in a charming older house that owner Ned Brown purchased in 1978. House specialties include the best rack of lamb in town, crab cream cheese stuffed mushrooms, freshly made Caesar salad, elk tenderloin and herb crusted trout. Two of the Blue Lion's desserts, Mud Pie and Russian Cream, have repeatedly been voted the top desserts in Jackson Hole in local newspaper polls. The restaurant offers catering, a private upstairs dining room, and 20% of the total bill to "early bird" diners. Reservations are strongly recommended.

Location/reservation information:
160 N. Millward St., Jackson
Phone: (307) 733-3912
www.bluelionrestaurant.com

Jedediah's Original House of Sourdough

One of the oldest log cabins in Jackson Hole houses Jedediah's Original House of Sourdough. Proprietor Mike Gierau and his staff whip up one of the best breakfasts in town, specializing (not too surprisingly!) in sourdough pancakes, waffles and biscuits. Mike's hearty, home-cooked meals and fresh preserves and jams are so good that he runs a thriving mail order business for folks that want to take a bit of Jed's home with them. Boxes of jams, sourdough stater and a sourdough cookbook are shipped nationwide. Jed's offers a casual, family-dining atmosphere inside and seasonal outside patio dining under its towering cottonwood trees.

Location/reservation information:
135 East Broadway, Jackson
Phone: (307) 733-5671
www.wy-biz.com/jedediahsourdough
For a free catalog, write Jedediah's Original House of Sourdough, Box 3857, Jackson, Wyoming 83001.

The Snake River Grill

The Snake River Grill is repeatedly mentioned when locals identify their favorite restaurant. Its intimate and comfortable dining rooms feature leather booths, a double moss-rock fireplace and log chinked walls. The SRG's innovative menu features fresh fish, free-range chicken and veal dishes, pastas, pizzas from the wood-burning oven, chops and prime rib from the grill, and creative fresh salads, side dishes and desserts. Diners peruse an award-winning wine list of 270 selections as well as microbrew beers, grappas, ports and single malt scotch. SRG is open nightly for dinner. Reservations may by made after 3 p.m.

Location/reservation information:
On the Jackson Town Square,
84 East Broadway, Jackson
Phone: (307) 733-0557
www.snakerivergrill.com

Food Columnists

Paul Bruun

Paul is a consummate sportsman, enthusiastic home chef and noted connoisseur of everything culinary. Over the years he has indulged his dual sportsman and food passions in award-winning columns and articles in both the *Jackson Hole Guide* and the *Jackson Hole* News, nationally recognized valley publications that merged into the *Jackson Hole News and Guide* in 2002. The recipes reprinted in this publication are from his famed *Jackson Hole News* "Exit Eating" column, where Paul once lucidly explained how to cook a fish in a dishwasher.

Therese Metherell, R.D.

Therese is a registered dietician who routinely featured great recipes in her long-running "Sound Bites" column in the *Jackson Hole News,* irrefutably proving to readers that food that is good for you tastes good, too. Many of her favorites are included in this publication. Therese, a professed chocophile, owns and founded Peak Nutrition, a successful nutrition education and counseling business. For information, call Therese at 307-733-5344.

Holly Herrick

For a number of years in the late 1990s, Holly penned the "Chef's Corner" column in the *Jackson Hole Guide.* Her hints for both experienced and aspiring chefs, accompanied by wonderful concoctions, were eagerly awaited by legions of readers. Holly is a grand diplome graduate of Le Cordon Bleu cooking school in Paris, France.

Tamalpais Roth-McCormick

Tamalpais upheld Holly's high standards when she took over the *Jackson Hole Guide's* "Chef's Corner" column in 2000. A local chef who is a graduate of the California Culinary Academy, Tamalpais' fun, informal style and on-target tips put gourmet results within reach of the average home chef.

Carole Travis Henikoff

Carole was taught to cook by her father, Carl Anderson, a world-class chef who operated the famed Chatam restaurant in Hollywood. Her "Cooking with Carole" column in the *Jackson Hole Guide,* which ran from the late 1970s to the early 1980s, was one of the first food columns in Jackson Hole. Carole published her first cookbook, *Star Food,* in 1981. The successful cookbook showcased Chatham and Hollywood's Scandia recipes that Carole had adapted for home use. Her second cookbook is currently under contract to be published.

J.C. Whitfield

J.C. became the *Jackson Hole Guide* food columnist in 1981 when Carole resigned to finish her cookbook. Her "Second Helping" column featured tasty recipes that homemakers could prepare with great results. Her most popular columns may have been the "Best Christmas Cookies in the Valley" series. Many of those recipes are included in this publication. J.C. is an accomplished amateur cook and a licensed professional counselor.

Chefs, Caterers and Food Professionals

Claudia Burkhardt

Claudia owns and operates one of the oldest catering businesses in the valley. Her culinary skills have shone at innumerable gatherings since her start in 1976. Claudia has provided food service for the cast and crew of many of the films and commercials shot in Jackson Hole. For information, call Claudia at 307-733-5016, or write Catering by Claudia, Box 311, Wilson, Wyoming 83014.

Jeff Drew

A graduate of The Culinary Institute of America, Jeff opened and operated four restaurants and was the executive chef of Santa Fe's famed Coyote Café before moving to Jackson Hole with his family to become chef for the Snake River Grill. He has been featured in various television spots, including CNN and the Disney Channel. Publication credits have appeared in many professional journals, including *Nations Restaurant News*, *Food Arts* and *Restaurant & Institutions Magazine*.

Carole Travis Henikoff
See Food Columnists

Holly Herrick
See Food Columnists

Mary Howley, R.D.

Mary Howley is a registered dietitian with an MS degree in Foods and Nutrition. Beyond Broccoli is her nutrition counseling and education business. She has developed over 100 recipes as part of her "Lunch and Learn" classes and other educational endeavors. Some of her favorites are shared in this publication. Contact Mary at 307-690-5785 or mhowley@wyoming.com.

Therese Metherell, R.D.
See Food Columnists

Karen Norby
Karen has been a "food fixture" in Jackson Hole for many years. She ran the professional kitchen at Teton Science School in Grand Teton National Park in the 1990s, catering many gourmet meals for special events, before signing on as a chef at the Yellowstone Garage. Her culinary home is presently Patos on East Broadway. Her innovative spring rolls draw many repeat customers! Karen is in the process of compiling her creative recipes into a cookbook.

Pat Opler
Pat operated the "At Home on the Range" cooking school in Wilson, Wyoming and Hinsdale, Ill. She authored two popular cookbooks, *At Home on the Range* and *Something's Chocolate* while simultaneously writing a cooking column for the *Jackson Hole News* in the 1980s. She generously granted permission to use four of her recipes in this publication in June of 2002. Sadly, Pat died of a pulmonary artery embolism while flying to Chicago from South Africa on July 30, 2002. The community of Jackson Hole misses her spirit and generosity.

Tamalpais Roth-McCormick
See Food Columnists

The Spice Merchants
Dave Bigge loves Asian cookery. He has shared his adept skills in numerous community education cooking classes, convincing a large meat and potatoes crowd to replace French fries with sushi rice and egg rolls. Frustrated at not being able to find the

ingredients he needed for his creations, Dave located sources of Asian spices and food items, and decided to share his knowledge by starting his own business on-line. Thus, The Spice Merchants was born. Visit it at http://66.113.152.50

Publications

Every effort has been made to secure permissions of copyrighted material. In the event questions or concerns arise regarding use of any material, the publisher expresses regret for inadvertent error and will gladly make necessary corrections in future printings. Thanks is extended to the organizations and companies below who granted permission to include their material.

The Artistry of Sourdough Cooking
Permission granted to include French Bread on page 37, Sourdough Buttermilk Biscuits on page 38 and Molasses Bran Bread on page 38. *The Artistry of Sourdough Cooking* is published by Jedediah's Original House of Sourdough. For ordering information, write Jedediah's Original House of Sourdough, Box 3857, Jackson, WY 83001.

At Home on the Range
Permission granted to include Focaccia on page 41, Potato Soup with Asparagus on page 134, Chicken with Hazelnuts and Mushrooms on page 162 and Ed Opler's Strawberries Romanoff on page 198. *At Home on the Range Cooking School Cookbook* by Pat Opler was published by Gibbs Smith in 1992. It is presently out-of-print.

Cooking in Wyoming: 1890-1965
Permission granted to include Honey French Dressing on page 108 and Imperial Beef Tenderloin on page 172 by recipe contributor Martha Hansen. Both recipes were included in *Cooking in*

Wyoming: 1890-1965, published by the state of Wyoming in 1965. The publication is out-of-print.

Feeding the Herd
Permission granted to include Vietnamese Shrimp with Rice noodles, on page 180. *Feeding the Herd* is a collection of favorite recipes compiled by The Jackson Hole Cowbelles, an organization formed in 1954 to promote beef. For ordering information, write The Jackson Hole Cowbelles, P.O. Box 1044, Jackson, WY 83001.

Historical Recipes from the Pure Food Club of Jackson Hole
Permission granted to include Basil Tomato Tart on page 163. *Historical Recipes from the Pure Food Club of Jackson Hole* by Judy Clayton includes both classic and contemporary recipes from the women of Jackson Hole, plus lots of fun historical tidbits and photos. For ordering information, log on to www.teton views.com, write Teton Views Publishing, P.O. Box 832, Jackson, WY 83001, or call (307) 733-7161.

The Hole Thing
Hot Buttered Rum on page 54 is reprinted from the *Jackson Hole Guide*. It was also included in a fund-raising cookbook published by St. John's Hospital Auxiliary called *The Hole Thing*. To order the new edition of this popular local cookbook, write to St. John's Hospital Auxiliary, P.O. Box 428, Jackson, WY 83001.

Jackson Hole A La Carte
Permission granted to include Pumpkin Cheesecake with Caramelized Walnuts on page 245. *Jackson Hole A La Carte*, edited by Jane Camenzind, is a wonderful cookbook compiled by the Jackson Hole Conservation Alliance, a nonprofit organization that works to protect the wildlife, scenic and recreational resources of Jackson Hole. For information on the Alliance, or to order a copy of the cookbook, write JHCA, P.O. Box 2728, Jackson, WY 83001, or call (307) 733-9417.

Peak Bloom
Permission granted to include Marilyn's Pesto on page 83 and Green Devil Cake on page 234. *Peak Bloom: Honest Advice for Mountain and Northern Gardeners* by Marilyn Quinn contains recipes that showcase a garden's bounty. For ordering information, call White Willow Publishing at (307) 733-0674.

Teton Temptations
Permission granted by recipe contributors to include Peanut Butter Bread on page 30, Honey dressing on page 103 and Oatmeal Fudge Bars on page 212. All were included in *Teton Temptations*, compiled by Teton County Extension Homemakers in 1977. The publication is out-of-print.

Teton Views
Permission granted to include Chicken Marsala on page 164. *Teton Views* is a weekly paper distributed free throughout the valley; it routinely features recipes from local residents. To subscribe, write to Editor Judy Clayton at Teton Views Publishing, P.O. Box 832, Jackson, WY 83001, or call (307) 733-7161.

The Vegetarian Epicure
Permission granted to include Creamed Tomato Soup with Cognac on page 138. *The Vegetarian Epicure* by Anna Thomas was published by Vintage Books, a division of Random House, in 1972. Publication rights are presently owned by Alfred A. Knopf, Inc.

www.recipes2.alastra.com
A few recipes in this publication are adapted from this large recipe database. Check it out!

Individual Recipe Contributors

Sloane Andrews
Anne Band
LoyDean Barney
Candy Bayer
Wyatt Beard
Lisbeth Beise
Dave Bloom
Jane Bloom
Linda Bourett
Gertrude Brennan
Betty Caesar
Janie Camenzind
Lucey Carissa
Nancy Carson
Hunter Christensen
Jed Christensen
Simone Christensen
Donna Clinton
Erin Dann
Marion Dolge
Linda Drumm
Emily Duggan
Judy Eddy
Sue Enger
Nicola Esdorn
Cindy Fischer
Dr. William Fogarty
Jo Gathercole

Janet Graham
Mary Gridley
Thelma Hamby
Putzi Harrington
Dick Hays
Jan Hayse
Deb Hibberd
Sunny Howell
Caroline Janney
Sherrie Jern
Jean Jorgensen
Linda Kaess
Marcia Kunstel
Ann Laubach
Doris Laubach
Val and George Lefebre
Frank Londy
Jolene Loos
Kay Loos
Joyce Lucas
Lokey Lytjen
Martha MacEachern
Louise Murie MacLeod
Elaine May
Elizabeth McCabe
Alyssa McCormick
Sherri McFarland
Kim McGregor

Sue McGuire
Bertie Millward
Muffy Moore
Mardy Murie
Erika Mushaweck
Linda Nousianen
Jayne Ottman
Alisan Peters
Keith Peters
Marilyn Quinn
Susie Rauch
Margie Reimers
Anne Whiting Richardson
Elizabeth Richardson
Lisa O. Robertson
Sami Robinson
Dana Rogers
Latitia Roskatool
Joyce Rudd
Lois Ruosch
Judy Schmitt
Paul Scialabba
Pat Siegel
Donna Spurlock
Dean and Julie Staynor
Rita Stephanou
William Stirn
Echo Taylor
Pierce Tome
Teton Views
Barbara Trachtenberg
Christy Walton
Eva Marie Watson
Rhonda Watson
Happy Weston
Charles Wheeler
Becky Woods
Georgia Woods
Joey Woods
Louise Woods
Marcia Woods

Margin Information Sources

Allan, Esther, *History of Teton National Forest*, unpublished, 1973.

Armstrong, David M. Rocky Mountain Mammals. Boulder, Colorado: Colorado Associated University Press, 1987.

Betts, Robert. *Along the Ramparts of the Tetons: The Saga of Jackson Hole, Wyoming*. Boulder, Colorado: Colorado Associated University Press, 1978.

Bonney, Lorraine. *Bonney's Guide to Jackson's Hole and Grand Teton National Park*. Moose, Wyoming: Homestead Publishing, 1995.

Craighead, John and Frank and Ray Davis. *A Field Guide to Rocky Mountain Wildflowers*. Boston, Massachusetts: Houghton Mifflin Company, 1964.

Daugherty, John. *A Place Called Jackson Hole: The Historic Resource Study of Grand Teton National Park*. Moose, Wyoming: Grand Teton Natural History Association, 2002.

Diem, Kenneth L. and Lenore L. *A Community of Scalawags, Renegades, Discharged Soldiers and Predestined Stinkers*. Moose, Wyoming: Grand Teton Natural History Association, 1998.

Fisher, Chris C. *Birds of the Rocky Mountains*. Vancouver, Canada: Lone Pine Publishing, 1997.

Hayden, Elizabeth Wied. *From Trappers to Tourists in Jackson Hole*. Moose, Wyoming: Grand Teton Natural History Association, 1981.

Kershaw, Linda and Andy MacKinnon and Jim Pojar. *Plants of the Rocky Mountains*. Vancouver, Canada: Lone Pine Publishing, 1998.

Olson, Linda and Tim Bywater. *A Guide to Exploring Grand Teton National Park*. Salt Lake City, Utah. RNM Press, 1991.

Ortenburger, Leigh and Reynold G. Jackson. *A Climber's Guide to the Teton Range*. Seattle, Washington: The Mountaineers, 1996.

Platts, Doris. *The Pass: Historic Teton Pass and Wilson, Wyoming*. Wilson, Wyoming: Self-Published, 1988.

Righter, Robert. *Crucible for Conservation: The Creation of Grand Teton National Park*. Boulder, Colorado: Colorado Associated University Press, 1982.

Turiano, Thomas. *Teton Skiing: A History and Guide to the Teton Range*. Moose, Wyoming: Homestead Publishing, 1995.

Photo Credits

Courtesy of Bridger-Teton National Forest
> pgs. 1, 34, 43, 54, 55, 58, 71, 75, 78, 79, 85, 97, 107, 116, 121, 126, 128, 131, 152, 156, 157, 159, 163, 171, 174, 176, 181, 197, 206, 209, 211, 214-216, 218-220, 247-250, 254, 258, 263, 281.

Courtesy of the Natonal Park Service
> pgs. 36, 88, 111, 210, 230.

Courtesy of the Historic American Buildings Survey/Historic American Engineering Record Collection, Library of Congress, Prints & Photographs Division
> pgs. 46, 47, 191, 194, 195, 232, 233

Courtesy of The Murie Center
> pg. 115

Public Domain
> Unless current rights/ownership are held by a private party, most historic photos taken on or before 1923 are in public domain. These photos are collected from a variety of public domain sources.
> pgs. 7, 9, 12, 14, 15, 35, 82, 101, 102, 130, 151, 175, 201, 203, 226, 227, 244, 245.

Rebecca Woods and www.clipart.com licensee
> pgs. 3, 4, 10, 13, 16, 17, 19, 20, 21,23, 24, 26, 28, 30-32, 38, 40, 42, 45, 49, 51, 52, 57, 58, 60, 62, 65, 66, 68, 70, 72, 74, 76, 80, 83, 84, 87, 91, 96, 108, 133, 135, 136, 138, 141, 142, 147, 148, 153, 154, 158, 160 -162, 169, 173, 177, 183, 185, 189, 192, 199, 200, 205, 207, 208, 212, 225, 228, 231, 234, 235, 237, 238, 241, 252.

Favorite Recipes/Notes

Order Form

To order additional copies of this book, please check with your favorite Jackson hole nonprofit organiztion or bookseller, or send a copy of this form with your personal check or money order to: White Willow Publishing, PO Box 6464, Jackson, WY 83002.

Jackson Hole Cooks Order Form

Please send _____copies of Jackson Hole Cooks

at $18.95 each _____

WY. Residents add 6% sales tax of $1.14 each _____

U.S. Shipping charge of $2 per book _____

Enclosed is my check or money order for $_____

Name _____

Mailing Address _____

City/State/Zip _____

Make checks payable to White Willow Publishing
PO Box 6464 • Jackson, Wyoming 83002

Jackson Hole Cooks Order Form

Please send _____copies of Jackson Hole Cooks

at $18.95 each _____

WY. Residents add 6% sales tax of $1.14 each _____

U.S. Shipping charge of $2 per book _____

Enclosed is my check or money order for $_____

Name _____

Mailing Address _____

City/State/Zip _____

Make checks payable to White Willow Publishing
PO Box 6464 • Jackson, Wyoming 83002

If you are interested in publishing a cookbook,
or would like to contribute a recipe for future editions,
please contact:

White Willow Publishing
PO Box 6464
Jackson, Wyoming 83002
307-734-7002
whitewillow@bresnan.net